IN SEARCH OF DEITY

John Macquarrie

IN SEARCH OF DEITY

An Essay in Dialectical Theism

The Gifford Lectures, 1983

Crossroad   New York

1985
The Crossroad Publishing Company
370 Lexington Avenue, New York, N.Y. 10017

© John Macquarrie 1984

Printed in the United States of America

Library of Congress Cataloging in Publication Data

Macquarrie, John.
  In search of deity.

  Bibliography: p.
  Includes index.
  1. God. 2. Theism. 3. Natural theology.   I. Title.
II. Series: Gifford lectures; 1983-4.
BT102.M273   1985   211'.3   84-23133
ISBN 0-8245-0682-0

To My Teachers

Contents

Preface

My first duty is to express thanks to the University of St Andrews for the great honour it has done me in inviting me to give this course of Gifford Lectures. Let me admit that from my youth I have been an admirer and an avid reader of Gifford Lectures. As an undergraduate, I believed that those who were invited to give these lectures must be persons of supernatural wisdom. I became more doubtful of this as I grew older and the critical faculty developed. The final disillusionment took place when I was myself invited to lecture on this Foundation, and it was brought home to me in a personal way how slender are our human resources for facing those great topics which Lord Gifford proposed.

I feel doubly honoured that the invitation to give these lectures has come from the most ancient and illustrious of the Scottish universities. How fortunate this small country of ours was when back in the fifteenth century she acquired three great centres of learning – the University of St Andrews first, then the University of Glasgow (my own *alma mater*), and, towards the end of the century, the University of Aberdeen. These three stretch across the country from the south-west to the north-east like the three bright stars in the belt of the constellation Orion, and although they have been joined by some newer and very distinguished universities, no one would grudge the primacy to these old Renaissance foundations. To one who, like myself, has lived for many years furth of Scotland, it is a great privilege to come back for even a short time and to spend it here at the very wellspring of Scotland's academic life.

I have mentioned the sense of inadequacy which I felt on receiving the University's invitation. In a situation like that, we turn to our teachers. I remembered that my own revered teacher, the late Professor Charles Arthur Campbell, had given the Gifford Lectures here at St Andrews in 1953, exactly thirty years ago. The series was entitled *On Selfhood and Godhood*, so I took it down from the shelf. As I more than half expected, I was reminded that he said, much better than I could hope to do, many of the things that I might have said in these lectures, and since I probably learned them from him in the first place, there will no doubt be echoes of his teaching in what I have to say. I could not help noticing, however, that Professor Campbell, at the beginning of his lectures, had paid tribute to his own teacher, Sir Henry Jones, whose name was still honoured at Glasgow University when I went there as an undergraduate many years after his death. Before going to Glasgow, he had taught at St Andrews. Sir Henry Jones gave the Gifford Lectures in 1921, with the title, *A Faith That Enquires*. I took down his volume, and found tucked into the back of it notes which I had taken many years before and which speedily reminded me of its contents. But what intrigued me now was to notice that Sir Henry began his lectures with some glowing words of appreciation for his teacher, no one else than another Glasgow professor, Edward Caird. His Gifford Lectures, too, were on my shelves, similarly annotated. They had been given in 1892, again in St Andrews, with the title, *The Evolution of Religion*. The trail broke off at that point, for the Gifford Lectures do not go back beyond 1888, but my inadvertent researches had brought to light two interesting points: the first is the close tie which the Lectureship has established between the University of St Andrews and the University of Glasgow; and the second, which is almost like a law of nature, is that pupil succeeds teacher at an interval of approximately thirty years. It is tempting to speak here of a doctrine of apostolic succession, but I think that belongs to revealed rather than to natural theology, and so is excluded by Lord Gifford.

My visits to St Andrews were made pleasant by the kindness and hospitality of many people, both in the University and in the wider community. To them I express my thanks. I wish also to thank a number of friends and colleagues with whom I had valuable discussions while preparing these lectures – in particular, the Revd Dr Wayne J. Hankey, Professor Eugene T. Long, the Revd Dr A. Meredith, SJ, Professor Steven Rockefeller and the Revd Professor Maurice Wiles.

It has for long been a custom among Gifford Lecturers to expand considerably the original lectures in the printed version, and I have followed this precedent. What was orally delivered at St Andrews consisted of the first three paragraphs of this Preface, by way of Exordium, followed by Lectures (now Chapters), II, III, IV, V, VII, X, XII, XIII, XIV, XVII.

Christ Church, Oxford,   John Macquarrie
December 1983

Part One

Classical Theism and Its Alternatives

I

The Idea of Natural Theology

The railway traveller in Scotland is likely sooner or later to find himself with time to spare, changing trains at Edinburgh's famous Waverley Station. That great monument to the Victorian age is almost a city in itself – indeed, the story used to be told of the countrywoman who was persuaded to go for the first time in her life to spend a day in the capital city, and came home full of admiration and with the surprising information that the whole town was covered over with glass. Most travellers, I expect, will find enough comforts and amusements within the station precincts, but for those who are more adventurous and desire to make a sally into the regions outside, even half an hour is long enough for an interesting excursion. A few minutes walk eastward brings you to the old Calton burial ground, a quiet and very likely deserted spot in the heart of the city. On going in, you will find the grave of David Hume, whom one of my teachers claimed to have been the greatest Scotsman who ever lived. He died in 1776 at the zenith of the Enlightenment. Among other things, he is generally supposed to have dealt a mortal blow to natural theology, and in addition he stimulated the thought of Kant, who dealt some further blows to that already dying subject. So it is something of an irony to find only a few yards from where Hume was laid to rest the tomb of Lord Gifford. He died in 1887, more than a century after Hume, and is chiefly remembered for his munificence in founding the Gifford Lectureship in this very subject of natural theology; for almost one hundred years philosophers, theologians, scientists and many others have devoted enormous intellectual energies to wrestling with the problems of natural theology under the auspices of this foundation. So it would seem that Hume and Kant did not quite finish it off.

Still, I do not wish to minimize the serious questions that Hume and Kant raised for any subsequent practitioners of natural theology. Further questions were raised in the nineteenth century, especially in the light of the theory of evolution with its idea of natural selection, which struck hard at the argument from design, often regarded as the strongest of all the arguments in the arsenal of natural theology. The position is further complicated by the fact that there have always been theologians, including the greatest theologian of our present century, Karl Barth, who have attacked natural theology with just as much vigour as have sceptical philosophers.

The position of natural theology is a precarious one. The methods of its older exponents, such as William Paley who had such a great influence at the beginning of the nineteenth century, seem to have been almost totally discredited. Yet natural theology keeps coming back, restating its positions, refining its arguments, adapting itself to new knowledge. Many of the series of Gifford Lectures demonstrate this point, and belong to a different world from Paley. I suppose one might say that the very fact that an intellectual enterprise is carried on vigorously, persistently and sometimes persuasively is a justification of that enterprise. I think there is some truth in this contention, and quite a substantial part of the present treatment of the subject will be devoted to the study of a particular tradition of thinking about God, a tradition which has persisted through many changes, shown itself capable of new developments, and still has, I believe, much to teach us. But I would not wish to lay too much stress on the fact that natural theology is still actively pursued, for I might give the impression that I believed that because a language game is in fact played, that in itself is a sufficient vindication for it. This view – or one very close to it – is in fact held by some philosophers of religion, but it entails what to my mind is an unacceptable and, indeed, irresponsible fideism. This Wittgensteinian fideism, as it is sometimes called, is in principle no different from the Barthian fideism which starts from the givenness of a particular revelation and refuses to inquire into the grounds for accepting that revelation. In both cases there is a fundamental scepticism about the powers of the human mind. This scepticism ill consorts with faith, and fideism in any form seems to me a very shaky basis for religious belief.

So I do not believe that anyone who commends religion can escape the obligation of providing a natural theology. Yet I am aware of the problematic nature of the subject, and accept that anyone who does venture into this field must begin by stating just what he understands natural theology to be and how he thinks it possible to go about it.

I think we should notice first of all that, despite the stringency of their criticisms, neither Hume nor Kant was entirely negative about natural theology. Hume seemed willing to acknowledge that 'the whole of natural theology resolves itself into one simple, though somewhat ambiguous, at least undefined proposition: That the cause or causes of order in the universe probably bear some remote analogy to human intelligence.'[1] Hume thought that this is a very meagre result, that it has no importance for human life and that it tells us very little about the ultimate reality on which natural theology is supposed to throw some light. There is no doubt at all that Hume believed that natural theology lends no support to traditional supernatural theism, if by that we understand a transcendent God who is able to intervene in the world's affairs by miraculous acts – that is clear from his writings. Nor would he agree that even what we may call the general order of the world proceeds from some external agency – the world, he suggests, is more like an organism than an artefact, so that its order is immanent to itself, not imposed from outside.[2] But Hume does not pause to consider what would be needed for such an order to evolve. The potentiality for worldhood must have been there, and that means that the elements of form and mind must have been there. Any reductive materialism is the more implausible, the more reductive it is. Out of what is merely a chaotic swirl of particles nothing structured will ever emerge, unless the basic structures are already there – as, in fact, modern theories of matter concede. Time and chance alone will never produce the form of a world. It has been said by someone that a billion apes banging on a billion typewriters for a billion years (let a few noughts be added to each billion if required!) would produce the works of Shakespeare. Apart from the fact that a true reductionist would scarcely begin from such intelligent animals as apes and such sophisticated machines as typewriters, the entire analogy is misleading. Even if the apes produced marks on paper down to the very punctuation corresponding to Shakespeare's plays, these would be senseless marks on paper and no more, in the absence of an intelligent being who could read them and in so doing enter into the world of Shakespeare. So even if Hume's criticisms were damaging to the popular conception of a transcendent deity, they do not touch the possibility of an immanent creative power to which some philosophers might be willing to ascribe the attribute of divinity. Hume's own conclusion was to make the grudging concession that there may be a remote analogy between the causes of order in the universe and the human mind, on the rather slender ground that the arguments for such an analogy exceed the objections against. But he considered the analogy to be so remote and ill defined that his own position is probably best described as a profound agnosticism.[3] Still, one is bound to remember that there have been philosophers and theologians who would have accepted most of Hume's critique of traditional theism, but who developed the view of an immanent deity, perhaps verging on pantheism, and these philosophers have also sometimes claimed a mystical experience confirming their belief that at the heart of things there is a reality that is more than material, though transcending our understanding. Of course, they would still have to face Hume's question: 'How do you mystics, who maintain the absolute incomprehensibility of the deity, differ from sceptics and atheists who assert that the first cause of all is unknown and unintelligible?'[4] But surely the mystic, as indeed we shall see in later discussions, does not maintain the '*absolute* incomprehensibility of the deity' (though his rhetoric may come close to suggesting that he does), but acknowledges what Hume himself calls a 'remote analogy' between the human mind and the forces at work in the world. The *via negativa* is always in practice eked out by the *via eminentiae*.

When we turn from Hume to Kant, we face a very diffferent situation, but one that is even more ambiguous. Kant's acknowledged aim was 'to deny knowledge in order to make room for faith',[5] and this involved exposing what he called the 'transcendental illusion' of natural theology. Certainly, his criticisms of the traditional theistic proofs have a thoroughness and penetration that are, perhaps, without equal. The main point is that the categories of understanding are limited in their application to the phenomena encountered in space and time, and that if we attempt to extend their scope to realities supposedly lying beyond these phenomena, then we fall into contradictions. In this negative part of his undertaking, Kant's conclusion is not very far from Hume's, that is to say, it is a positivism or agnosticism which declares that if there are any supersensible realities, they lie beyond the grasp of our minds. We should notice too that the concept of God which Kant has in mind in his criticisms is the same concept as Hume criticized, namely, a God separate from and external to the world, admittedly, the God of most traditional theism, though even more like the distant God of Enlightenment deism. But even in the *Critique of Pure Reason* Kant's negative conclusions are to some extent modified. He concedes that even when we have been shown the limitations of the human mind, 'the human reason has a natural tendency to transgress these limits'.[6] In its quest for a scientific and systematic understanding of the world, the mind posits a principle of unity which holds everything together in a totality. This is the idea of God. It is not, in Kantian language, a 'constitutive' idea, that is to say, we cannot show its objective reality, though this cannot be disproved either. It remains, however, as a 'regulative' idea, a *focus imaginarius* or ideal limit, conducting the mind towards a unified understanding of the world. The point is made more affirmatively in the *Critique of Judgment*, where Kant asks whether teleology proves the existence of a divine intelligence, and replies: 'No. It proves no more than this, that by the constitution of our cognitive faculties and therefore in bringing experience into touch with the highest principle of reason, we are absolutely incapable of forming any conception of the possibility of such a world unless we imagine a highest cause operating designedly.'[7] But if the idea of God is virtually a necessity of thought, can we be content to think of it as only a subjective regulative principle? The whole tendency of Kant's philosophy is towards a kind of rational monism, an immanent principle of reason pervading everything that is, and in which the human mind participates. This is not the God of traditional theism, but might it not merit the name of God, albeit a somewhat abstract God, purged of all anthropomorphisms?

We have still to incorporate into our account the findings of the *Critique of Practical Reason*. There are at least three points to be considered here. The first of these seems to me the least important, though it is often mentioned. It is the view that the existence of God is a postulate of the practical reason, because morality demands that happiness be proportioned to virtue and so there must be a supreme moral governor who will ensure this.[8] It seems to me that here Kant is falling far below his own best insights – he is introducing into morality a prudential element which elsewhere he rigorously excludes and, worse still, he is reverting to an anthropomorphic view of a monarchical God to whom is being assigned a far from exalted function. Long ago A. S. Pringle-Pattison remarked that

'God seems to be introduced in Kant's moral theory almost as an afterthought, and he is connected with the [moral] law not as its inspirer or author, but in the merely administrative capacity of paymaster.'[9] A second point is much more important. Although Kant had shown that speculative reason cannot establish the reality of freedom, he now maintains that freedom, too, is a postulate of the moral life, for it would be senseless to speak of duty unless we had the power to do our duty. More than that, this freedom is a breach in the phenomenal order, giving access to the noumenal realm. A moral being, according to Kant, 'belonging to the world of sense, belongs also to the supersensible world, this is also positively *known*, and thus the reality of the supersensible world is established, and in practical respects *definitely* given, and this definiteness, which for theoretical purposes would be *transcendent*, is for practical purposes immanent'.[10] At this point, Kant is coming near to saying that in the moral experience of duty, we have something like an experience of God, but this God is the objective rational order immanent in the world though also in a sense transcendent, not the anthropomorphic God who proportions happiness to virtue. It is true, of course, that Kant insisted on the autonomy of the moral law, as a law which man gives to himself in virtue of his rational nature, and that he always opposed heteronomy. But one could only speak of heteronomy in the case of God conceived as divine governor or in some other one-sidedly transcendent way, not when he is conceived as an immanent order in which human beings participate. Thirdly, in the *Groundwork of the Metaphysic of Morals*, Kant makes use of the feeling of respect. Usually he distances himself as far as possible from emotion, and he apologizes for introducing such a topic: 'It might be here objected to me that I take refuge behind the word "respect" in an obscure feeling, instead of giving a distinct solution of the question by a concept of the reason. But,' he continues, 'although respect is a feeling, it is not a feeling *received* through influence, but is *self-wrought* by a rational concept and therefore is specifically distinct from all feelings of the former kind, which may be referred either to inclination or to fear.'[11] Nevertheless, in spite of these cautionary words, I suppose that respect is not very far removed from reverence, and is about as close as Kant comes to acknowledging anything like a religious sentiment. But the feeling is inspired by the immanent rational principle of the world, and if this can be called

'God' or if it has a function similar to God, it is not an anthropo-morphic or monarchical God.

It is true that in the *Critique of Judgment* Kant declares in one place that 'religion is morality in relation to God as lawgiver'.[12] This talk of God as lawgiver might seem to suggest a more personal conception of God and to imply that respect for the moral law rests on reverence for its giver. But one should not make too much of an expression like the one quoted, and in any case I do not think that Kant had now abandoned the autonomy of the rational will for some form of heteronomy. At the most, he is recognizing that reason in the human being has its source in a universal reason. A similar view of the relation of morality and religion is found in the later work, *Religion within the Limits of Reason Alone*, where we read: 'Religion is (subjectively regarded) the recognition of all duties as divine commands.'[13] A long footnote to this sentence and still more the whole tenor of his book on religion make it clear that for Kant religion is virtually absorbed into morality. His rationalistic mind was insensitive to and distrustful of religious experience in its emotional and imaginative aspects. Worship, prayer and dogma are valued only to the extent that they contribute to the performance of moral duty. Even so, they are suspect, and in the completely rational religion which Kant holds up as the ideal for the future, they would be virtually eliminated. Certainly, he has no thought that communion with God might be a good thing in itself – indeed, could one have communion with the kind of God of whom or of which Kant speaks? He was also hostile to mysticism, which he regarded as illusory, claiming that the human being has no capacity for intuiting the immediate presence of God.[14]

Yet religion is not simply superseded, and his contemporaries have testified that in his way Kant was profoundly religious. The need for religion emerges in his refusal to countenance the belief in human progress and perfectibility, a belief that had gained much popularity at the time of the Enlightenment and had been passion-ately propagated by such rationalists as Lessing. In opposition to this view, Kant declared that there is a radical principle of evil in human nature, what the religions call 'sin' or even 'original sin'. The function of religion is to strengthen man's pursuit of the good in the face of moral weakness and even corrupt propensities. Kant frankly acknowledges the human need for divine assistance in fulfilling moral duties, but this is all so contrary both to this theoretical agnosticism and his championing of practical autonomy that he cannot come to terms with it. It is little short of painful to see this great intellect struggling with the concept of divine grace as something he acknowledges to be necessary to the human condition, yet something for which his general philosophy (and perhaps also his temperament) cannot find a place. We find him writing:

> The concept of a supernatural accession to our moral, though deficient, capacity and even to our not wholly purified and certainly weak disposition to perform our entire duty, is a transcendent concept and a bare idea, of the reality of which no experience can assure us. Even when accepted as an idea in nothing but a practical context, it is very hazardous and hard to reconcile with reason, since that which is to be accredited to us as morally good conduct must take place not through foreign influence but solely through the best possible use of our own powers. And yet the impossibility thereof (that is, of both these things occurring side by side) cannot really be proved, because freedom itself, though containing nothing supernatural in its conception, remains, as regards its possibility, just as incomprehensible to us as is the supernatural factor which we would like to regard as a supplement to the spontaneous but deficient determination of freedom.[15]

Here it may be enough simply to comment that God's grace will be a 'foreign influence' only for one having a deistic conception of God, and that freedom is neither more nor less a mystery than grace.

I have thought it desirable to discuss Hume and Kant at some length, because they are often cited as if they had discredited the whole enterprise of natural theology, and I do not believe that this is the case. They did certainly raise serious difficulties for the traditional theistic proofs, and, more than that, they raised difficulties for the traditional concept of a transcendent personal God, so that any subsequent natural theology is bound to take note of the work of Hume and Kant and their successors, and to try to avoid the difficulties which they exposed. But we have also found that there are ambiguities in the positions of both these philosophers, and that some ways to natural theology remain open. If, for instance, one were to pay more attention to the notion of divine immanence, some of the difficulties might be overcome. In other words, it is not simply a case of trying to reply to the criticisms of Hume and Kant, but asking first of all whether the idea of God which they were rejecting is really an adequate one. It seems to me that they oscillate between an anthropomorphic quasi-mythological idea of a God who keeps interfering in the world by miracles or by handing out appropriate rewards and punishments, and an attenuated deism in which God is conceived as a distant being beyond the universe which he leaves to run its course as best it is able. I would not wish to defend either of these conceptions of God, and I have the impression that few contemporary theologians would be upset by their disappearance. I find myself in large measure of agreement with Keith Ward when he writes:

> For the theist, God is not an inference, an absentee entity. He is not an object apart from the universe, of which we can only detect faint traces. On the contrary, he is the mind and heart of the universe itself. To believe in God is to believe that at the heart of all reality, of this very reality in which we exist, is spirit, consciousness, value, reason and purpose. We are not trying to convince people by sheer logic that there is some extra object, far beyond the limits of the cosmos, but to get them to discern the existence of objective spirit, *in and through* the things around them. We are seeking to evoke a way of seeing this world, not to assert the abstract existence of some merely theoretical object.[16]

It should be noted, too, that it is not only a defective conception of God that Hume and Kant criticized. Their idea of knowledge was equally unsatisfactory. For them, the paradigm of knowledge was knowledge of objects or of facts. But if there is any reality that is designated by the word 'God', one must suppose that this reality is supremely active and could not be an object passively submitting to investigation but would itself have the initiative in communication. The nearest analogy in our ordinary human experience would be knowing another person, and we can know another person only to the extent that that person lets himself be known by us.

When we look at the actual terms of Lord Gifford's foundation,[17] we see that the conception of natural theology expressed there does go beyond the narrower forms criticized by Hume and Kant, and, of course, this is confirmed when we consider the lectures that have in fact been given in the past without for the most part ceasing to be recognizable as natural theology. One could say that the Gifford Lectureship has by itself brought about a vast development and enrichment of the conception of natural theology in respect of method, scope, sources and content. Lord Gifford spoke of natural theology 'in the widest sense of that term', to quote his own words, and it can be understood in a much wider sense than Hume and Kant understood it, without, however, becoming so wide that it loses definition.

But when Lord Gifford goes on to say, 'I wish the lecturers to treat their subject as a strictly natural science, the greatest of all possible sciences,' or when he says, 'I wish it treated just as astronomy or chemistry,' it might seem that he is here imposing rather a severe limitation on the lecturers. But this is not so. When he says that the subject is to be treated as a 'natural science', he cannot mean that God is to be treated as a phenomenon of nature, but that the inquiry is to be carried out by the natural human faculties that are common to all, without appeal to some special source of knowledge. This is how the word 'natural' was tradition-ally understood in the expression 'natural theology'. We should not be misled either by the mention of chemistry and astronomy. Clearly, no one could suppose for a moment that God could be observed or investigated in the manner appropriate when we are inquiring about chemical reactions or planetary motions. Natural theology is to be like chemistry and astronomy and the other natural sciences in its openness, its intellectual integrity and its determination not to rest on authority alone. Lord Gifford in fact makes the distinction crystal clear when he says that natural theology is the science of 'infinite being'. A science of infinite being would be *toto coelo* different from any science that concerns itself with some limited area of beings. In an alternative terminology, it would be ontological science as distinct from all ontic sciences.

It is also stated in the trust deed founding the Lectureship that there should be no 'reference to or reliance upon any supposed special exceptional or so-called miraculous revelation'. The oper-ative words here, I think, are 'special exceptional or so-called miraculous'. This does not exclude the possibility that there may be ways in which God universally communicates himself to his creatures, ways which can be properly called 'revelation', though not the special revelation of any one particular religious tradition. At this point the borderline between natural and revealed theology surely becomes blurred. There is a sense in which all natural theology is revealed theology, for if God is the source of everything, he must also be the source of the knowledge of himself, and there is no 'unaided' knowledge of God, any more than there is unaided knowledge of my neighbour. But there is also a sense in which all revealed theology is natural theology, since it comes through persons, things and events in this world and is appropriated by our universal human faculties.

In the light of these remarks, I think I can also define my position with regard to those theologians who question the legitimacy of natural theology. I can agree with Karl Barth that God cannot properly be turned into an object and that there is no 'unaided' or purely human knowledge of God, at least, not any that would have significance or value. But where I cannot go along with him is in his contention that the only genuine knowledge of God is that communicated by the Christian revelation. Still, I can acknowledge Barth's concern lest the knowledge of God be treated as a purely theoretical concern, so that one loses sight of its significance for human life or even human salvation. The religious significance of natural theology must not be neglected. It seems to me one of the great weaknesses in Kant's treatment of religion that he tried to keep pure reason and practical reason in separate compartments, and obviously considered that pure reason has some superiority over practical reason, certainly in questions of truth. How much richer his philosophy of religion might have been, if he had overcome this dualism and been able to consider the human being in his wholeness! Certainly, it was not Lord Gifford's intention to separate natural theology from religious interests. On the contrary, one can discern almost a missionary motive in his foundation – the mission of disseminating a knowledge of God that would not rest merely on tradition or authority but one that would have taken root in the minds of men and women, and would be all the more efficacious because of that. Thus we find him saying: 'The lectures shall be public and popular, that is, open not only to students of the universities but to the whole community without matriculation, as I think that the subject should be studied and known by all, whether receiving university instruction or not. I think such knowledge, if real, lies at the root of all well-being.'

I have in these introductory remarks offered a preliminary defence of natural theology against some of its most famous critics, but I have also indicated that the kind of natural theology I would seek to develop would be different at many points from the kind which Hume and Kant criticized. The detailed working out of this natural theology will be our concern throughout the remainder of the book, but at this point it may be useful to give an outline of the path that will be followed.

Since it is not only natural theology but all theology that has been under fire in modern times, our first task will be to examine the key-word of all theology, the word 'God'. It is, of course, a word of our language and in every human language there is some corresponding word. But innumerable meanings have at one time or another been given to the word 'God' or its equivalents. Is it possible to form a coherent concept of God that would be meaningful in the contemporary world?

The quest for such a concept inevitably leads us to give serious consideration to the criticisms that have been directed in the past two hundred years or so against what I have been already calling 'traditional theism'. Why has belief in God, not only as he is understood in the popular mind but as he has been represented in much orthodox theology, declined so steeply in the intellectually advanced societies of the world, particularly the societies of the Western world? Are these criticisms, which today are heard not only from avowed atheists but even from believers, indicative of defects in some of the traditional ways of understanding God, so that they call for some radical rethinking if talk of God (theology) is to continue as a serious and important area of discourse, still more, if the reality of God is to have that significance for human well-being which, as we have noted, Lord Gifford supposed it to have? We shall see that some of the criticisms of traditional theism are in fact well founded. The alternative, however, is not necessarily atheism. Indeed, I shall criticize atheism, too, for its own inadequacies and incoherence. But there is not a stark disjunction between theism, in the traditional sense, and atheism. There are alternatives, and I think that on the broad spectrum of beliefs there are many people today occupying positions which are neither atheistic nor yet orthodoxly theistic.

The alternative I shall develop I am calling 'dialectical theism'. I am using this expression because, as it seems to me, the traditional theism has been too one-sided in its account of God. It has stressed one set of divine properties to the neglect of others. To give just one example, God's transcendence has been emphasized at the expense of the almost total neglect of his immanence. I know, of course, that the best theologians have always made some mention of immanence – Thomas Aquinas, for instance, affirms that 'God is everywhere in substance, power and presence'.[18] But in practice it has been transcendence that has been stressed, certainly in the Judaeo-Christian tradition of the West.

When I speak of 'dialectical theism', I am not thinking of some weak compromise. 'Dialectic' is to be understood in the strong sense of the clash of opposites; for instance, God is not half transcendent and half immanent, but wholly transcendent and wholly immanent. This may sound like a contradiction. It is so in terms of the logic of the finite, but not of the logic of the infinite.

In natural theology, one may suppose, there is nothing new under the sun. What is here called 'dialectical theism' has had a long history. It originated in pre-Christian philosophy, it continued through the history of the Christian church as an alternative to main-line theism – an alternative that was sometimes suspected of heresy – and it continues in what some would regard as the post-Christian philosophy of the present. The middle part of the book will be devoted to a study of this alternative teaching about God, so that we can learn from both its achievements and its errors. I cannot, of course, attempt a complete history of the tradition, so I have chosen eight representative figures. The first four among them are unmistakably neo-Platonists; the second group belong to the modern world and yet are in continuity with the others. I begin with the pre-Christian Plotinus, and we may be reminded that more than sixty years ago a former Dean of St Paul's, W. R. Inge, devoted an entire series of Gifford Lectures in St Andrews to expounding the thought of Plotinus. I have chosen Dionysius the Areopagite as the thinker who effected the most radical union of the neo-Platonist and Judaeo-Christian traditions. We shall then study that profound but neglected thinker of the early Middle Ages, John Scotus Eriugena, without doubt the greatest Celtic philosopher who has ever lived. As the Middle Ages pass into the Renaissance, we come to Nicholas of Cusa applying the logic of infinity to God. Coming into modern times, we find some novel contributions in the philosophy of Leibniz at the dawn of the Enlightenment. German idealism is represented by the master of dialectic, Hegel. It was a contemporary of his in the same idealist tradition, Karl Krause, who invented the term 'panentheism' for a philosophy which seeks to find a path between theism and pantheism, so doing justice both to divine transcendence and divine immanence. The term is roughly synonymous with what I am calling 'dialectical theism', and I shall sometimes use it, but because it is so easily confused with pantheism, I shall in the main avoid it. Finally, I come to two twentieth-century figures, Whitehead and Heidegger, and I think we shall see that there are good reasons for including them.[19]

Having completed this historical survey and, I hope, having learned some of its lessons, we come back in the concluding chapters to our main task of constructing a natural theology for the present day. In the light of it, we shall reconsider the traditional proofs of God's existence and then ask about the consequences of this natural theology for ethics, for spirituality, for Christian theology and for the emerging dialogue among the world religions.

II

Towards a Concept of God

Who or what is God? Perhaps this question ought to have been asked even before we discussed the viability of natural theology, since all theology presupposes God as its subject-matter. However, as has already been pointed out, 'God' is a word of our language, and there is a corresponding word in every language. Presumably we have some general idea of what the word means. But here is the difficulty. There was a time in Western society when 'God' was an essential part of the everyday vocabulary. The word was on everyone's lips. What God demanded determined the way in which people lived; what God was doing explained the events taking place in the world around them; prayer to God was the safeguard against misfortune. This state of affairs still holds in many societies. But in the West and among educated people throughout the world, this kind of God-talk has virtually ceased. For two or three centuries, the process of secularization has been going on. The demands of society rather than of God determine our patterns of conduct; events around us are explained in terms of other events within the world; prayer is only the last uncertain resort when more mundane methods of coping with problems have failed. People once knew, or thought they knew, what they meant when they spoke of God, and they spoke of him often. Now in the course of the day's business we may not mention him at all. The name of God seems to have been retired from our everyday discourse. Even a believer, if he is asked 'What do you mean when you speak of God?', may find himself stumbling over an answer. The word that for thousands of years held a central place in language has become elusive.

When we are uncertain about the meaning of a word, we usually look up the dictionary. This is in fact the method recommended by Gordon Kaufman for getting theology started. Its basic terms including 'God', belong to the common stock of words, so we may at least begin with the dictionary definitions.[1] I am not sure myself that one could get very far along this road – that would depend on whether the lexicographer consulted happened to be also a good theologian. Still, it is an interesting experiment to look up two leading dictionaries, one British and one American: to be precise, the *Oxford English Dictionary* and *Webster's Third International Dictionary*, and see what they think the word 'God' conveys to contemporary post-Enlightenment men and women of the English-speaking world. Both dictionaries have separate entries for 'god', as the word is used in respect of the divine beings of polytheism, and 'God', as the word is used in monotheistic faiths or in philosophy. On the first usage, they are in fairly close agreement. *Oxford* defines a god as 'a superhuman person who is worshipped as having power over nature and the fortunes of mankind', while *Webster* tells us that a god is 'a being of more than human attributes and powers, especially a superhuman person conceived as the ruler or sovereign embodiment of some aspect, attribute or department of reality, and to whom worship is due and acceptable'. In the case of the God of monotheism, *Oxford* has: 'the one object of supreme adoration; the creator and ruler of the universe', while *Webster* has: 'the supreme or ultimate reality; the deity variously conceived in theology, philosophy and popular religion as . . .' and then follow half a dozen brief descriptions of God as he is understood in the Christian, Muslim, Hindu and other traditions, including some philosophical traditions. Let us consider these definitions for a few moments.

Perhaps the first point to impress itself upon us is just the sheer variety of meanings that have been assigned to the word 'God', as is evidenced in these definitions. God has been understood – or possibly misunderstood – in many ways by different human beings at different times and in different places. No doubt there has been development. Some ways of thinking about God are obviously more reflective than others. But the differences are not to be explained only in terms of greater or less maturity, deeper or shallower penetration. In different traditions, reflection has taken different directions, and distinctive ideas of God have emerged. The reason for this may be that God is a reality with such rich or even infinite content that any idea of God can only encompass some of his characteristics. Each tradition seizes upon certain attributes that have been important in the formation of the tradition, and in all probability will develop these in a one-sided way, to the neglect of others that have been missed. I am not, of course, saying that all the differences in the ideas of God that are held or have been held can be resolved in a single unified idea. We may well discover that God surpasses all human understanding. Yet I do believe that some of the differences, at first sight quite sharp differences, can be overcome in a more inclusive view. It is surely significant that those who hold different ideas of God nevertheless assume that they are talking about the same God. Even if one thinks that a person in another tradition has got it all wrong or has seriously distorted views about God, it is assumed to be the same God. And here at least is a point of agreement. As soon as people have got beyond the polytheistic stage, they realize that there can be only one God. We should notice, too, that although each tradition claims some more or less determinate knowledge of God, it is doubtful if any would claim that its knowledge is exhaustive. They are agreed in recognizing that there is a mystery of God. If in each case there is an idea of God, and this idea tends to be made more definite, in each case it also shades off into a hidden depth. It is possible that what has been brought into the clear focus of one idea of God remains hidden in another, and that once again this may suggest that different ideas of God are not necessarily in sheer contradiction with one another.

Let us first of all go back to the gods, since it is in that early polytheistic phase that recognizable God-talk begins, though of course religion had already had a long history before that, in animistic and possibly pre-animistic forms. In typical polytheistic religions, the gods were the great powers of nature: sun, wind, sea, rain, mountain, river and so on. Human life was dependent on them and sometimes destroyed by them. Certainly the idea of power – power of a superhuman order – featured prominently in the understanding of the gods. But I question if this was the important feature. It was not the power of these forces that made them gods, it was the belief, perhaps originally just the feeling, that somehow these powers were personal or quasi-personal, that they had a being which, to recall David Hume's phrases about natural theology, 'bears some remote analogy' to the kind of being that we know in ourselves. I am suggesting that God-language, even in its earliest usage, arose from the sense of affinity that human beings had with the cosmic forces around them. Indeed, has this not been of the very essence of belief in God from early times down to the most sophisticated forms of theism – that the believer has had a sense of affinity with an environing reality which he believes to be of a higher order than his own? The atheist, on the other hand, acknowledges no such affinity. For him, that environing reality is indifferent to the human spirit and belongs to an order of being that is essentially mechanical and sub-personal.

At the level of the polytheistic religions, talk of the gods takes the form of mythology. Stories are told of the gods, and in these stories they take on more definite personal characteristics. They may be represented in the visual arts as human or quasi-human beings, usually with some special feature that relates them to the particular force of nature or department of human life over which they severally preside. They are still considered to be immanent in the world and perceptible in the world, just like the natural forces which they represent. But surely, as indeed I have already indicated, human beings never worshipped the powers of nature simply as such. The notion of a merely natural phenomenon is a modern one, and is reached only by a gigantic effort of abstraction. For the archaic religious mind, the sun or the lightning flash or the river was more than a natural phenomenon – even if they had had the conception of a merely natural phenomenon. All these things were already sacramental. Through them, the worshipper believed, a reality at least in some ways analogous to his own inward being, was touching his life.

Of course, someone may say this was just pure superstition, and so are all the more sophisticated religious beliefs that have developed subsequently. The sun is nothing but a gigantic nuclear furnace, the lightning flash is nothing but a discharge of electrical energy in the atmosphere, the river is nothing but a dynamic configuration of water; in short, the reality that surrounds us and from which we have ourselves arisen has long ago been de-divinized, and we know it now to be nothing but a vast congeries of physical particles acting and reacting on one another. This language of 'nothing but', sometimes called 'nothing-buttery' or, more respectfully, 'reductionism', enjoys, of course, great prestige in the scientific age. One could not for a moment deny the value of methodological reductionism in the sciences. Arthur Peacocke, for instance, says, 'The progress of the sciences has certainly been in part due to their successful propensity to break down, for purposes of exploration, unintelligible complex wholes into their experiment-ally more manageable component units.'[2] As an illustration, he mentions the famous discovery of the molecular basis of heredity.

But to go from methodological reductionism to ontological reductionism may well be a quite fallacious move. It would be obviously false to say that heredity is 'nothing but' the behaviour of certain complex chemical substances, and the falsity of reductionism becomes even more obvious if one seeks to extend it to a general view of reality. The richness and concreteness of the world of human experience has to be taken on its own terms as a world in which meaning and value and spirit and possibly God himself are not considered any less real or less ultimate than physical process. The philosopher who has in recent times made the best case for interpreting the world in its concreteness rather than in the abstractions proper to specific scientific enterprises was Whitehead, and we shall be examining his thought in more detail at a later stage.[3] For the present, it is enough to say that the polytheist's intuition of a numinous or divine aspect in the powers of nature cannot be summarily dismissed as mere superstition. It was an attempt, however unsatisfactory, to express the mystery of being that is already raised by the occurrence of the simplest phenomenon.

In polytheistic religions, many gods are recognized, sometimes very many indeed, representing the multiplicity of natural forces and human affairs. It is probably that multiplicity that first of all impresses itself on the human mind. But sheer multiplicity would be chaos, and the mind seems to seek a unity in the multiplicity. This is true above all of the religious mind. 'If it is allowed that the existence of the many gives rise to a problem,' writes Frederick Copleston, 'synthesis takes the form of a movement of the mind towards The One, conceived as the source of the many and as the ultimate reality.'[4] The unity of God, of course, has more than one meaning. We have already noted that when people begin to reflect on the idea of God in any depth, they see that there can be only one God. Still, even the assertion of God's unicity has to be qualified. It is not a numerical unicity, but rather the realization that if there is divine being, the category of number is not applicable to it. This was clearly recognized already by such thinkers as Plotinus. But the unity of God is also understood as his unity within himself. The very idea of God implies an unimaginably rich and inclusive content, but this content belongs to God as that which has been perfectly unified.

Precisely how the advance from polytheism to some form of monotheism comes about historically is not clear, and no doubt it has happened differently in different cultures. Sometimes the appearance of a religious genius like Zarathustra or Mohammed would seem to have been the occasion for the transition, but the seeds are already there in polytheism itself, in the form of both religious and logical tendencies. The gods of polytheism are often imagined as constituting a family, and within the pantheon one god usually comes to have a position of dominance over the others. Thus, either explicitly or implicitly, polytheism moves towards monotheism.

Monotheism takes two fairly distinct forms – the religious and the philosophical. Since these are sometimes in tension with one another, we shall begin by considering them separately.

The classic example of religious monotheism is surely the faith expounded in the Hebrew scriptures. These scriptures, of course, were written over several centuries and retain some primitive features, but the difference from polytheism is striking. The unity of God is central: 'Hear, O Israel: The Lord our God is one Lord.'[5] This oneness has the two senses distinguished above. God is unique. The polemic against the gods runs all through Hebrew religion. These pretended gods are unreal and ineffective. Only the one God acts. This God, moreover, is faithful; that is to say, he is no capricious God but a God who can be trusted because all the attributes of deity are united in him. The common Hebrew word for 'God' is a plural form, *elohim*, though it is considered as singular and used with singular verbs and adjectives. It has been suggested that, whether consciously or unconsciously, this usage implies that all the gods are included in the one God of the Hebrews; all deity is comprehended in him.

In some ways, however, this monotheistic God retains features that were found in the polytheistic gods as well. He is very definitely a personal God, and his personality is portrayed in quite anthropomorphic ways. He speaks to patriarchs and prophets, he makes covenants and promises and can also utter threats. He experiences passions and emotions and is frequently angry or displeased. In spite of what was said above about his faithfulness, he sometimes repents or changes his mind. He is usually character- ized by images rather than concepts, and these images are taken from human society – king, judge, shepherd, warrior, father – though sometimes natural or material objects are used as images: rock, tower, light.

But over against this anthropomorphic tendency we find that God is in many ways contrasted sharply with man and the world.

The God of the Bible is very much a transcendent God, unlike the immanent gods of polytheism. This is implicit in the doctrine of creation, which now stands at the beginning of the Bible. God is prior to the world and independent of the world, which he has brought into being by his commanding word. Again, the typical language of the Bible is not mythology, in which the gods appear within the world, but a form of history in which events are seen as under the control of God. Certainly, God is involved in the history of Israel, but not as another item within the world. Even the anthropomorphisms are neutralized: 'For my thoughts are not your thoughts, neither are your ways my ways. For as the heavens are higher than the earth, so are my ways higher than your ways and my thoughts than your thoughts.'[6] God is not exhausted in anthropomorphic descriptions, and the Bible certainly leaves room for the mystery, otherness and even hiddenness of God. When Moses inquires about the name of God, he gets the enigmatic answer, 'I am who I am.'[7] Admittedly, the writer of Exodus presumably did not foresee the subtle ontological speculations that would be reared upon these words, but he must have been aware that he was safeguarding the ultimate incomprehensibility of God, and he succeeded pretty well, as is evidenced by the fact that the most learned scholars are still arguing about the meaning of his words!

It is a noble picture of God that emerges in the Hebrew Bible, in spite of occasional lapses. It has been an inspiration for centuries, and in a sense it cannot be superseded. Yet for centuries there has been developed alongside the religious monotheism a philosophical monotheism. Although the concrete imagery of kingship, fatherhood and so on cannot be superseded in the actual life of religion, in prayer and liturgy for instance (who ever addressed a prayer to necessary being?), and although the strongly personalist and even anthropomorphic language serves to keep before the worshipper that sense of affinity with the divine being which we have seen to be essential to belief in God and which it is the business of religion to encourage and enhance, reflective members of the religious community have looked for ways of expressing theism that would be more satisfying intellectually. In general, they have tried to move away from images to concepts and to express theism as a philosophical doctrine.

The immediate occasion for the development of a philosophical concept of God was the confluence of the religious monotheism of the Hebrew tradition with the metaphysical speculations of Greek philosophy, but I think we should recognize that philosophical reflection on religious belief was not just the result of contact with the Hellenic world but is fundamentally a demand of our own rational nature, so that if Greek philosophy had not been available for the task, it would still have had to be done sooner or later in some other philosophical idiom.

The Jewish scholar, Philo of Alexandria, led the way in developing the new philosophical theism, and the task was continued by the early Christian writers and their successors right into the Middle Ages. The personal God who had been represented as king or shepherd became a distant transcendent principle of being. The 'I am' of Exodus had been translated ὁ ὤν in the Septuagint, and this becomes the philosophical name for God – 'He who is', or, in the Latin translation, *Qui est*. In course of time, names even more distant from the religious tradition were used, for instance, 'self-subsistent being' and 'necessary being'. Whereas the biblical tradition had been content to apply to God such adjectives as 'righteous', 'merciful', 'faithful' and the like, new semi-technical expressions were introduced, such as 'omnipotent', 'immutable', 'impassible' and many others. In order that God might not be brought too closely into contact with the world, Philo developed the idea of the Logos as the intermediary between God and the creation, and, of course, this idea came to play a major part in Christian theology. So, for instance, it was not God himself who had spoken to Moses at the bush, but the Logos. Philo and his imitators also developed the method of allegorical interpretation as a way of handling stories in which God was involved in affairs within the world. Again, whereas the biblical tradition (like other religious traditions) simply assumes the reality of God, philosophical theism began to search for arguments that would prove the existence of God.

It is not easy to see how the religious and philosophical forms of theism can be integrated. As I mentioned, they have in fact often been in tension with each other. Pascal, Kierkegaard and Barth are obvious examples of very acute men who regarded philosophical theism with very profound suspicion. The God of such theism, whether we call him 'unmoved mover' or 'supreme intelligence' or something else, seems a pale abstraction alongside the God of Abraham, Isaac and Jacob. Attempts to prove the divine existence may only sow doubts, rather than providing certitude. The whole enterprise may seem to have become a theoretical matter and to be cut off from the practical business of living – an artificial separation of which we were inclined to think that Kant was guilty in his treatment of religion.

Yet there is something to be said on the other side, too. There are minds which cannot rest unless they have inquired, as far as their powers allow, into the very foundations of belief. They would consider it irresponsible not to conduct such an inquiry. I do not think it is fair, either, to say that such persons end up by putting an abstraction in place of the living God. The American philosopher Paul Weiss writes: 'Behind the Gods of the various religions is an ultimate, inescapable being which is irreducibly real and effective here and now, no matter what men may think or say or do. This is not a mere being, a "God beyond God", but God himself, freed from the particulars added by particular religions, but not freed from an involvement with man and other realities.'[8] If one reads the book from which this quotation is taken, I think it is perfectly clear that the author has not turned some abstraction of thought into a God. He has a genuine religious relation to God, but his intellectual integrity demands that his concept of God must be clarified and criticized as far as possible.

I have to stress the words, 'as far as possible'. Philosophical theism does not in most cases claim that we can arrive at a comprehensive concept of God. Indeed, most of the thinkers who have been mentioned in the preceding paragraphs took the view that God transcends our understanding. We can apprehend him up to a point, we can make some affirmations about him, we can even say (and we shall have to ask how this is possible) that God *must* be such and such, if he is a reality at all.

An interesting question arises at this point. What is the relation of concepts to images in talking about God? The philosopher who tries to express belief in God as metaphysical theism would seem to have given concepts priority over images. This was certainly the case with Hegel, whom we shall be considering at a later stage. Hegel placed absolute philosophy above absolute religion, precisely on the grounds that the former deals in concepts, the latter in images. Hegel, however, was a panlogist, that is to say, he believed in the competence of reason to understand everything, even God. But if, like some of Hegel's own followers, including the English philosopher F. H. Bradley, we make a more modest claim for reason and acknowledge that the ultimate reality is beyond the grasp of reason, then we may wish to answer the question about concepts and images rather differently. If God is finally a mystery, our conceptual grasp of him will take us only part of the way. Is it not the virtue of an image that, although it lacks the precision of a concept, it has a certain creative and imaginative power which allows it to point beyond the strictly knowable, stretching both our language and our minds? In religious discourse, we shall never be able to dispense with images, symbols and metaphors, perhaps not even with myth and story. These are the primary modes of expression of the religious consciousness, bringing to words the obscure knowledge that is already there and at the same time pointing beyond what the words are able to express. Yet as responsible rational beings, we have to guard against becoming lost in a world of luxuriant fantasy, and this means that we have to ask critical questions about the meaning of the images and symbols, to clarify them conceptually and judge their truth. Perhaps there will always be a tension between images of God and concepts of God, between religious or biblical or revealed theology and philosophical or natural theology, and perhaps different types of mind will always lean towards the one side or the other, but we would make a mistake if we tried to eliminate either one of them. They belong dialectically together within theological reflection on God.

The reason for this becomes apparent if we think back for a moment to those dictionary definitions of God from which we took our departure. They spoke of God in both existential and ontological terms, that is to say, as the reality that is known primarily in the religious consciousness and as the reality that is posited by the intellect as the ground of all that is. If we remind ourselves of one example, the *Oxford English Dictionary* told us that God is 'the one object of supreme adoration, the creator and ruler of the universe'. In the history of religious thought, we find that often God has been defined in only one of these two ways. Luther is strongly existential: 'That to which your heart clings and entrusts itself is, I say, really your God.'[9] In this he has been followed by many Lutheran theologians, including Ritschl in the nineteenth century and Bultmann in the twentieth. But this way of thinking of God is far too subjective. God may very well end up as just an ideal in the mind of the believer. Luther himself was aware that his definition of God would apply equally well to an idol. How then does one distinguish God from idols or from subjective ideals? It is at this point that we need an ontological definition which will claim for God a reality beyond either my mind or the mind of the believing community, indeed, an ultimate reality. And we may note that although the existential definition of God arises from the religious consciousness, that consciousness itself refers its awareness of God to a reality beyond itself. But it is to theologians like Thomas Aquinas who names God 'He who is',[10] or Anselm, who defines him as 'Something than which no greater can be thought,'[11] that we must turn for a concept of God which affirms primarily his ontological reality, his objective being as distinct from the subjective being which God undoubtedly has within the religious consciousness. But having said that, we now have to make the opposite correction to the one which we deemed appropriate in the case of Luther. There we had to guard against a subjectivizing of God; now we have to guard against severing his association with the religious consciousness and turning him into a merely metaphysical entity.

As our exploration of the concept of God proceeds, I think it is becoming increasingly clear that there is a dialectic built into the very idea of God. Whatever we say about him, it seems we are bound to correct it by saying something of opposite tendency. This may be traceable to the double meaning that is always present in the word 'God' – highest value, from the point of view of the religious consciousness, highest reality from the point of view of the intellect. Yet the division is not so neat as this might suggest. The religious consciousness demands reality as well as value; the intellect, unless it has been forcibly detached from the entire range of personal existence, is never value-free.

We have, I think, an inherent tendency to see things in a one-sided way, and perhaps we are especially prone to this error when we try to think of God. The so-called 'swing of the pendulum' in theology is usually to be explained in terms of one one-sided idea succeeding another that had been equally one-sided and whose very one-sidedness carried within it the seed of its dissolution. Yet the two sides belong together, and each needs the other. We have just been touching on the dialectic of subjective and objective elements in the conception of God. Obviously, however, there are many more oppositions – transcendence and immanence, impassibility and passibility, eternity and temporality, to mention only a few – and in each case we have to resist the temptation to be onesided and try rather to give due weight to each side of the opposition. I do not think, however, that one has to give *equal* weight to each side, for one may be more fundamental than the other. If we accept the traditional analysis of thesis, antithesis and synthesis as a guide to the structure of dialectic, one may say that the thesis is fundamental, and though it needs to be qualified by the antithesis, the final synthesis will be closer to the original thesis than to the antithesis.

Dialectic requires us to say that if God is transcendent, he must also be immanent; if he is impassible, he must also be passible; and so on. What is the meaning of this 'must'? How can we say that God 'must' be this or that? I think we are simply saying that if God-language is appropriate, then certain conditions must be satisfied. These conditions correspond to the requirements of the religious consciousness and of the intellect. Is the idea of God, then, *a priori*? In a sense, I think it is. There is a quest for God in the human being, and we have seen at an earlier stage how this issues in both a sense of affinity with the environing reality and a sense of a unity which makes that reality more than just a collection of contingent items. On the other hand, it is no doubt the broadening and deepening of experience which supply an ever richer content to the concept of God, while at the same time making us aware of that vast hidden area of Godhood that has not yet been opened to thought and experience.

Does God exist? The fact that the religious consciousness and the intellect together frame a conception of God is in itself no guarantee of his reality. He might be, in the Kantian phrase, no more than a *focus imaginarius* or a regulative idea. The ontological proof for the existence of God is open to too many objections for anyone to invoke it by itself. On the other hand, the fact that human beings do seem to have an *a priori* idea of God and a predisposition to believe in him has at least some significance.

It has been said that the correct procedure for natural theology would be first of all to form a coherent concept of God and then produce evidence that there is a reality corresponding to it. This is much too naive a suggestion. It might be the right way of settling the question about the existence of some object within the world, but does not touch the complexities of the question of God. If someone asks whether unicorns exist, the procedure would work quite well. One would first of all consult zoologists, and ask whether a unicorn is a conceivable form of life. It might well turn out that there is nothing biologically impossible about a unicorn. Then one would institute a search for an actual specimen. But the case of God is clearly very different. Even to speak of the 'existence' of God can be very misleading, for if he can be said to 'exist' at all, the mode of existence is quite different from that of any finite being. To say that unicorns exist means that they can be found within the world. God, by definition, is not an item within the world, so he does not exist in that sense. Incidentally, the world itself does not exist in that sense – the world is not an item discoverable within the world. It is an *a priori* idea implicit in our recognition of any object. In fact, the logic of the concepts 'God' and 'world' is very similar. Both are inclusive concepts for quite unique realities. The question of the relation between God and the world and the question whether the word 'God' means anything more than the word 'world' (the question of pantheism) will have to be discussed later.

We cannot discuss the question of the reality of God by asking whether there exists an entity corresponding to the concept. The method must rather be as follows. The concept of God is an interpretative concept, meant to give us a way of understanding and relating to reality as a whole. There are other possibilities, of which the most obvious is atheism, but although theism and atheism are the extreme opposing interpretations, there are other possibilities between them. We can compare these different interpretations, and although we are not likely to get beyond probability, we ought to be able to judge which interpretation is most coherent and best accords with experience.

III

A Critique of Classical Theism

I have several times referred in mildly critical terms to what I have called 'traditional' theism. Though I have committed myself to the position that natural theology is possible and significant, I have also indicated that the concept of God at which a contemporary natural theology might arrive would be different in some respects from the one which was taught by traditional theism, and that, in particular, it would be more dialectical. It is now time to define more sharply what is meant by 'traditional' theism and then to make explicit those criticisms of it which seem to call for quite a radical rethinking of the concept of God.

First, let me say that the expression 'traditional theism' is itself too vague and general. It was sufficiently clear to indicate what I had in mind when I used it on earlier occasions, but it would not be sufficiently clear to be made the object of detailed criticism. When one sets out to criticize a position, whether it is theism or anything else, there is a great temptation to direct one's criticisms against some generalized form of the theory which may in fact be a mere caricature or straw man, set up precisely for the purpose of criticism. 'Traditional theism' includes not just the theistic formulations of great philosophers and theologians of the past, but a vast penumbra of popular beliefs about God, many of them wide open to criticism – indeed, many of them already criticized by responsible philosophers and theologians who were themselves theists. Some highly influential atheists have in fact been guilty of directing their shafts against aberrant forms of belief in God and have produced the impression of bringing all belief in God into disrepute, though in fact they have failed to touch the strongest forms. A good example would be Freud's contention that belief in God is a form of neurosis. Every pastor knows that there is a great deal of neurotic religion around;

he would be as critical of it as Freud, but his criticism would not lead him to atheism but to what he would consider a healthy theism, of which the neurotic form of belief would be a degenerate misrepresentation. For the purposes of the following criticism, therefore, I shall tighten up the concept of theism and consider it in its strongest form as expounded by its best representatives, especially Thomas Aquinas. To indicate that it is this strict form of theism that I have in mind, I shall call it 'classical' rather than 'traditional' theism. This expression not only acknowledges the strength and balance of Thomas' theistic teaching but conforms to the usage of writers among whom are both critics and admirers of his work.[1]

But unfortunately, no matter how carefully classical theism is formulated, it still tends to present a distinctly 'monarchical' view of God, that is to say, God as one-sidedly transcendent, separate from and over or above the world. The transcendence and majesty of God are not sufficiently qualified by recognition of his immanence and humility. The intellect demands a more dialectical concept of God, while the religious consciousness, too, seeks a God with whom more affinity can be felt, without diminution of his otherness. The problems that are inherent in the classic statements of theism by Aquinas and others are magnified in the various popular forms of belief in God that are derived from them. On an earlier occasion,[2] I quoted with approval Keith Ward's disavowal, *as a theist*, of the view of God which sees him as 'an inference, an absentee entity, an object apart from the universe'. Yet this distorted understanding of God, which he rightly rejects, is all too easily derived from classical theism, and I shall try now to show that this happens because of defects in the classical formulation itself.

Aquinas begins his discussion of God with the fairly basic question, 'Does God exist?'[3] We have already taken note that this question is misleading. When we talk of something 'existing', we normally mean that it occurs somewhere in space and time or that it belongs to the real world, and it seems clear that God does not 'exist' in that sense. Of course, what Aquinas actually asks is *'an Deus sit'*, 'whether God is', and although this use of the word 'is' has become somewhat archaic in English, this formulation of the question is less misleading than the more natural, 'Does God exist?' It is so because the word 'is' has a richer semantic range than the word 'exists'. We have seen that the most natural interpretation of 'existence' is 'occurrence in a spatio-temporal context', and clearly

God does not 'exist' in that way. There are many ways in which something can *be*, and when we claim that God *is*, we understand that to him belongs a mode of being quite different from the inner-worldly existence of finite things. We could say that God supplies the context for finite existence, but has himself no context. His being may be remotely analogous to the being of finite entities, but it must be altogether more active, original and ultimate. God's being is 'letting-be'; it is being, raised to a higher power, so to speak. This is not clearly expressed by Thomas, although I think it is implicit in his thought. Nevertheless, when he tells us that *Qui est*, 'He who is', is the most appropriate name for God, there is a grave danger of thinking that God is another being or entity in addition to those that we meet in the world, or in addition to the world itself, if it can be considered an entity. As I shall say later, Thomas at this point is less subtle than Eriugena, who speaks of God as *Qui plus quam esse est*, 'He who is more than being'.[4] Eriugena is more subtle because he is more dialectical and expresses more clearly than Thomas that if one says that 'God is' or 'God exists', one must also say that 'God is not' or 'God does not exist', for the mode of being that belongs to God is not what we usually mean by 'being', so that Eriugena has to resort to the paradoxical expression, *plus quam esse*, 'more than being'. What sense we can make of such tortured language is a question that we defer for the present.

Unfortunately, in the famous five ways by which Thomas seeks to answer the question whether God exists, the ambiguity steadily deepens. In the first of the five ways, it is said that we plainly see processes of change going on in the world; anything that is changing must be changed by something else; as we trace this process back, we arrive eventually at a 'first cause of change, not itself being changed by anything' (*aliquod primum movens quod a nullo movetur*).[5] This, we are told, is what everybody understands by 'God'. The second way is similar, and is based on the nature of causation. Everything, we see, has a cause, and if we trace back any series of causes, we shall come to the point where it begins. 'One is therefore forced to suppose some first cause, to which everyone gives the name 'God'.[6] The third way begins from the notion of contingent being. The things that we see in the world might not exist. But if everything were merely contingent, then, it is argued, there would be nothing at all. So we are led to conclude that there is something which must be, a necessary being which has the cause of its being in itself. The fourth way notes the fact of gradation in the world.

Whatever quality we imagine, we can think of a higher degree of that quality, and the higher the degree, the nearer it approaches the superlative. 'Something therefore is the truest and best and most noble of things, and hence the most fully in being (*maxime ens*).'[7] This is the source of the good qualities of everything else, and is again identified with God. The last argument is from the order and design of nature. 'Everything in nature is directed to its goal by someone with understanding (*aliquis intelligens*) and this we call "God".'[8]

It is not my intention to discuss the validity of these arguments, but simply to draw attention to two points which are relevant to my critique of classical theism. The first point is that in all the arguments, except perhaps the fifth one, God is considered as one other item among the things that exist. In the first, he is a mover among the things that are in motion; in the second the first cause in the series of causes and effects; in the third the one necessary being among all the contingent beings; in the fourth the summit of a hierarchical universe. Admittedly – and we shall have to come back to this point in a later discussion[9] – each of the descriptions of God is fundamentally qualified: he is *unmoved* mover, *first* cause, *necessary* being, the superlative which is also the *source* of qualities in other things. It could be argued, I think with justification, that in each case the adjective introduces such a radical qualification that God is removed by it from the series of items among which he appears. But this remains unclear and is at best only implicit. The impression conveyed is that everything that exists may be traced back to something else that exists, to one being among other beings, though admittedly the being which *is* in an eminent sense (*maxime ens*). The second point draws attention to the use of the expression 'what everybody understands by "God" ' or equivalent expressions. It reminds me of what was said earlier to the effect that 'God' is a word of our language, and that a possible approach to the problem of God-talk is to look up the dictionary to ascertain the usage of educated people. But I did say that such a procedure would be helpful only if the lexicographer happened to be a good theologian![10]

Popular ways of understanding the word 'God' may already conceal in themselves popular misunderstandings from which God-talk needs to be purified. A commentator claims that in the first four ways, Thomas thinks of God in terms of ultimate causality, and in the fifth way as an overruling providence. He questions whether in fact the being at whom Thomas arrives would be recognized by the ordinary man as God.[11] Certainly the word here seems to have been abstracted from the context of prayer and worship, which is its immediate home. Yet, as soon as there is any reflection about God, people seem to arrive speedily at the idea that he is the efficient cause of the universe and also its intelligent ruler. We may recall that the definition quoted earlier from the *Oxford English Dictionary* was 'the creator and ruler of the universe', though these words were rightly put in apposition to a prior description in specifically religious terms, 'the one object of supreme adoration'.[12] The desire of Thomas to relate the God of the five ways to 'what everybody understands by "God" ' must make us question whether we were justified in distinguishing 'classical' theism from 'traditional' and supposedly more popular theism. The former is admittedly more refined and sophisticated, but does it really overcome the weaknesses of the popular version? Is not the way already open to that view of God criticized by Keith Ward – God as 'an inference, an absentee entity, an object apart from the universe'? Unhappily, these suspicions become confirmed as we work through the various doctrines which together make up classical theism. These simply amplify the monarchical idea of God as creator and ruler of the universe, first cause and providence.

We turn now to the doctrine of creation. According to the teachings of classical theism, God created the world out of nothing by a free act of his sovereign will. Creation is an act without any parallel among finite beings, though indeed we sometimes speak of the 'creativity' of the artist. The nearest analogy to creation is making, but of course a human being who makes anything must have some material out of which to make it. A carpenter can make a table only if he has wood on which to work. So at a very important point the parallel between creating and making breaks down, for the divine creator brings into being the very material out of which he forms the world. The world owes its origin and its continuing existence solely to the divine will. This is often held to differentiate the Judaeo-Christian doctrine of creation from the Platonic view in which the creator works on a pre-existent matter. However, since this matter was entirely formless and without any determinate characteristics, it might be hard to say how it differed from nothing at all. The theistic understanding of creation can be more clearly distinguished from the neo-Platonist view that the world is an emanation from God. The analogy corresponding to emanation is not making but flowing forth, and that which flows forth from its origin obviously maintains a closer relation to that origin. It participates in the origin, and the origin participates in it, and when we are thinking of the relation of God to the world, this clearly demands a strong doctrine of immanence. As we shall see, emanationism does not necessarily lead to pantheism, but it does imply that in some sense God is in the world and the world is in God. Creation out of nothing, as understood by classical theism, places the world outside of God. The creation is external to the creator, and it has its own reality and even a measure of independence, though these are derivative and limited. But this sharp separation of God and the world already contains within itself the possibility of such distorted developments as deism and dualism. Deism is in fact a dualism, for it has widened the gap between creator and creation to the infinite distance between an absentee God unconcerned about his creation and an entirely autonomous and self-regulating universe to which God has no access. Of course, deism is a sorry departure and deterioration from classical theism, just as much as is pantheism in the opposite direction, but any doctrine which stresses the total otherness of the creator, the complete externality of the creation, and the infinite difference between them has a concealed tendency towards deism or even, eventually, atheism.

I do not think I have been guilty of any caricature in this presentation of the view of creation found in classical theism, and I think the points can be all found in Aquinas.[13] He does in fact use the word *emanatio* in the title of the *quaestio* which relates to creation: *de modo emanationis rerum a primo principio*, but the word is not used here in its neo-Platonist sense, but in a very general way. We might translate: 'Of the Manner in which Things Take their Rise from the First Principle.' There is no question that the teaching which follows is thoroughly creationist. It is asserted that creation is out of nothing, that everything that exists has been created by God, he himself being the only uncreated being. Furthermore, it is held that the world has not always existed, but was brought into being by a free act of the divine will and that there was no need for God to create. Thomas' words are worth quoting, though I shall abridge them slightly: 'Nothing apart from God has been from all eternity. We have shown that God's will is the cause of things. So then the necessity of their being is that of God's willing them. Next it has been established that there is no need for God to will anything but himself. Hence there is no necessity for God to will an everlasting world. Rather, the world exists just so long as God wills it to, since its existence depends on his will as on its cause.'[14]

This is a strong statement of what I call the 'monarchical' view of God. With all respect to the Angelic Doctor, it does seem to me that his words convey a sense of arbitrariness, as if God were not only a monarch but a somewhat capricious one. 'There was no need for God to will anything but himself . . . there is no necessity for God to will a world . . . the world exists just so long as God wills it to.' Of course, there could be no talk of God finding it *necessary* to do anything. That would imply that there is some force that can compel God to do things, and if there were, he would not be God. Whether one can properly talk of either necessity or freedom in respect of God is doubtful. In any case, however, freedom has nothing to do with randomness or arbitrariness. Freedom is structured and purposeful, and to be free is to be able to move towards the goals that one has chosen for oneself. To be free is not to be able to act otherwise or to refrain from acting at all. The truly free person would not dream of acting otherwise than his own nature has determined. Freedom has nothing to do with unpredictability – that is caprice, and is typical not of the free person whose character is rational and stable, but of the unfree person who is blown off course by impulse and passing desires. If God is a God of love, then he would not do anything other than create. It would be a misuse of language to say that it is necessary for him to create. He freely creates because in so doing he is following his own nature, which is loving and giving. There is nothing seriously wrong in saying God 'freely' creates, provided that the word 'freely' is understood in the sense explained, and has been purged of every hint of arbitrariness and of the idea that in order to be free, one would have to claim, 'I could have acted otherwise'.

Emanationism does think of the world as the overflowing of the divine love and generosity, and that God really does put himself into his world and has a stake in it. The creationism which we have just been considering traces the origin of the world not to love but to will. The creation is a product of the will. It has been brought into being and at any time it may go out of being. It is external to its maker; it does not enhance his being, nor would its disappearance diminish his being. I think there is some justice in the complaint of Lynn White that the biblical doctrine that the created order is a product of divine will external to God and, as has sometimes been said, 'dedivinized', has been a factor encouraging the reckless exploitation of nature, for nature is surely devalued if it is only a product of the will of God and intended for subjection by the will of man.[15]

I should perhaps say, to guard against misunderstanding, that I am not advocating emanationism as a rival view to the biblical doctrine of creation. Creation itself is a mystery to which, as I have said, we have no exact parallels in human activity. We have two analogies that have been used in theological and philosophical thought – the analogy of 'making' and the analogy of 'emanation'. All I am asking is that we do not think of these as mutually excluding one another. To take any one of them by itself and to develop it in a one-sided way leads into distortion, and I have tried to show this in the case of 'making' and the classical theistic account of creation. But we would do no better with emanation on its own. What we need is a dialectic embracing both 'making' and 'emanation', each of these analogies complementing and, if need be, correcting the other. I doubt if there is any other way by which one may glimpse something of the meaning of the mystery of creation.

We pass on from creation to the question of God's action in the world. If indeed God is first cause, so that everything flows from him, it might be supposed that all that happens is the action of God, and no doubt, in an ultimate sense, this is the case. But we have seen that in classical theism (as opposed for instance, to various forms of monism) the created world has a measure of independence, and is certainly not illusory. On the other hand, classical theism is different also from deism, for although God creates the world 'in the beginning', he does not just leave it to its own devices, but continues to govern it in his providence. His government, however, must be such that he leaves to the world a certain openness and autonomy appropriate to the measure of reality and independence which it possesses. Classical theists have allowed for this relative independence of the world by positing what they call 'secondary' causes as well as the first cause. These secondary causes (*causae secundae*) are the ordinary agencies that we see at work around us. Heat is such a cause when it brings about the melting of wax, and human volitions would also count among secondary causes.

Some classical theists (Calvin is the example that comes to mind) sometimes came close to asserting that every single event that occurs in the world is directly caused by the express command of God, though even Calvin, whether consistently or not, did not believe that he was abolishing the role of secondary causes. Thomas, for his part, was quite definite that events in the creation normally result from the agency of secondary causes. In reply to the claim that God's action alone is sufficient to account for the events that go on in the world, he writes: 'God does act sufficiently within things as the first agent cause, but that does not imply that the activity of secondary causes is superfluous.'[16] Even material things, he believed, have some causal properties, and there would have been no point in creating them if they had not had some manner of operating.

So the universe goes along for the most part according to the laws of nature, that order of secondary causes which is inherent in the world, though ultimately originating from the first cause of all, namely, God. But when the question is asked whether God has the power to do anything outside the order inherent in nature, Aquinas, and with him the classical theistic tradition in general, returns an affirmative answer. God, as sovereign ruler, will occasionally intervene by a supernatural act to overrule the ordinary processes of the universe in order to attain some desired end. Such an act is usually called a 'miracle', that is to say, an event which causes those who witness it to wonder (*mirari*).

This brings us to one of the most serious difficulties that a modern person is likely to have with classical theism. The idea of a God, external to and transcendent of the universe but nevertheless intervening in it from time to time to achieve some particular purpose, has become quite foreign to most of us. The whole of modern science is built on the assumption that there are laws of nature universally operating, and nowadays we would think of human history too as the product of inner-worldly (though not mechanical) agencies. In addition, from a religious point of view, we might question whether a *deus ex machina* role has a place in any worthy conception of God. Already in the nineteenth century, the difficulty of admitting direct divine agency in the world was forthrightly expressed by David Friedrich Strauss as follows:

> A main element in all religious records is sacred history; a history of events in which the divine enters, without intermediation, into the human; the ideal thus assuming an immediate embodiment. But as the progress of mental cultivation mainly consists in the gradual recognition of a chain of causes and effects connecting natural phenomena with each other; so the mind in its development becomes increasingly conscious of those mediate links

which are indispensable to the realization of the ideal; and hence the discrepancy between the modern culture and the ancient records becomes so apparent that the immediate intervention of the divine in human affairs loses its probability.[17]

Strauss summed it up in the dilemma: 'The divine cannot so have happened; or, that which has so happened cannot have been divine.'[18]

Of course, the human mind does not want to give up entirely the belief that God acts in the world. Just as Thomas maintained that if things have no causal efficacy, there would have been no point in creating them, so it may be said with even more force that if God has no power to act, there would be no point in believing in him. The reluctance to give up belief in direct divine intervention may be illustrated from the fact that Newton, who had amply shown in principle that the solar system can be explained as a self-regulating physical system without introducing metaphysical agencies, still wished to maintain that certain irregularities in the system need to be corrected from time to time by the direct action of God.[19] But if we are to find a meaning for divine action in the world, I think it must be on other lines than the view of classical theism, that is to say, belief in a God external to the world, but nevertheless able to intervene in its affairs. To hold such a belief, and at the same time to assent to the basic assumptions of the scientist, does not seem to me to be logically possible. Some people do want to do both, just as Newton wanted to in his day. But it imposes too great a strain on credulity. Bultmann was doing little more than restating what Strauss had said more than a century before him when, in his plea for demythologizing, he declared that 'it is impossible to use electric light and the radio and to avail ourselves of modern medical and surgical discoveries', and at the same time to believe in divine interventions of the kind described in the New Testament and other ancient religious writings reflecting a mythological mentality.[20] When confronted by a very conservative colleague who did want to go on believing in supernatural interventions, Bultmann is reported to have asked him: 'If you were thrown into prison in eastern Europe for your Christian faith, would you really expect an angel to come and let you out?'

Much of the difficulty, I believe, is due to the one-sidedness of classical theism, especially its one-sided stress on the transcendence of God. If we could understand the world-process as more closely integrated into the being of God, then it might be possible to reconceive the belief that God acts in the world. But this would be only part of a more general reconception of theism in dialectical terms, and since this is the main enterprise that lies before us, we shall have to delay the fuller discussion of God's action in the world until we have made further progress with the main question.

But there is one other point that may be noted at this stage. In classical theism, God acts on the world, but the world does not act on God. He affects the world, but is not affected by it. This, of course, is consistent with that view of creation in which it is held that God is not in any way increased by the world, nor would he be diminished by the world's disappearance. This again is, of course, a thoroughly one-sided and undialectical view of the relation between God and world. Is the relation quite so asymmetrical as it is here represented to be? Or are there elements of symmetry and reciprocity in the relation of God and the world? If we cannot allow for some reciprocity, then we seem to have taken a further step along the road that leads to a complete devaluation of the cosmos, even to a kind of acosmism, where, strangely enough, transcendent theism would come out at the same place as certain forms of monism. Only the invisible God or spiritual being is real; all else is illusion. Is that not the true position of those theologians of transcendence who expressed their teaching in the twofold formula:

The world minus God = 0; God minus the world = God? Certainly, one could not quarrel with the first of these two statements. Without that creative, dynamic source, that fundamental letting-be which we call 'God', the world would not exist. But the second statement must surely be challenged. Does the world make no difference to God? Would he be unaffected by the world's going out of existence? If so, what was the point of creation at all? Or is there no point to it? Was it just part of the divine sport, a capricious act with no further significance? If so, is there any difference between theism and atheism, for a capricious act of God would seem no different in quality from what nineteenth-century material-ists used to call a 'chance collocation of atoms'.

These reflections lead to further criticisms of classical theism. Its upholders used a whole battery of words to express the basic attributes of God, but most of the words so employed were very one-sided indeed. They contributed to strengthen that strongly monarchical idea of God which we have already found occasion to criticize. The kind of words I have in mind are 'impassible', 'immutable', 'eternal', 'perfect'. There are others, but it may be enough to discuss the four mentioned. It should be remembered, too, that I am not denying that God is any of these things, but only that they should not be applied in a one-sided way but dialectically. If we apply any one of these ideas to God, we have to correct the picture by recognizing that an opposite attribute is also applicable.

Let us begin with the idea of the divine impassibility. We have already touched on this idea in our discussion of divine action in the world. The traditional belief is that God is active but not passive, that he affects the world but is not affected by it. But what kind of God would that be? A God without *pathos*, an apathetic God, which is indeed a literal translation of the expression which some of the Greek fathers used about God. Such a God could not be a God of love, for to love is to be vulnerable and to lay oneself open to suffering. If God is supremely love, must he not also be supremely touched by suffering, grieved by the countless pains of all the creatures whom he loves? Indeed, could we rightly apply the name 'God' if God were totally untouched by suffering? A God of sheer power would hardly command our worship. Of course, a God who merely suffered and shared the unhappiness of his creatures would not deserve the name of 'God' either. Paradoxically, any God who can be adored *as God* would have to be one who is both afflicted in the afflictions of his creatures, and yet one who can rise above the affliction. The right attitude to a God who could only share our suffering would be, as Eric Mascall wittily said, 'not one of adoration so much as of sympathy'.[21] God, we may believe, does suffer, yet because he is God, no suffering overwhelms him but is absorbed and transformed in the divine being. This is the truth in the doctrine of divine impassibility, dialectically understood.

Let us consider next the ideas of 'eternity' and 'perfection'. Stated in a one-sided way, as they generally are in classical theism, these ideas suggest a static God outside time totally self-contained with all perfections in himself. To call such a picture in question does not mean that one rushes to the opposite extreme and begins to talk of an evolving or emerging God who will only attain perfection – indeed, we might say, who will only become God – in some distant consummation of history. It is rather to say that if God is truly involved in his creation, as we have argued, then in some respects he must be involved in time and history, even if in others he is above time. In our own experience, we have an analogy, since we know what it is to live in time, but also what it is to transcend mere successiveness. Furthermore, if the creation is really significant to God, will not the bringing of the creation to its highest level increase God's bliss or happiness, if we may so speak, and so his perfection? For perfection is not necessarily a static idea. What is perfect at one point or in one set of circumstances may be surpassed in a new and wider perfection. The related idea of 'immutability' need not mean a frozen changelessness, but rather that utter constancy with which God pursues his end, for himself and for his creation.

One last point in classical theism has to be questioned. God has been represented as personal, even to the point of anthropomorphism. This is entirely appropriate, provided once more that one does not present it in an exclusively one-sided way. Of all the modes of creaturely existence, personality is the highest and so the fittest to serve as an analogy of divine being. Also, we have seen that the very beginnings of religion are possibly to be found in a sense of affinity between the human being and the environing reality. Yet personality cannot exhaust the mystery of the divine being which stretches away into the region of the incomprehensible. No merely impersonal force could merit to be called 'God', but perhaps he is best called 'suprapersonal', and this is obscured in much classical theism, which speaks of him in exclusively personal terms. But at this point we can pay our tribute to Aquinas. If we have criticized some aspects of his theistic teaching, we have to acknowledge that he was fully sensitive to the ultimate incomprehensibility of deity. 'It is impossible,' he writes, 'that any created mind should see the essence of God by its own natural powers.'[22]

IV

Alternatives to Classical Theism

We have examined classical theism with particular attention to the formulation it received from its most celebrated advocate, and we have found it to be problematical at several points. Our findings receive something like an empirical confirmation from the fact that so many people in recent times have apparently turned away from the God who was for many centuries worshipped in the Western world. The defection may appear to be greater than it actually is. Vast numbers of people have ceased to worship God or to give any visible manifestation of a belief in God. Nevertheless, opinion polls regularly inform us that a majority in the West still claim to believe in God. No doubt if one were to inquire into this widespread belief, it would turn out to be very vague, and probably only a minority would define God in terms which we could recognize as characteristic of classical theism. But this penumbra of ill-defined belief is not to be ignored. In an earlier volume, I tried to show that the very existence and nature of the human race is evidence for the reality of God, and I even developed an anthropological argument for God.[1] So although the conception of God in classical theism is at some points questionable, this certainly does not mean the end of God. There may be other and better ways of conceiving God, which is also to say that there may be other and better forms of theism than the classical one. I say this deliberately, because classical theists are often inclined to monopolize the term 'theism', and to deny that those who have departed from the classic formulations are really theists at all. For instance, not only Tillich but even Whitehead have been branded as 'atheists'. This seems to be quite ridiculous. These men, let us agree, were not classical theists, and possibly their ideas of God are theoretically defective at various points. But it was certainly their intention to expound a doctrine of God, and their

formulations were backed in each case by genuine religious sentiment. An interpreter has a duty to be as sympathetic as possible in
his interpretation, and no one with a shred of sympathy would call
either Tillich or Whitehead an atheist.

An opposite error is to be seen in those theologians (Tillich,
Rahner and John Baillie are examples) who have claimed that there
are no true atheists and that wherever we see a person seriously
responding to the claim of moral values, there is at bottom in that
person a tacit faith in God; he is an 'anonymous Christian', or
however it may be expressed. In several earlier writings, I have
attacked this arrogant pretension of the theologians.[2] One has to
accept at its face value the atheist's disavowal of God, which may
have come only after painful conscientious wrestling with the
problems of belief and unbelief. The atheist claims *as an atheist* to
have values, and though one may question whether these are
securely founded, it is wrong to question the sincerity of his
profession or to argue that if only he understood himself as well as
the theologian understands him, he would see that he is a secret
believer.

Admittedly, in this area of belief or disbelief in God, the complexities and variations are so great that one cannot be sure where the
boundaries lie between classical theism and other forms, or between
theism and pantheism, or between pantheism and atheism. Some
cases are especially ambiguous. Hegel is a case in point. To many
in the nineteenth century, he seemed to be the great defender of
God and religion. To others, he was a pantheist, while still others
have taken him to be an atheist. Hegel considered himself to be a
theist, a Christian and even a Lutheran! At least, we must do him
the courtesy of beginning from the assumption that a man of such
profound and subtle intellect was not mistaken about his own
beliefs.

But with these cautionary remarks on interpretation, we must
turn to the main problem of the present chapter. What are the
alternatives to classical theism? I have said that the most we can
hope from natural theology is to be able to compare some of the
fundamental options in the question of God, and decide which is
most coherent and in accordance with our experience.[3] I have
argued that classical theism does not quite measure up to the
requirements. Where then do we look?

It might seem that atheism is the most obvious alternative to
theism, and no doubt many people in the world today would claim

to be atheists, or, at least, agnostics, and agnosticism is a practical atheism, since the agnostic understands himself and his world as if there were no God. Atheism has a long history. There were atheists in the ancient world, not only in Greece but also in India and China. Yet here we come to a difficulty. Atheism is so complex and variable a phenomenon that it is hard to know whether some of these ancient atheists would qualify as atheists in the modern world. In the early centuries of the church, for instance, Christians were sometimes accused of atheism because they did not recognize the pagan deities, but they certainly believed in God and would never be reckoned atheists today. Again, it has often been said that primitive Buddhism was atheistic, but this has been challenged by some scholars. John Bowker declares: 'It is a fundamental mistake to attempt to "explain away" theism in Buddhism as though it is peripheral to the Buddha's insight or intention.'[4] I cannot go into the details of his argument, but his view is that there are 'arguments in the Buddhist canon against false opinions about the gods, but not arguments against the gods as such'.[5] Obviously, much depends on what is to count as 'God' or 'theism'. Bowker, however, is drawing attention to what may be accepted even by the theist as an abiding merit of atheism or quasi-atheism, namely, it criticizes false opinions of the gods. False opinions have certainly abounded in the history of religions, and the spur of atheism has served, even if unintentionally, to purify and deepen theistic beliefs.

Although atheism is ancient, it is not as ancient as belief in the divine. As the negative form of the word indicates, atheism is a secondary phenomenon which arose as a critique or denial of prevailing religious beliefs. But in the modern world, atheism has taken on a more positive aspect. For many centuries, atheists were a minority and even a very small minority. Today, atheism, either explicitly or implicitly, is very widespread in human society. Even where it is not engaged in any overt polemic against religious belief, atheism may be present as an attitude to life and to the world. Those who adopt such an attitude see no need to bring God into the picture, and may even think that the idea of God is harmful to human welfare. This modern, positive kind of atheism is often called 'humanism', in one of the several senses of that word. The atheistic humanist considers himself to be committed to the pursuit of human welfare, but he also believes that there are no 'super-human' or 'transhuman' realities and that man must pursue his destiny solely in his own wisdom and with his own resources.

This modern atheism involves deeply intertwined strands, some theoretical, some emotional and some moral. It is this kind of atheism which presents itself to contemporary society as the major rival to theism, whether classical theism or some other variety of theism.

Let us consider first the theoretical strands. We have noted that modern science seeks to explain phenomena in terms of other phenomena within the world, and excludes any supernatural agency. This methodological atheism tends to transform itself into an ontological atheism. It is not so much that God is explicitly denied as that he has been made redundant. He is no longer needed as a principle of explanation. We took note that even as late as Newton, divine intervention was still invoked because certain irregularities in the solar system could not be fully explained in physical terms. But these lacunae in the texture of the physical universe have been more and more filled up, and as this has happened, no place is left for the 'God of the gaps', as he has been called. This very expression, however, might indicate that God was not much honoured by being assigned the minor role of occasionally functioning where it was impossible to discover 'secondary causes'. Science has relieved God of many functions once attributed to him by classical theism, but we may think that God is well rid of many of them. In the Anglican Prayer Book, bad weather ruinous to the crops and epidemics of 'any common plague or sickness' are both supposed to be visitations of the divine wrath against a sinful people, and the remedy is prayer and penitence. Nowadays, both the weather and the public health are understood, at least partially, in quite other ways, and any problems which they cause must also be differently handled, suggesting that not only is God otiose but that prayer and penitence are not important either. Thus, in many areas of life where one would once have spoken of God and perhaps have sought his aid, there will be no thought of God at all. The absence of God in these areas may suggest that he is absent in all areas, that, in the famous words of Laplace, 'we have no need of that hypothesis', and so what begins as a methodological principle which is proper in the sphere of the investigation of natural phenomena is inflated into metaphysical atheism.

The theist might reply that although God is not needed to explain any particular phenomenon or group of phenomena within the world, he is needed to explain the world as a whole. This was the point of Leibniz' famous question, 'Why are there beings at all, rather than just nothing?' – a question, incidentally, which we shall have to look at more closely in later parts of the book. But the person who has accepted the methods of modern science as the surest road to reliable knowledge may be also something of a positivist, that is to say, he may be unwilling to entertain any questions which do not clearly lie within the competence of the scientific method to answer. So he may not be impressed by the contention that perhaps God is needed to explain the cosmos as a whole. He may take the line that questions about a creative reality beyond the cosmos are unanswerable. Even if he conceded that there might be a creative reality which we may call 'God' and which is the source of the physical universe, there would still be a question whether such a concession went any length towards satisfying the concern of the theist. Would it not as best yield a kind of deism – there was a reality called 'God' responsible for the creation of the cosmos, but God has not been at all involved in its subsequent history? So does it really matter how it began?

The theist might think that it does matter, for he would at least have wrung from his opponent the admission that the material universe is dependent on a superior reality. It is not self-explanatory. This is a difficult point to establish, but it would seem to be vital in the dispute between theists and atheists. The believer in God holds that the universe needs an explanation beyond itself. The atheist maintains that the universe is itself the ultimate reality.

But I do not think that the physical universe can be accepted as the ultimate or absolute or self-existent being. In the words of J. N. Findlay, 'the world points ineluctably beyond itself; it not only is not, but cannot be, all that there is'.[6] The second part of this sentence may remind us of the third of Aquinas' five ways – the way which leads the mind from an awareness of the contingency of every fact or set of facts within the universe to the conclusion that there must be a reality which is not contingent but necessary and dependent on nothing else for its existence. The atheist might reply that while every fact or set of facts within the world is contingent and might not have been at all, the universe itself is necessary, and it is a logical error to treat the universe as if it were the same kind of entity as the innumerable facts of which it is made up. We may well sympathize with this argument, which is very similar in its main thrust to what I have said about the logic of 'God' and the error of conceiving God as if he were another entity comparable to entities within the world. But if one were to argue that the universe itself is some kind of absolute or ultimate being, one would have to ascribe to it a unity, structure and solidarity which is precisely what the naturalistic or materialistic atheist denies. He regards the world as simply a collection of contingent facts. Can he get away from the conclusion that the sum of these facts is no less contingent than any single one of the facts themselves? Perhaps he will claim that at least the framework of space-time remains when all the facts have been thought away. This might have been a possible line to take in the days of Newtonian physics, when space and time were regarded as a kind of receptacle or container, even a kind of divine matrix. But in an Einsteinian universe we have abandoned that idea of the spatio-temporal container, absolute time and space. Augustine had already seen that time comes into being with the world, for there can be no time that is empty of events. Nowadays, something similar would have to be said about space – there is no space without the physical phenomena disposed in it. The infinite eternal spatio-temporal universe imagined in the nineteenth century is no more than imaginary. Indeed, we now have good evidence for believing that the physical universe, including space and time, came into existence in some primaeval burst of energy some fifteen billion years ago. So far from being the ultimate existent, it seems probable that the universe derives from a reality beyond itself.

The atheist has another move he may make. Abandoning the view that the universe is a mere collection of contingent facts, he may import into it creativity, organism, emergence, even certain 'values' which it seeks to achieve. Nietzsche's will to power is an example of this, and there is something similar in Marxism, especially in some of its more recent varieties, such as Bloch's philosophy of hope. In such cases, pure atheism has been abandoned, and there has been smuggled into the theory a creative power with at least some of the traditional attributes of God. No wonder that Bloch was accused by hard-line Marxists of 'mysticism'! Admittedly, the quasi-God of such theories is not the transcendent God of theism, but an immanent sub-personal force, at most a kind of godward trend in the universe. But nowadays any atheism, when we recognize the enormous complexity and mystery that lie even in a hydrogen atom, is bound to begin much higher up the scale of being than the older atheisms. There is no matter without form, and form is what is characteristic of mind or spirit. So theoretical atheism has fallen into a dilemma and perhaps cannot be stated as a coherent position. The more thoroughly reductionist and materialist, that is, the more truly atheistic it tries to be, the less plausible it is, for, as philosophers from Plotinus[7] to Whitehead[8] have pointed out, inert formless matter cannot evolve into such a universe as we know. (As some contemporary atheists now freely admit, that would need a miracle which even many billions of years would not bring about.) On the other hand, the more atheism imports into matter in the way of form, creativity, direction and so on, the nearer it moves to pantheism and an immanent quasi-God. So theoretical atheism is open to very serious objections.

Let us now turn to those forms of atheism in which emotional factors play a considerable part, though these forms are reinforced by further theoretical considerations, especially of an epistemological nature.

According to Patrick Masterson, 'the atheism of our day consists chiefly in asserting the impossibility of the coexistence of finite and infinite being; it is maintained that the affirmation of God as infinite being necessarily implies the devaluation of finite being, and, in particular, the dehumanizing of man'.[9] I think this is true of the mainline of atheistic philosophy during the past two centuries. The thinkers who obviously exemplify this protest in the name of humanity against an allegedly oppressive God are Feuerbach, Marx, Nietzsche and Sartre. I call this 'emotional' atheism because it arises from feelings of human dignity and commitment to ideals of human freedom and transcendence. But it also has its theoretical aspects. Its theoretical foundation, it has been claimed, is the *cogito ergo sum* of Descartes.[10] That famous argument marks the 'turn to the subject' in the history of European philosophy. The one centre of certainty upon which truth can be built is the human consciousness. It is true that Descartes himself was a theist and invoked God as the guarantee that our perceptions of the physical world are veridical. But the balance had been decisively tipped towards the subjective consciousness. Man had been made the measure of all things, and this has tended to become part of the modern Western outlook. The feeling that human freedom and transcendence are frustrated by the existence of God has some validity if one holds a monarchical conception of God, and so these atheistic objections have some force against classical theism, which did indeed encourage a monarchical view of God, often coupled with a legalistic morality supposed to be based on the commands of God. However, I have tried to show at length in an earlier volume[11] that, rightly understood, God is not the enemy but the encourager of human transcendence and its goal.

But in using the words 'rightly understood', I have in mind a conception of God different from that of the 'monarchical God', and different from that of classical theism. So I do not think that the kind of atheism which professes to speak in the name of human freedom is any more successful than the theoretical atheism whose inadequacies we have already noted. This contention is borne out by Masterton's careful analysis, which shows that the attempt to overcome alienation by abolishing God has resulted not in an advance in human transcendence but in an increased alienation and frustration. The way from Feuerbach to Sartre has given not the slightest support to the atheistic hopes of emancipation.

I come finally to the atheism that is morally motivated, though I should say that once again the motivation is mixed, and that intellectual and emotional considerations are also involved. This is perhaps the oldest atheism of all, the sense of outrage that God or the gods should have contrived a world in which there is so much suffering, injustice and evil of many kinds. Do not all the senseless, negative features of existence tell against the existence of a divine and presumably benevolent creator? This type of atheism has been examined by Stewart Sutherland, who takes as its representative the fictitious character Ivan Karamazov, portrayed by Dostoyevsky in his celebrated novel, *The Brothers Karamazov*.[12] Ivan's point quite simply is that a world which includes as part of its normal process the senseless suffering of children is an enterprise in which he wishes to have no part. He respectfully returns his ticket, as he puts it. In a sense, he is not so much atheistic as anti-theistic, anticipating the position of Albert Camus, who felt that the only proper response to this world is what he called 'metaphysical rebellion'. In both cases, we may note that the God who is indicted is the God of classical theism, the monarchical God whose impassibility is in sharp contrast to the sufferings of the creation. But if one were to visualize a God who is passible and shares in the sufferings of his creatures, then the moral argument for atheism would lose much of its force.

Incidentally, it is in Dostoyevsky's discussion of atheism that we are forced to face the disturbing question whether, if God does not exist, everything is permissible. The ultimate expression of atheism was the philosophy of Nietzsche, in which everything is contingent and relative, and we stand on the verge of nihilism. There is no longer a forward or a backward, an above or a below, a good or evil, except what we determine these shall be. There is no centre of reference, no absolute, and we have to ask ourselves seriously whether the logical working out of atheism must not of necessity lead to nihilism. Of course, many atheists have values, and some of these values may not be very different from the values of religious believers. Again, there are undoubtedly cases where atheists show themselves more faithful in pursuing their values than many of the nominally religious. But if all is contingent and relative, what are the foundations for the atheist's values? One suspects that they are the inherited values of a culture that was shaped by religion, and that in course of time they will grow weaker and may eventually vanish.

I conclude that the case for atheism is much weaker than is often supposed. The more reductionist (or godless) atheism becomes, the less plausible it is. Such attractions as it may have arise only when we contrast it with classical theism, and disappear when we introduce other forms of theism that are immune to the atheistic critique. So if we are looking for an alternative to classical theism, we do not find it in atheism.

What about pantheism? Here is a third possibility, and at first sight it might seem to be more satisfactory than either classical theism or atheism. Pantheism is the view that all things in their unity constitute God, or that God is all things or is in all things. The difficulty of finding a simple formulation indicates that the idea of pantheism is an elusive one and that it is hard to make sense of it. If God is identified with the universe so that 'God' and 'universe' are merely alternative names for a single reality, how does pantheism differ from atheism or how would it escape the objections to atheism already noted? It is indeed true that the best known of modern pantheists, Spinoza, wrote of *deus sive natura*, as if God and nature were interchangeable terms. However, he also held that the one infinite substance, God or nature, is both extended and thinking, so I do not think he could rightly be called an atheist, though that epithet has often been applied to him. An alternative and opposite description, the 'God-intoxicated' man, is more apposite. Pantheism is usually religious, frequently mystical, and therefore it may be said to lean more towards theism than to atheism. If we think of the so-called 'higher pantheism' of the poets, we are led to much the same conclusions. Wordsworth had an intense awareness of the beauty and unity of nature, but his feelings were not directed simply to the physical universe. There was 'more' to the world than its physical being. His sentiments were not only aesthetic and directed to that highest pitch of beauty which we call the sublime and which, in its overwhelmingness, is not far from the holy. His feelings were definitely religious, they had a sense of affinity with the surrounding reality, and we have seen that something like that lies at the heart of religion. No one could have been more sensitive to the beauties of the natural scene than Wordsworth, but it was something more than that that touched him and to which he tried to give expression;

> And I have felt
> A presence that disturbs me with the joy
> Of elevated thoughts; a sense sublime
> Of something far more deeply interfused.

What is this 'something far more deeply interfused'? It is what, for want of a better name, we call 'spirit', a deeper level of reality than the material, though perhaps found only through the mediation of the material. And we may remind ourselves that, according to one witness, 'God is Spirit'.

Pantheism, therefore, is not the simple identification of God and the universe. The physical universe is not, in itself, worshipful. At an earlier stage I noted that even if religion began with the worship of natural phenomena, these phenomena were already regarded as more than natural – indeed, the primitive mind did not have the idea of the *merely* natural. So in pantheism the natural world is not as such identified with God. The world may be mysterious and awe-inspiring, but it is hardly adorable. It becomes divine only when a new dimension of being has been introduced and the world is seen as the manifestation of an indwelling spirit. Ninian Smart has pointed out that the so-called idolater does not 'bow down to wood and stone'.[13] When he does bow down before some physical object of wood or stone, that object is already for him more than wood or stone and has acquired a sacramental status as the dwelling-place of a divine spirit. In pantheism, the world is not mere world which may also be called God; it is world inseparably conjoined with an indwelling spirit, and it is the presence of spirit that divinizes the world.

It is sometimes said that in pantheism, God is supposed to be equally present in every part of the physical universe. This may be an implication of the literal meaning of pantheism, that everything is God or God is everything. In practice, however, some things are accepted as more fully manifesting the presence of God than others.

But God would be present to some degree in everything, so that pantheism often combines with a doctrine of panpsychism, the view that there is some presence, however minimal, of mind or spirit in everything that exists.

But the fact that some things are more obviously material, others more obviously physical, introduces an instability into pantheism. The pantheist tries to hold together matter and spirit in an indissoluble union, but in any given case, one or the other tends to predominate. Either mind becomes a mere adjective of the physical universe, a passive indwelling, in which case 'God' is primarily an alternative name for the material world and pantheism seems to collapse into atheism. Such was the case with the pantheism of Ernst Haeckel,[14] whose monism was quite naturalistic, in the old-fashioned sense of being materialistic and mechanistic. It is hard to see how one could apply the name of God to a universe governed by 'the great eternal iron laws' of nature, as Haeckel conceived it. At the other extreme, the pantheism of Indian religion makes the universal spirit the ultimate reality, with the result that the physical world is seen as *maya* – not exactly illusion, but certainly appearance having an inferior degree of reality. So pantheism, in spite of its attraction for certain types of people, tends to break down, being either reduced to atheistic materialism or else dissolving the world in a mystical acosmism. We can see why the teaching of Spinoza was so ambiguous and susceptible to opposing interpretations.

If we reject both atheism and pantheism as alternatives to traditional theism, what is left to consider? No doubt there are many finely nuanced views, each shading into the next, but there is one other major position which we have still to examine. It is sometimes called 'panentheism', and regarded as standing somewhere between pantheism and classical theism. According to the panentheist, the pantheist and the classical theist really share the same fundamental error, though they have developed it in opposite directions. That error is one-sidedness. In the critique of classical theism, we have seen that it does in fact stress one series of divine attributes – transcendence, externality, immutability, impassibility, eternity and so on – to the virtual exclusion of the opposite qualities. I say 'virtual exclusion', for although some recognition may be given to the ideas of divine immanence and divine participation in history and the events of the created order, these points are not taken very seriously. In pantheism, on the other side, all the stress is on immanence and we have the virtual identification of deity with the world-process. The champions of panentheism hold – rightly, I think – that theism and pantheism are alike over-simplications. The being of God, they claim, is both transcendent and immanent, both impassible and passible, both eternal and temporal, and so on with other divine attributes. This may look like contradiction, but the panentheist would reply that the logic of God is different from the logic of the created order, just as the logic of the infinite is different from the logic of the finite. Obviously, of course, we shall have to consider this claim in much more detail before we can decide whether it is acceptable. There can be no doubt, however, that panentheism has won a great many adherents in recent decades. Among contemporary philosophers and theologians who have either themselves adopted the panentheist label or had it applied to them by others are Whitehead, Hartshorne, Jaspers, Tillich, Moltmann and Robinson.

I am not myself intending to make much use of the term 'panentheism', though it must be already apparent that I have a good deal of sympathy with the position for which it stands. The word 'panentheism' is too close in its formation to the word 'pantheism', with the result that there can easily be confusion between them. I think that in the minds of many people, panentheism is assumed to be a modification of pantheism, though sophisticated advocates, such as Charles Hartshorne, tell us that panentheism is closer to theism than to pantheism.[15] For my own part, I am content to call this position 'dialectical theism', thereby stressing that it is essentially a species of theism and closer to theism than to pantheism, while the adjective 'dialectical' makes it clear that I intend to avoid the one-sidedness of classical theism and the difficulties which it brought with it. When I first introduced the notion of dialectic, I said that one does not have to give equal weight to each side of the dialectical opposition.[16] In the case of dialectical theism, we shall find that the weight is towards classical theism rather than towards pantheism, yet there is also a decided departure from the one-sidedness of classical theism.

But if one talks of a 'decided departure' from classical theism in some matters at least, can one still honestly go on using the words 'God' and 'theism'? Are the theologians and philosophers of religion whom I mentioned a moment ago really theists, or are they, as some of their critics have claimed, really atheists or crypto-atheists, or perhaps crypto-pantheists? Whether dialectical theism can yield a concept of God that is religiously and intellectually satisfying is a question that will only receive its answer at the end of our inquiry. Nevertheless, even at this stage, I think it could be said that no insuperable objections stand in the way, and that we might even arrive at a more satisfying conception of God than the one that we have inherited from classical theism – certainly it is my hope and intention that we may do so.

It comes back to the question, what must God be, if he is to be both the focus of human worship and aspiration, and at the same time be seen as the source, sustainer and goal of all that is? There is nothing in dialectical theism that would prevent the framing of a conception of God that would meet these conditions.

In the first place, such a God must be spiritual. Only that which is spirit or even above spirit (if we can attach a meaning to this expression) could be an object of worship for the spiritual beings that we ourselves are. Our earlier reflections led us to believe that the physical universe points beyond itself, so at this point dialectical theism is lined up with classical theism and with many forms of pantheism as over against any materialistic atheism in claiming that there is an ultimate spiritual reality. Dialectical theism is no less committed to the supremacy of the spiritual than is classical theism.

In the second place, such a God must be both the creator and the goal of all finite beings. At this point, dialectical theism is aligned with classical theism over against pantheism. In pantheism, God and the world are coequal aspects of a single reality. In dialectical theism, God is the source of the world, and there is a doctrine of creation, though, as we have seen, the relation between creator and created will be more intimate than was the case in classical theism, and there will also be no trace of any arbitrariness in the creation. Not only does dialectical theism stand with classical theism against pantheism at this point; the two of them stand also against those views in which God is only in process of emerging so that perhaps one can only speak of God at the end. Dialectical theism does not, however, entertain the belief that God possesses some frozen immutability, and acknowledges that if the creation is real and matters to God, then God's being will be enriched and his bliss increased as the creation is brought to the consummation which he desires for it.

As I have said, the justification for these assertions can come only at the end of our inquiry. But before we proceed directly to the detailed exposition of a natural theology of dialectical theism, we have to make a detour through history. There has in fact for many centuries been an alternative to atheism, pantheism and classical theism alike – an alternative to which the names of panentheism or dialectical theism might fairly be given. We shall now enter into discussion with some of the leading representatives of that altern- ative tradition, in the hope of learning enough from both their achievements and their errors to reach a position where we may attempt to construct a version of theism appropriate to the under- standing and the needs of our own time.

Part Two

Representatives of an Alternative Tradition

V

Classical: Plotinus

It could be claimed with some reason that Plotinus was the greatest philosopher of religion to emerge in the Graeco-Roman world. He is said to have been born in AD 204 in the city of Lycopolis in Egypt. His disciple, Porphyry, composed a brief account of his life and writings, and this is usually placed at the beginning of editions of Plotinus' works. We learn that in his late twenties, he took up the study of philosophy under Ammonius Saccus in the famous school of Alexandria. He was so fascinated by this teacher that he continued to frequent his lectures for eleven years. After travels in the East, he opened his own school in Rome in 244, but he did not write anything until he was over fifty years of age. Once he had begun, he was very prolific and produced a long series of tractates dealing with questions in logic, epistemology, spirituality and metaphysics, and in these he brought to expression a more or less systematic philosophical position. After his death in 270, the faithful Porphyry collected his writings. Like many of his contemporaries, Porphyry was interested in the significance or supposed significance of numbers, so he was delighted to find that the number of tractates left by his master was exactly fifty-four. Thus he was able to arrange them, roughly according to subject-matter, in six groups of nine, and from this circumstance these writings received the title *Enneads*.[1]

Plotinus is usually considered to be the leading representative of neo-Platonism, but this should not be misunderstood as implying that his philosophy is a new edition or modification of Plato's. Plotinus drew not only on the philosophy of Plato (though he alludes to him often, and with great respect), but on the whole philosophical tradition of Greece, and out of it he produced something new and distinctive. A. H. Armstrong does not hesitate to call him 'an original genius of the first rank'.[2] I do not think that this verdict is an exaggeration.

Still, it will be necessary to offer some defence of the choice of Plotinus as our first exemplar of that type of theism which seems to me both intellectually and religiously the most satisfying, whether one calls it 'dialectical theism' or 'panentheism'. It is true that more than sixty years ago an Anglican scholar, W. R. Inge, devoted a complete course of Gifford Lectures at St Andrews to an exposition of the philosophy of Plotinus, and confessed that he spoke not just as a student but as a disciple. 'I have steeped myself in his writings,' he said, 'and I have tried not only to understand them, as one might try to understand any other intellectual system, but to take them, as he assuredly wished his readers to take them, as a guide to right living and right thinking. In Plotinus, the fusion of religion, ethics and metaphysics is almost complete. He must be studied as a spiritual director, a prophet and not only a thinker.'[3] Of course, these words might be dismissed as one more instance of Anglican eccentricity, and I certainly would not myself wish to make such a sweeping claim for Plotinus. But I do hope to show that we can discern in his philosophy the basis for a concept of God which has in fact had a continuous history of development and presents itself today in new guises as a viable and, indeed, convincing form of theism.

Let us admit right away that there are some aspects of Plotinus' thought that belong to the past and have no validity for us today. These aspects, however, can be disregarded, and the main structure of his philosophy can stand without them.

For one thing, he believed that there are many grades of spiritual beings in the cosmos above the human level. This in itself might not seem incredible to our own age, in which the vastness and complexity of the universe has been opened up as never before. Plotinus, however, like many people of his time, identified these superior beings with the sun and stars. But, on the other hand, we have to notice that he rejected the popular astrology of his day. He held it absurd to suppose that the events of our human history are caused by the stars.[4] So the fact that he shared a widespread belief in the divinity of the celestial beings does not really affect the substance of his philosophy or his understanding of the human condition.

Another difficulty is raised by his negative attitude towards matter, and this might seem to be especially telling in an age so preoccupied with the natural sciences as ours is. But two points may be made in Plotinus' defence. The first is to remind ourselves that by 'matter' (ὕλη) Plotinus understood something very different from what the word conveys to us. For him, matter was without form, had no qualities and was virtually indistinguishable from nothing. So he held that materialism is an impossible theory, for out of matter, as he understood it, there could never arise an ordered and formed universe.[5] For contemporary physical science, on the other hand, matter is already formed – indeed, it is formed in a most intricate manner – and if a case can be made for materialism today, this is because complex form is deemed to be present in matter. But the concept of matter has changed so much that probably one should no longer speak of 'materialism'. The second point is to draw attention to Plotinus' hostile comments on the Gnostics, who believed that the material world is positively evil and the product of malevolent powers. No one, Plotinus claims, seeing the order and the beauty of the physical universe, could reasonably hold that it had been brought into being by demonic powers rather than by The Good. 'Even in the world of sense there are things of a loveliness comparable to that of the celestials.'[6]

However, if we leave aside such problems in Plotinus as the place of superior spiritual beings and the low estimate of the material world, there are other severe difficulties that seem to stand in the way of taking him as representative of a viable and satisfying doctrine of God. Some writers have denied that he was a theist at all, and have said that the Absolute which heads his system is so remote and impersonal that it could not possibly be identified with God. Others have considered him a pantheist who makes no distinction between God and the cosmos or who thinks of God as no more than a World-soul. Admittedly, one could find passages which, taken in isolation, might seem to support one or other of these interpretations, but they both miss the dialectic of Plotinus and fall into onesidedness. This dialectic is no mere compromise, but an attempt to hold together a strong sense of the transcendence, otherness and mystery of God with an equally strong sense of his immanence, kinship and accessibility. However difficult it may be to reconcile these two sides, they both belong to any adequate concept of deity.

Plotinus himself devotes one of his tractates to this very theme of dialectic.[7] He distinguishes it from logic, holding that whereas logic treats of propositions and syllogisms, dialectic is concerned with the realities of the world. Perhaps this is his way of saying that these realities will often prove to be more untidy and more resistant to one-sided ways of thinking than the propositions and theories we construct about them. In any case, he does say that in dialectic we consider things in their identity and difference, we alternate between analysis and synthesis, we explore one path and then follow another in the opposite direction so as to traverse the whole reality that is being investigated, and to see it from many points of view. Though there was a long way to go from the dialectic of Plotinus to that of Hegel, Marx and other philosophers of recent times, the origins of later conceptions of dialectic were already there in Plotinus and, as we shall see, there has been a continuous process of development through a succession of thinkers who all stand in a broadly neo-Platonist tradition.[8]

The centre of the Plotinian dialectic is the opposition between the one and the many, unity and multiplicity. The idea of unity would seem to be *a priori* and deeply rooted in our being. We know unity and identity in ourselves. We perceive the beings around us as unities. We even ascribe unity to the world, for we call it a 'universe' or a 'cosmos'. The first of these words obviously implies unity, while the second expresses the notion of order, and order is possible only where, in the midst of multiplicity, there is found repetition, identity, system, organization. But over against our awareness of unity is the awareness of multiplicity. The universe confronts us with a bewildering variety of contents, and even within ourselves we are aware of diversity and sometimes conflict. But if all were difference, if there were merely a collection of contingent items, we could not be, we could not know, there could not be a universe; indeed, it seems doubtful if there could 'be' anything at all. Plotinus believed that unity is prior to being. He declared: 'If unity is necessary to the substantial existence of all that is – and nothing exists which is not one – unity must precede being and be its author.'[9] Thus, in the dialectical opposition of the one and the many, Plotinus assigns priority to unity, but he does not go to an extreme monism in claiming that only The One is real, and that the moving multiplicity of things and events in the world is illusion or mere appearance. The multiplicity, too, is real and the world of sense is real, but their reality is admittedly of a relatively low degree, compared with the eternal realities.

Plotinus' solution of the problem of the one and the many was, very briefly, that The One, because of the superabundance of its being, has brought forth that which is other than itself, though when one says 'has brought forth', this does not mean that there was an initial moment of creation in the past but speaks only of the derivation of all things from The One. 'We hold,' he writes, 'that the ordered universe in its material mass has existed for ever, and will for ever endure.'[10] But everything that has come forth from The One seeks to return into union with its origin, so that there is an eternal going forth and returning. The cosmos of Plotinus is neither the unbroken unity of Parmenides nor even the eternal realm of ideas of Plato, but, as Inge expresses it, 'a world of life, activity and ceaseless creativeness'.[11]

It is clear that the question of unity in Plotinus lies very close to the question of God, though it may also be the case that the very important place given to the concept of unity would lead to an understanding of God rather different from that found in traditional theism. We should not forget, however, that one of the central affirmations of biblical religion is: 'Hear, O Israel! The Lord our God is one Lord.'[12] Still, it may be asked whether the biblical God is not more typically represented under other attributes of a more concrete and personal kind, especially the attribute of righteousness.

A more significant difference from biblical theism is found in Plotinus' understanding of the relation between The One and the beings which it has brought forth. Plotinus certainly does not have a doctrine of creation as that has usually been understood, and I am referring not so much to the fact that he thought of the world as having existed from eternity as to the fact that The One has brought forth everything else by a kind of overflow from its own being. The English word generally used for this relation is 'emanation', a flowing forth. Several words are used in the Greek of Plotinus: ἀπόρροια is literally a 'flowing forth', and is nearest to the English 'emanation;' πρόοδος is a more general word, with the sense of 'proceeding' or 'going forth'; another word used is ἔκλαμψις, 'radiation', the metaphor being that of light shining forth from the sun. Curiously enough, it is in a deutero-canonical Jewish writing from the first century BC, The Wisdom of Solomon, that we find what is said to be the earliest use of the word ἀπόρροια in the sense of an 'emanation' from God.[13] Wisdom is said there to be 'a pure emanation of the glory of the Almighty'.[14] In this passage, we may suppose, wisdom is regarded as a divine hypostasis, proceeding from God and sharing in the divine nature. Likewise in Plotinus, the two highest emanations from The One, namely, Mind or Intellect and Soul, are regarded as divine, and constitute with The One the triadic Plotinian Godhead. But the great difference between neo-Platonist and biblical teaching in this matter of emanation is that for Plotinus the whole universe of finite beings is also considered to be an emanation, albeit a more remote one, from the ultimate source of being, whereas for the Bible finite beings are creatures, that is to say, they are made by God and external to him. It might seem then that Plotinus, with his teaching on emanation, cannot help falling into pantheism.

But is the opposition between emanation and creation an absolute one, or is it justifiable to speak of theism only in connection with a strongly creationist doctrine and to assume that emanationism is inevitably pantheistic? I would like to answer both of these questions in the negative.

If we take the idea of creation first, it is surely worthy of note that in biblical Hebrew, a language with a somewhat limited vocabulary, a special verb is used for the creative activity of God. This is the verb *bārā'*, which is used only with God as subject, so that it would be fair to call it a metaphysical verb. Certainly it has a much deeper meaning than simply that of 'making', which would be expressed by the common Hebrew verb *'āśā*. It is true, of course, that in speaking of God's creative work, the Bible does say that he 'made' various creatures, including human beings.[15] But the word 'made' in such cases is, strictly speaking, an analogy for the unique idea of creation, and sometimes other analogies are used. Important among these is talk of God's 'breathing', and clearly the analogy of his imparting his own living breath[16] understands his relation to the creatures in a far more intimate way than the analogy of making. So one could hardly say that the biblical idea of creation must be interpreted as meaning that God makes the world as a product entirely external to himself. His relation to it, or at least to some parts of it, is much closer than that. Many theologians have suggested that the relation is more like that of an artist to his work, for while the artist has indeed made that work, it is also in some sense an extension of the artist himself. I have myself maintained elsewhere that the dominant analogy of 'making' used to interpret the idea of creation in Christian theology needs to be balanced and corrected by some use of the analogy of 'emanation'.[17] The question nowadays is more than an academic one, for there is good evidence to suggest that the idea of a 'dedivinized' universe, entirely external to God, has encouraged the reckless exploitation of the earth and can hardly be corrected without some recognition of the divine presence in the creation.

If we return now to Plotinus, I think it is a mistake to suppose that his doctrine of emanation leads to pantheism. It is true that in his teaching everything flows ultimately from The One but it is also true that there is a sharp differentiation between the world of spirit and the world of sense, though the latter, too, is good and not evil. Armstrong declares it 'impossible to call Plotinus a pantheist', and he gives as his reason 'the very marked separation of the material universe from even the lowest of the great hypostases'.[18]

At this point we must examine more closely the concept of deity found in Plotinus. We have already seen that at the apex of the hierarchy of beings stands a triad: The One, the absolute reality or ultimate source; next to it is Mind or Intellect; the third place belongs to Soul. The One stands higher than Mind, while Mind ranks above Soul, so that there are relations of superordination and subordination among them, yet we must not separate them, for they also constitute a unity. In Plotinus, it is the triad which is divine being, not any single hypostasis in isolation.

The One (τὸ ἕν) is the ultimate reality, and is also called The First (τὸ πρῶτον) and The Good (τὸ ἀγαθόν). But, strictly speaking, this ultimate is nameless, and the titles we give it are only pointers. To call it 'The One' is not to assert numerical unity, but simply to deny that here we have anything that can be numbered. 'If we are led to think positively of The One, there would be more truth in silence.'[19] Likewise, it is called 'The Good' only in a metaphorical sense. For the most part, we can speak of it only in negatives. We cannot even say that it is, for it is rather the condition or ground that anything may be. 'It is by The One that all beings are beings.'[20] Thus, The One is not to be found among the beings, for 'in order that being be, The One must be not being but being's begetter'.[21] The language here seems like an anticipation of Heidegger, and I think we shall eventually see that the resemblance is not just accidental. Plotinus can also say: 'That which stands as primal source of everything is not a thing but is distinct from all things; it is not then a member of the total, but earlier than all, earlier thus than intellect.'[22] Again, we are told that The One does not know, but this is not to be reckoned a defect: 'It is no weakness in it not to know itself, since, as pure unity, it contains nothing which it needs to explore.'[23] The One has no memory, for everything is present to it. The One cannot aim at anything or desire anything, for it is already fulfilled. The One is both everything and nothing: 'It can be none of existing things, yet it is all; none, in that beings are subsequent, yet all, as the wellspring from which they flow.'[24] So far we have a markedly negative theology, but as happens in all negative theology, Plotinus allows himself to say a good deal more about the Absolute than the strict application of his own praise of silence would seem to admit.

We can know something of The One through the beings which it begets. If we ask why The One should trouble to beget anything when it is already fulfilled, two answers appear to be given. The first is that The One 'must not be solely the solitary, for if it were, reality would remain buried and shapeless, since in The One there is no differentiation of forms'.[25] This cannot mean, of course, that The One is mere potentiality, for, as we noted in connection with Plotinus' view of matter, he believed that out of mere potency nothing actual or formed could emerge. What it does seem to mean is that The One would remain dark and unknown if it did not go out of itself – and here we have something like an anticipation of Hegel. And this leads into the second of the two answers to the question of why The One begets beings. This answer refers to the generosity of The One in producing beings that can have communion with it. In a remarkable passage, we read: 'Seeking nothing, possessing nothing, lacking nothing, The One is perfect, and, in our metaphor, has overflowed, and its exuberance has produced the new. This product has turned again to its begetter and been filled and become its contemplator.'[26]

It is important to remember that in Plotinus The One, though ultimate, is not by itself God. As we have seen, God is the Triad comprising The One, Mind and Soul. This must be remembered, for some critics of Plotinus, such as H. P. Owen,[27] have claimed that his God is unintelligible, impersonal, indifferent and so on. This is to take Plotinus' teaching in a one-sided way that misses the mark, rather as if one were to take a single person of the Trinity in Christian teaching, and treat that person in isolation as God. It seems to me that Plotinus' teaching about The One conveys a truth that belongs to any adequate understanding of God, namely, that there is in God a region of otherness, mystery and transcendence, beyond all our categories, even the category of personality. But that is not the whole truth about God, and certainly Plotinus did not think it is the whole truth. The One has to be seen in the context of the Triad.

So we pass on to the second member of the Triad, Mind or Intellect (ὁ νοῦς).[28] Mind is an emanation from The One, and it is the emanation that stands nearest to The One. We could say that with the begetting of Mind, the wealth that lay buried and as yet without differentiated form in The One is now brought into the light of intelligibility. The fullness of reality remains one, but its unity is now the unit of an ordered cosmos or organic system. We are speaking, however, of a cosmos of intelligibles or ideas, not yet of the sensible or material universe. The Mind beholds 'a higher reality from which this [sensible] world derives'.[29] There is a close analogy between the way the Mind beholds intelligibles and the way in which our senses perceive objects. In both cases, there is immediacy. Mind intuits the intelligible realities directly, unlike Soul, for as we shall see in a moment, the latter proceeds by discursive reasoning from one point to another. 'The Soul's action is successive . . . the Mind, however, embraces all.'[30] There is the further distinction that whereas Soul directs its reasoning on objects outside of itself, Mind possesses in itself the intelligible realities which it intuits. These intelligible realities or ideas are not so much objects of Mind as its very structure.

At this point we have to face the question whether Plotinus, with his heritage from Plato, is committed to idealism. Of course, 'idealism' is a very slippery and inexact term. Presumably in some sense it implies the priority of the mental to the material. This has sometimes been taken to mean that the fundamental reality is some kind of mental or spiritual substance, but such a view has few advocates today and probably involves the category mistake of thinking that mind and matter are two entities of the same order. But if that which is mental or ideal is no substance or stuff, but rather form, and if idealism means that form is fundamental to being, then this would seem to be correct, for a formless matter could never evolve into anything else such as a world or cosmos. Without form, there could be neither order nor knowledge nor, perhaps, being. It is this second and acceptable kind of idealism that we find in Plotinus, that is to say, his recognition of the primordial and essential presence of form in reality. This interpretation of Plotinus is supported by Inge, who attributes to him the view that 'reality is neither thought nor thing, but the indissoluble union of thought and thing, which reciprocally imply each other'.[31]

Next after Mind comes Soul (ἡ ψυχή). 'So divine and precious is the Soul,' writes Plotinus, 'be confident that by its power you can attain to divinity . . . yet the Soul is no more than an image of Mind.'[32] The relation of Soul to Mind is analogous to the relation of

Mind to The One. Soul is inferior to Mind because, as we have noted, Mind grasps everything intuitively and simultaneously, whilst Soul proceeds by discursive reasoning (διάνοια) from one thing to another. Furthermore, although there is a universal Soul or World-soul, there are also individual finite souls. Again, there are grades within soul – indeed, the Greek word ψυχή is often better translated 'life' than 'soul'. The highest part of the soul reasons, but there are also sentient soul and even vegetable soul, present in animals and plants. In some passages, Plotinus seems to come near to a doctrine of panpsychism, that there is soul in everything: 'The Soul is of so far-reaching a nature – a thing unbounded – as to embrace the entire body of the All in the one extension; so far as the universe extends, there Soul is.'[33] But the presence of Soul and the grade of soulishness decrease as one moves down through the levels of beings. Plotinus is prepared to admit 'some shadow of soul' in bodies 'holding animal or vegetable life'.[34] But beyond this, it would seem, Soul does not reach.

An interesting question concerns the relation of individual or finite souls to the World-soul. Plotinus has a strong sense of the unity and sympathy that bind all souls together. 'If the soul in me is a unity, why need that in the universe be otherwise? And if that, too, is one Soul, and yours and mine belong to it, then yours and mine must also be one.'[35] From this the conclusion is drawn that when one soul suffers, other souls must suffer with it, even the World-soul must suffer too. But this unity does not abolish the distinctness of souls.

Nowadays one often hears the complaint that in Christianity God has been conceived in almost exclusively masculine and patriarchal terms, and this draws attention to another interesting feature of the Plotinian Triad. Though grammatical gender does not always coincide with distinctions of sex, it does suggest that the entity designated by the word has been imaged one way or another. In the Plotinian Triad, The One is in the Greek neuter, and the reality it designates is beyond the distinction of sex, as, indeed, it is beyond all other distinctions. The other two members of the Triad, Mind and Soul, are designated by Greek nouns which are respectively masculine and feminine. I am not suggesting, of course, that this was a deliberate policy on Plotinus' part, but it could well reflect a subconscious tendency to achieve a balanced concept of God in which both masculine and femine elements are present, with the recognition that the ultimate reality of deity lies beyond the distinctions of sex.

Both in ancient and modern times, attempts have been made to relate the Triad of Plotinus to the Trinity of Christian theology. There are some obvious differences. The three persons of the Christian Trinity are equal, whereas the Triad of Plotinus is hierarchical. Still, the notions of 'begetting' and 'procession', as used to express relations within the Trinity, are surely not too far from the Plotinian notion of 'emanation'. Further differences become apparent when we compare the several members or persons in the two conceptions of Godhead. The One of Plotinus lacks the concreteness, to say nothing of the anthropomorphic features, of the Father. Indeed, Plotinus says explicitly that we would think of The One inadequately if we thought of him as God – to think of The One as Mind or even as God is to think too meanly.[36] Presumably we think too meanly because some traces of finitude and anthropomorphism cling to even the most refined ideas of God.

Passing to the second member of the Plotinian Triad, Mind, there might be a better case for comparing this with the Word (Λόγος) or Wisdom (Σοφία) in Christian thought, though, as Augustine pointed out, neo-Platonism could not have conceived of the Word's becoming flesh.[37] Perhaps the comparison is closest in the case of the third member or person, the universal Soul of Plotinus and the Holy Spirit of Christianity. Both are a ground of communion for individual finite souls, and both share with these souls in their striving, as the immanent power and presence of deity in the world. It may be the case, of course, that any dialectical theism must eventually come to think of God in a threefold way, and this would explain why triune deities appear in many unrelated forms of religion.

Plotinus himself makes an interesting comparison between the Triad of his own sophisticated philosophy and some of the gods of ancient Greek mythology. He claims that his own doctrine is no novelty, having been foreshadowed in the old stories of the gods.[38] Though Zeus was the principal God in classical times, the mythology told that he had usurped supreme rule from his father, Kronos, and that the latter had in turn taken the place of his own father, Ouranos. Plotinus identifies The One with Ouranos, for Ouranos is the sky, the empty, infinite, nameless, featureless matrix, which symbolizes the goal of the mystic's quest for the divine. Kronos was associated with a primitive Age of Gold, which

Plotinus sees as symbolizing the archetypal realm of ideas before the descent into the universe of time and space and matter, so that Kronos represents Mind or Intellect. Zeus, in turn, is the Soul of the world and governs our earthly affairs.

What is the position of the human being in this scheme of things? Already we find something like the idea of man as the microcosm, containing in miniature all the hierarchical structure of reality, from vestiges of the divine from which he has come to involvement in the material at the other end of the scale. Elmer O'Brien declares that in Plotinus 'ontology is the extrapolation of psychology'.[39]

The human being, like everything else, has come forth from The One, and his highest destiny is to return to union with The One. For Plotinus, this means that he must turn from the body and the things of sense to cultivate the soul and to ascend to the intellectual realm. He rises above the beauties of the sensible world to the beauties of virtue and knowledge and noble deeds.[40] He reaches a stage when he has not only got beyond the attractions of the sensible world but when the greatest bodily and material afflictions can no longer distress him. 'His light burns within, like the light in a lantern when it is blowing hard outside, with a great fury of wind and storm.'[41] The highest reach that he can attain takes him even beyond Mind to a mystical, ecstatic union with The One, but this last stage, we are told, is achieved only by a leap.[42] According to Porphyry, Plotinus attained that union four times while he was with him in Rome.[43] The ideal of human life is 'detachment from all things here below, scorn of all earthly pleasures, the flight of the lone to the Alone'.[44] By modern standards, this seems an austere and world-negating aim, yet in spite of the talk of the flight of the lone to the Alone, it is not individualist or escapist. We have already seen that in Plotinus' teaching there is a sense in which all souls are one. So we find him doing more justice to the sociality of human life in a passage where he offers an alternative expression of his belief that human lives are transformed and enhanced by their relation to transcendent being. 'We are like a chorus grouped around a conductor, who allow their attention to be distracted by the audience. If, however, they were to turn towards their conductor, they would sing as they should, and really be with him.'[45] In this harmony, we forget ourselves in the contemplation of The Good, but this does not mean that individuals are simply absorbed.

The question may be asked whether Plotinus faces up to evil with sufficient seriousness in developing his philosophical system. We have seen that he rejected any Gnostic doctrine of a dualism of ontological principles, or of the inherent evil of matter. Matter is next to nothing, but it is not evil and, indeed, it is necessary. Evil does not belong to matter as such, but to the preferring of the lower to the higher. Sometimes it seems to be suggested that this is the best of all possible worlds, and that in the divine providence even the evil is made to serve an ulterior good. So we find Plotinus writing: 'Perhaps even the less has its contributory value in the All. Perhaps there is no need that everything be good . . . Matter is continuously overruled towards the better.'[46] He can even declare: 'All is just and good in the universe in which every actor is set in his own quite appropriate place. Even as things are, all is well.'[47]

It is true that Plotinus constantly contrasts things as we know them with what he calls simply 'There' or 'Yonder' (ἐκεῖ). But 'There' is not a region beyond the sky or an eschatological age that will come in the distant future. When we turn to the realities of Soul and Mind and The One or The Good, and see things as they are and in their true relations to one another, we are already There. He says: 'We do not need to bring real beings down into ourselves, for we are There among them.'[48]

VI

Patristic: Dionysius

Even if he had no other claim to fame, the person known as Dionysius the Areopagite would deserve to be remembered as the perpetrator of one of the most successful literary hoaxes in history. However, it is probably unfair to speak of a 'hoax'. Our author simply did what many other ancient authors did: he chose the name of a well-known personage as a pseudonym, no doubt hoping that by doing so he would gain for his writings an authority and a readership that they would not have had if he had written under his own name. Our particular author chose as pseudonym the name of a man who was not too famous – Dionysius the Areopagite, mentioned in the New Testament as having been converted by Paul on the occasion of his preaching on Mars' Hill,[1] and said by later tradition to have become the first bishop of Athens. Although Dionysius is not an important figure in the New Testament, it is obvious that if any writings of his had survived, they would possess great authority as coming from an immediate disciple of Paul and giving first-hand information about the church in its earliest period. Our author encourages the fiction of sub-apostolic authorship by addressing himself to Timothy as a fellow presbyter and by claiming Paul himself as his preceptor. The deception worked (if that is not too harsh an expression) and for centuries the Dionysian corpus was highly esteemed in both East and West.[2] Only with the emergence of the critical spirit in the sixteenth century did doubts begin to arise, and these have, of course, been decisively confirmed by modern scholarship. The writings show the influence not only of neo-Platonism but of a relatively late neo-Platonism, from a period not only centuries after Paul but even long after Plotinus. It seems certain that the author knew the writings of Proclus, who died about 485. Likewise, the writings reflect a highly developed ecclesiastical order, not to be found in the early formative period of the church's life. It is also significant that these writings, destined to become so famous, are not mentioned by anyone until early in the sixth century. So the consensus of opinion is that Dionysius the Areopagite (if we may call him by the name which he chose) flourished around the year 500, and that the principal influence upon him was not Paul but a certain Hierotheus whom he mentions with great respect and who was presumably a Syrian mystic, teacher and philosopher, at home in neo-Platonist speculation.

I have mentioned these matters in some detail, because I think they have created a strong prejudice against Dionysius or pseudo-Dionysius or whatever we may call him. It may well be the case that in earlier times he enjoyed an exaggerated reputation, and this was no doubt due in large measure to his supposed connection with Paul. But the modern reaction against him has been extreme, and no doubt it, too, has been largely inspired by the extraneous consideration that he was not who he claimed to be. Let us agree that this would be important in some contexts, for instance, if someone were using the picture of the church found in Dionysius as evidence of its institutional form in the earliest period. But no such consideration applies concerning Dionysius' philosophical teaching. This has to be considered on its intrinsic merits, and unless it had such merits, I do not think it would have commended itself to such persons as Maximus the Confessor and Thomas Aquinas. Philosophical and theological teaching does not derive its worth from the status of the teacher but from the wealth of its insights and the cogency of its arguments.

Of all the ancient Christian writers, Dionysius is surely the one who attempted the most complete union of neo-Platonism and the biblical tradition. Two concepts of God, in many respects very different, were brought together in a dialectical synthesis, and opinions have differed sharply on the value of the result. According to Adolf Harnack, 'the Christian dogmas themselves appear merely as the dress of neo-Platonist ideas'.[3] An exactly opposite judgment is delivered by Louis Bouyer, who says of Dionysius' teaching that 'under its Greek clothing it is wholly biblical'.[4] Harnack, of course, had a nostalgic longing for what he believed had been the original Christian faith, a simple rationalist belief in the Fatherhood of God, uncomplicated by dogmas of the Incarnation or the Trinity. So in his eyes Dionysius stands at the end of a sad story of decline. He could not allow for the possibility that the encounter of biblical and philosophical ideas could be a genuinely reciprocal matter, in which both would be transformed and something new and more comprehensive would emerge. Bouyer is much nearer the mark than Harnack when he claims that 'one must recognize that far from having succumbed without resistance to the prestige of Plotinian, or even Proclusian, cosmology and theology, Dionysius put them on a new basis'.[5]

It may be useful to begin our discussion of Dionysius by sketching in a few broad strokes his concept of the universe. The ultimate reality is God or, as Dionysius prefers to say, the 'thearchy' (θεαρχία). Like many other philosophers and theologians, he may have thought the word 'God' misleading – perhaps too anthropomorphic or too much laden with popular connotations, or too vague and so lacking in the specific meaning he wished to attach to it. Next to the thearchy is the intelligible universe. This is the distinctively Platonic element in the Dionysian universe, a world of intelligences and ideas above the realm of the sensible and material. But in the marriage that Dionysius has effected between Plato and the Bible, this ideal or intelligible world is the world of angels. It is this relatively unimportant part of the Dionysian scheme that seems to have made the profoundest impression on subsequent generations. Everyone has heard of the nine choirs of angels, themselves arranged in three triads: seraphim, cherubim and thrones; dominations, virtues and powers; principalities, archangels and angels. These triads are emanations in descending order from thearchy. We notice, too, that they constitute an elaborate hierarchy, and indeed the term 'hierarchy' is very important in Dionysius' writings. In modern societies, with their egalitarian tendencies, 'hierarchy' is not a popular word, but we have to try to read it regardless, as far as possible, of modern ideologies. Whether or not one wants to call it 'hierarchical', there is no doubt that we live in a graded universe. There are many levels of beings – intelligent beings, sentient beings, vegetative beings, molecules, atoms, sub-atomic particles, to mention only the more obvious. But when Dionysius speaks of 'hierarchy', he has in mind something more than even the gradations of beings. Hierarchy is not the static stratification of reality, but something very dynamic, the reciprocal communication among the different grades of being. More exactly, hierarchy is the coming down from God through the various levels and, in reverse order, the rising up to God. Dionysius himself writes: 'The whole hierarchical function is divided into two holy tasks, those of receiving and transmitting purification free from mixture, divine light and the science (ἐπιστήμη) that makes perfect', and the aim of this active process of hierarchy is to bring all beings, so far as possible, into likeness to God or deiformity (θεοείδεια).[6] To complete the picture, the hierarchical universe is represented as extending below the level of the intelligibles into the sensible world, that is to say, the familiar world in which we human beings live.

Stated in this summary form, the Dionysian view of the cosmos can hardly fail to strike us as alien to our modern ways of thinking – more alien in some ways than even the cosmology of Plotinus, for although Plotinus did give a place to spiritual beings intermediate between God and humanity, it was among his disciples that the elaboration of this realm of intermediaries took place. The neo-Platonism of Dionysius has been transmitted through such later followers of Plotinus as Proclus, and the combination of an elaborate neo-Platonist doctrine of intermediate beings with Jewish angelology lies behind the luxuriant spiritual society depicted in *The Celestial Hierarchy*.

I am not suggesting, however, that Dionysius' speculations about angels are to be dismissed as of no value. They do make a certain contribution to the philosophy of mind, and therefore to philo-sophical theology which has to ask both about the mind of God and about finite minds and their capacity for knowing God. Even if no angelic beings exist (and in this mysterious universe, could anyone be certain about that?), we might still have something to learn from speculation on the possibility of intelligences more powerful than the human intelligence and freed from some of its limitations. Perhaps more than any other philosophical theologian of ancient times, Dionysius wished to emphasize the transcendence of God, and so he has a whole string of constantly recurring words and expressions designed to point to the otherness of the divine – 'above being' (ὑπερουσία), 'beyond intellect' (ὑπὲρ νοῦν), even 'above deity' (ὑπερθεότητος). I shall have more to say about this exuberant language later. At the moment, I simply want to say that the discussion of the angelic beings in Dionysius affords a clue to the interpretation of some of these expressions. One of the differences which Plotinus had made between Mind and Soul was that the former grasps ideas immediately and intuitively, while the latter reasons discursively from one point to another.[7] Dionysius draws a similar distinction between the angelic mind and the human.[8] The angelic mind grasps truth in the immediacy of pure intellectual contemplation, whereas our human minds use images and proceed discursively. A good illustration of this point is found in what A. J. Ayer says about mathematics: 'A being whose intellect was infinitely powerful would take no interest in logic and mathematics. For he would be able to see at a glance everything that his definitions implied, and could never learn from logical inference anything of which he was not conscious already.'[9] Of course, even the most acute human minds cannot take in the whole of mathematics at a glance, so we have to proceed painfully by lemmas, theorems, corollaries and the like. It is therefore not fruitless to speculate about higher orders of intelligences, for from such speculation we may learn both something of the limitations of our own minds and the possibilities that might belong to a divine Mind, if such there be. This also shows us that extravagant as Dionysius' language is, when he talks of 'above being' and 'beyond intellect' and so on, such expressions cannot be set aside without further ado as meaningless. Our finite minds cannot indeed *know* what it would be like to rise above the limitations of discursive thinking, but we can have *some idea* of what is meant.

So far I have been defending Dionysius against some of the common prejudices that militate against him. But if we are prepared to put up with his rhetoric of superlatives – 'above this' and 'beyond that' – and his compulsive artificiality in representing everything in triads – perhaps no worse than Hegel's – and his obsession with hierarchy – though I have shown that this is a less rigid concept than is often supposed – we may now penetrate more deeply into his thought and see if there is anything of substance in it. I think there is, and that at several points Dionysius was dealing in an interesting way with theological problems that are still with us.

We begin with his teaching about God or, better, the Godhead or thearchy. We have already noted some of the words he applies. Chief among them is 'above being', often rendered in English not too happily as 'superessential'. God or the thearchy is, of course, real above all else, but his mode of being is unique so that strictly speaking he cannot be reckoned among the beings. 'He is not contained in being, but being is contained in him.'[10] He may indeed be called 'true being', but since this true being is 'the one transcendent origin and cause of all things', its being is quite other than the being of all that exists in the cosmos.[11] Again, Dionysius teaches something like a doctrine of degrees of being, those beings which are closer to God possessing more being, so to speak, while those that are distant barely exist. Yet God is not the highest member in the series, but transcends it.[12] We noted also that God is 'above intellect', and I tried to indicate briefly what this expression might mean. Dionysius explains that 'the lack of mind must be predicated of God by excess and not by defect' and that 'the mind of God embraces all things in an utterly transcendent knowledge'. Things do not stand over against God as objects to be known external to himself. 'The universal Cause, in knowing itself, can scarcely help knowing the things that proceed from it and whereof it is the cause. With this knowledge, then, God knows all things, not through a mere understanding of the things but through an understanding of himself.'[13] We even noted that the thearchy is said in some sense to be 'above God', for the very word 'God' cannot convey the 'mystery beyond being'.[14] Perhaps it is too infected with images or with the experiences of finite personal existence. We find an echo of this austere teaching in Karl Jaspers, who includes the word 'God' among what he calls the 'ciphers', pointers to the incomprehensible Transcendence, which he explicitly compares to The One of Plotinus.[15]

The thearchy of Dionysius is also the Trinity of Christian theology, but he does not succeed well in incorporating the trinitarian doctrine into his concept. The most important attribute of God is unity, yet even this unity is an incomprehensible unity. 'No unity or trinity or number or oneness or fecundity or any other thing that either is a creature or can be known to any creature, is able to utter the mystery, beyond all mind and reason, of that transcendent Godhead which, as beyond being, surpasses all things.'[16] The various transcendent expressions, 'above being', 'beyond reason' and the like, belong to the undifferentiated thearchy, and apply equally to the three persons of the Trinity. In using the word 'persons', of course, one has to understand that it is not used in its modern sense. Father, Son and Holy Spirit are, like the thearchy in its unity, suprapersonal, just as they are beyond all other attributes. Yet the persons of the Trinity are not simply absorbed into an undifferentiated unity. While they all have the same attributes, they differ in their relations to each other. This introduces an element of differentiation into the thearchy, and although this is said to leave the unity undisturbed, it is the ground for a fecundity in which the thearchy goes out from itself in emanation and creation.

I have deliberately used both the words 'emanation' (πρόοδος) and 'creation' (κτίσις), for both are needed to express the way in which Dionysius understands the relation between God and the world. The higher spiritual beings are indeed emanations, yet all things to some extent participate in that Reality that is above being. 'The One is the elementary basis of all things . . . and you will not find anything in the world but derives from The One.'[17] But we have already seen that there are degrees of being, and those things which are furthest from the source have only a minimal participation. They may rightly be called 'created', provided that word does not imply that they are external to God, for everything that is is in God. It is strange to find that Dionysius has been said by some to teach the most extreme doctrine of divine transcendence among all the Christian Fathers, while others have accused him of pantheism! The same conflicting judgments have been made about Plotinus, and in both cases there is simply a failure to grasp the dialectical nature of their thinking about God, though admittedly language needs to be strained to the utmost to give expression to that dialectic, and neither Plotinus nor Dionysius are free from fault. But to call Dionysius a pantheist is surely mistaken. The charge is refuted both by our author's unrelenting insistence on the incomprehensibility and otherness of the Godhead – we might appropriately say, his 'hyperbolic' language – and the doctrine of degrees of being, for this does not acknowledge as pantheism does, a uniform diffusion of the divine through the cosmos.

When I used the word 'hyperbolic', it was meant to be a joking allusion to Dionysius' over-fondness for the prefix 'hyper'. But in the course of his exposition, he does himself introduce the Greek word ὑπερβολή in the sense of 'excess'. The thearchy which is above being, beyond intellect, above deity and so on possesses, as it were, an excess of being or of super-being which overflows in emanation and creation. God, he claims, was moved by this abundance to create the universe.[18] The world is like an overflow of the divine goodness. Creation is neither a necessary nor a voluntary act on the part of God, but simply a consequence of his own nature. Just by existing, he creates. Using a familiar comparison with the sun, Dionysius writes: 'For as our sun, through no choice or deliberation, but by the very fact of its existence, gives light to all those things which have any inherent power of sharing its illumination, even so the Good (which is above the sun as the transcendent archetype, by the very mode of its existence, is above its faded image) sends forth upon all things according to their receptive powers the rays of its undivided goodness.'[19] He has in mind here in the first instance spiritual beings, but the whole creation down to the lowest levels arises from the same outpouring.

So far this is very much like Plotinus. But there is a striking passage in which Dionysius seems to introduce a novel idea. Aware of his boldness, he writes: 'And we must dare to affirm (for it is the truth) that the Creator of the universe himself, in his beautiful and good yearning towards the universe, is through the excessive yearning of his goodness transported outside himself in his providential activities towards all things that have being, and is touched by the sweet spell of goodness, love and yearning, and so is drawn from his transcendent throne above all things to dwell within the heart of all things, through an ecstatic power that is above being and whereby he yet stays within himself.'[20] This language of transport and ecstasy, of God's going out of himself and leaving his transcendent throne, introduces a dynamic note and, more than that, the thought of God's self-emptying or self-humiliation. Could we even say that this is the true transcendence of God, a going beyond himself in generous love and self-giving, an active kind of transcendence analogous to what we understand by transcendence on the human level, rather than that static otherness and aloofness with which we seem to associate divine transcendence?

But then one may ask whether this bold idea of Dionysius is not cancelled out by his final remark that he continues to stay within himself. However, I do not think that this does cancel out the idea of a genuine self-humiliation which Dionysius is striving to express. It is the same kind of difficulty that Christian theologians have known in incarnational theology. They have never taught that the Godhead whole and entire descended into the creation in the incarnation, but that the Logos or second Person of the Trinity so humbled himself. Indeed, aware of the problem of how the divine can assume the human, some theologians have even claimed that the Logos itself could not wholly incarnate itself in Christ but continued to subsist in some transcendent mode – a famous example is *illud extra Calvinisticum* which caused such sharp controversy between Lutherans and Calvinists. The only case I know in which it was held that God had wholly resigned his Godhead to immerse and lose himself in creation was the teaching of the so-called 'death of God' theologians in recent times. So Thomas Altizer could say that 'the radical Christian claims that God has actually died in Christ, that this death is both a historical and a cosmic event, and, as such, it is a final and irrevocable event'.[21]

Obviously, Dionysius was thinking along different lines from Altizer, though I suppose that the neo-Platonist tradition might be susceptible to the kind of interpretation that Altizer does in fact read into Hegel. But I think the true interpretation of Dionysius is one that has reappeared in many subsequent thinkers, right down to Whitehead in recent times. God has two aspects. There is the aspect that is turned towards us and that manifests itself in creation, time and history. But there is also, as it were, the 'far side' of God, God as he is in himself, incomprehensible to our minds. Some such concept of God, if we can think it coherently, allows us both to accept his genuine self-immersion in creation, even his ecstatic coming forth from himself, and yet at the same time to acknowledge that God does not exhaust himself in this and that the eternal mystery remains. Perhaps the ecstasy of divine love of which Dionysius speaks is to be understood in analogy with the ecstasy of the Christian mystic. The mystic is taken out of himself or transported, but this, we are assured, does not mean that he is simply absorbed, still less that he is annihilated.

As in the system of Plotinus, so in that of Dionysius, the creatures that come forth from the Godhead seek to return into union or communion (ἕνωσις) with the Source, so there is a two-way movement, downwards from God into the creation in an ever-widening differentiation of being, and back towards the source as the creatures, according to their capacities, strive after likeness to the God from whom they have come.

It is this double movement of coming forth and returning that determines for Dionysius the dialectical shape of theology. There are three types of theology, or three ways of thinking theologically. The affirmative or cataphatic way reads the character of God from the creation; the negative or apophatic way denies that any predicates can be applied to God, who from the standpoint of our finite minds is nameless and incomprehensible; the symbolic way arises from the confrontation of the two other ways, and though it leans more to the negative in recognizing that any knowledge of God is symbolic and not literal, it is not empty but, so far as it goes, does yield a knowledge of God. Let us consider each of these three ways in turn.

The cataphatic way belongs to the descent, that is to say, to the coming down or coming forth of the hidden God into the created realm. God, though above being, is not wholly incommunicable. The divine reality 'lovingly reveals itself by illuminations corresponding to each separate creature's powers, and thus draws upwards holy minds into such contemplation, participation and resemblance to itself as they can attain'.[22] Just as God was not content to remain shut up in himself but brought into being the hierarchically ordered universe, so he is not content to remain silent, formless and unknown to the intelligent beings in the universe but reveals or declares himself (ἀποφάνσις) and grants them such illumination (ἐλλάμψις) as each is capable of receiving. Dionysius in fact devotes an entire treatise, *The Divine Names*, to listing and expounding the major attributes of God. He explicitly says that we should confine ourselves to the Holy Scriptures, in which God has communicated himself under such images as are appropriate to our needs and powers.[23] Among other topics, he discusses God as goodness, light, beauty, love, being, life, wisdom, reason, power, peace, holiness, perfection and unity. These are names of God sanctioned by God himself, so Dionysius believes, for his self-communication or revelation. But they necessarily belong to that aspect of God that is turned towards us. They tell us what we, with our limited powers, can learn of God as he has come out from himself.

So over against the affirmative theology there has to be the negative way. God, as unique, is incomprehensible in himself, and no images derived from created existence can properly express his nature. We speak of him as being, goodness, life, wisdom, unity and so on, but none of these words, not even 'being' or 'unity', can be taken literally. They all point to an inexpressible mystery, and so each one has to be denied as well as affirmed. It is the negation rather than the affirmation that is worthy of the divine reality. He is not this, not that. Yet the negation is not mere negation, but is meant to point beyond the affirmation to a mystery that eludes understanding. So we arrive at the paradox that the highest knowing (as far as God is concerned) is an unknowing and the highest illumination a darkness. But the unknowing is not sheer ignorance, rather the overwhelming experience of the mystic, while the darkness is the brilliance of a light that cannot be borne.

Dionysius, however, does not leave us simply with the paradox of two opposed theological ways. He brings them together in symbolic theology, and I think it is here that we find an important contribution to the epistemology of religion. He lays the foundation for a critical theory of religious symbolism, and what he says is still relevant to contemporary discussions. One cannot read his remarks on symbols without being impressed at various points by the way in which he has anticipated the views of twentieth-century writers. Let me name three such writers. Austin Farrer, in *The Glass of Vision*,[24] claims that the great images of the Bible have a revelatory quality which conducts the mind to an apprehension of divine truth that would be otherwise inaccessible, even through the rational operations of natural theology. Paul Tillich, in *The Dynamics of Faith*,[25] made large claims for the power of symbols to open up new areas of reality, on the grounds that they ultimately participate in Being or God, though he also warned against the danger of absolutizing any finite symbol and so turning it into an idol that would block the way to God rather than open it up. Ian Ramsey, in *Models and Mystery*,[26] distinguished between picturing and non-picturing models or symbols and argued that the latter, in both religion and science, may have a superior disclosive power in spite of their dissimilarity to the reality which they are claimed to symbolize.

Returning to Dionysius, we find that his symbolic theology is associated with the ascending way that leads back to God. Now the symbols that emerged in the cataphatic way have to be stripped down as the soul rises nearer to the hidden reality of God. We have already seen that Dionysius believed the great biblical symbols to be a genuine language of God, in which he communicates himself to his creatures in ways appropriate to them. Yet even this revealed language has to be criticized and the effort made to penetrate behind the symbols to the reality. He notes that two kinds of symbols are employed in the Bible. Some of these symbols are themselves such exalted entities – life, light and the like – that they may be thought to have a close resemblance to the still more exalted mystery which they symbolize. This could easily be misleading, and could cause us to stick at the symbol, for every symbol falls short of the divine reality. So he argues that a measure of superiority may belong to the type of symbol which makes no claim to resemble that which it symbolizes. Such a symbol is unlikely to establish itself as a substitute or idol between our minds and God, for its apparent remoteness from God is a continuing reminder of the inadequacy of all symbols, and thus the way to mystery is held open.[27] The criticism of symbols is likened to the work of the sculptor in chipping away the marble to reveal the hidden content: he removes 'all the impediments that hinder the clear perception of the latent image, and by this mere removal displays the hidden statue in its hidden beauty'.[28]

So theology moves in the dialectic of affirmation and negation, or, perhaps better expressed, it moves through affirmation to negation and then on to criticism and a constant process of refining. No doubt there are different points at which the balance may be struck. Dionysius leans towards the *via negativa* and the result is a fairly austere theology, tinged with a degree of agnosticism. Incidentally, this confirms that, however he may be described, Dionysius is no pantheist. His bias is rather towards a God of otherness and hiddenness. But whether he has the balance right or not, his intention is dialectical and aims at a vision of God and the world that will accommodate and do justice to the many polarities which all seem to have a just claim when we reflect on these questions. We shall see whether some of his successors did better.

The theology described here is closely linked with the ascent of the soul to God. In other words, theology is seen by Dionysius in the closest relation to spirituality, understood as the flowering and coming to perfection of the human person. We must finally therefore consider Dionysius' anthropology. Human beings, as creatures possessing both sense and intellect, come somewhere in the middle of the hierarchical universe, and the human race itself is taken by Dionysius to be hierarchically ordered. But we must remember that these hierarchies are not static stratifications. Human beings can and should ascend through the various stages to a culmination which Dionysius, in common with many other early Christian writers, does not hesitate to call 'deification' (θέωσις). The stages on the way are those described by many spiritual writers – purification, illumination and mystical union. It will be noted that these three stages of the spiritual life correspond exactly with the three ways in theology, though here they appear in a different order. But the order is not important, for although one speaks of stages, each one recurs and they are really distinguishable moments in a unitary process of development. Furthermore, each one engaged in this pilgrimage has a responsibility for others. The very notion of hierarchy implies both receiving and giving. Those who are purified help to purify others; those who are illumined give illumination to others; those who have attained to communion with the divine bring others to the same relation.[29] Human beings are unified with each other as they seek union with God. This ascent towards God is not to be understood as simply human improvement by human effort, though on the other hand it is not effected by God alone, regardless of the human contribution. God indeed draws us upwards. Dionysius is a believer in synergism – we have God as co-worker (συνεργός).[30] The end is that relation to God which, as we have seen, is called 'deification'. This is not absorption, though presumably it would include an immediate knowledge of God, like the intuitive knowledge of the highest ranks of angels. Such a knowledge would transcend the measure of separation character-istic of both the subject-object and I-thou patterns, for it would belong to a still deeper union or communion. One may suppose that this is the kind of knowledge attained by the mystic in the moment of ecstasy. It cannot be expressed in any language available to us, but the symbols of symbolic theology, provided we do not take them literally but hold open their symbolic character, point us to the mystery. Dionysius, however, is always careful to qualify what he has to say on these matters by reminding us of the limits of what is possible for the finite human being. So we find him giving a surprisingly restrained description of what 'deification' means: 'a process whereby we are made like to God and are united to him, so far as these things may be'.[31]

VII

Mediaeval: Eriugena

Johannes Scotus Eriugena has a good claim to be considered the greatest Celtic thinker who ever lived. Born about 810, he was known in his lifetime and for centuries thereafter simply as Johannes Scotus or John the Scot, but since there were many people so named, he eventually became known by the distinctive agnomen that he had himself used on the title page of one of his works – Eriugena or 'Irish-born'. We do not know anything about his education, but at that time Ireland boasted several great centres of learning, such as Clonmacnoise. It is also tempting to speculate that Celtic spirituality, with its strong emphasis on the immanence of God in nature and in daily life, has to be reckoned along with neo-Platonism as the source of Eriugena's later teaching about the manifestation of God in the things of this world – 'theophanies' was the word that he used.

Like many another Celt, he found the attractions of his homeland insufficient to keep him there, and before the middle of the century he was already teaching in France. He was noted as a linguist and grammarian, and translated into Latin the works of Dionysius the Areopagite. His own major work was a massive philosophico-theological treatise, *On the Division of Nature*.[1] Though he writes from the viewpoint of Christian neo-Platonism, he has a sturdy independence. Acknowledging that his teaching may sometimes 'horrify' his readers, he says: 'Do not be afraid. For now we must follow reason, which investigates the truth of things and is not overborne by any authority, and is by no means prevented from revealing publicly and proclaiming to all men the things which it zealously searches out by circuitous reasoning, and discovers with much toil.'[2] And while he acknowledges the authority of the Bible, he warns that it cannot be taken literally in all things. Actually his teachings speedily became suspect in the eyes of the ecclesiastical authorities, though they were not actually condemned until several centuries after his death. The main point in dispute was whether his emphasis on the divine immanence had not been carried too far in the direction of pantheism. We shall have to make up our minds on this point as we follow the train of his arguments.

Eriugena died in 877. If the legend is to be believed,[3] he had the distinction of being one of the very few professors who so upset his students that they murdered him, stabbing him to death with their styles at the end of an overly provocative lecture. But in recent decades, steps have been taken to rehabilitate Eriugena's reputation. According to preference, he has been hailed as a precursor of Spinoza, Schelling, Hegel and Whitehead. Perhaps he could hardly have been all these, but he remains one of the greatest thinkers of the Middle Ages and his ideas well repay our study.

Eriugena's starting point is to make a fourfold division of Nature. It should be said first of all that he uses the term 'Nature' in a very general sense to cover everything, both the things that are and the things that are not. The meaning of this curious phrase will occupy us later. But let us hear what the fourfold division is. It is very logical in a rather scholastic way. Nature, we are told, consists, first, of that which creates and is not created; second, that which is created and also creates; third, that which is created and does not create; and fourth, that which neither creates nor is created.[4]

At first sight, this fourfold division is somewhat unclear. Eriugena points out that the first and third divisions are opposites, that which creates and is not created being logically the exact opposite of that which is created and does not create. It is also clear in this case what each of the division includes, for God is obviously the one who creates and is not created, while the finite beings of the world, including human beings, come under the heading of that which is created and does not create. The second and fourth divisions, that which is created and also creates and that which neither creates nor is created, are likewise logical opposites, but it is not so easy to see what is the content of these divisions. The second division is meant to include the eternal ideas, species or forms, also called divine volitions and participations in the one Cause of all things. They are themselves primordial causes which determine what can possibly come into being in the universe. They thus have a creative agency, though themselves created by the divine will.[5] The fourth division would seem to include nothing at all,[6] but it actually turns out to be the same as the first; that is to say, its content is God, but God seen in a different way. From God as creator flows the differentiated creation, but in the end all things will return to God, he will cease to create and all things will be at rest in him.[7] Thus in the end it would be possible to say of God that he neither creates nor is created. At this point, however, Eriugena's division of nature seems artificial. It also appears to contradict what he says elsewhere, for he states that God and his making are co-eternal, that for God to be and to make are one and the same, that making is not accidental to God but essential, and even that God did not exist before he made all things, if one could suppose such a time.[8] These consequences seem to be entailed in any case by the inclusion of God in the first division of nature, for there he is defined in terms of his creating activity.

We have seen that God is included by Eriugena in Nature, which is co-extensive with reality. He can also use the term 'universe' in this inclusive sense and says that 'I use the term "universe" for both God and the creatures' (*universitatem dico deum et creaturam*).[9] Is this not clear evidence, then, that he is a pantheist? By no means. We have seen that God is not identified with Nature or the universe as a whole, but only with the first and fourth divisions in Eriugena's scheme. Moreover, since God is defined as the creator, he cannot be held to be simply a part of the universe. Eriugena is making every effort to bring together transcendence and immanence, not in any weakened compromising form, but thoroughgoing transcendence together with complete immanence. Both seem to be demanded by the very meaning of the word 'God', but to try to express this consistently may be impossible. Eriugena is himself well aware of the difficulties and knows that God cannot be encapsulated in some tidy concept. But as a philosopher and theologian, he must struggle as best he can towards a dialectical way of speaking about God that will be modestly agnostic in the face of deity which by its very otherness must surpass human comprehension and will yet at the same time express as clearly as possible such imperfect knowledge of God as we can attain.

Eriugena does in fact keep coming back to objections to including God in Nature, but he sticks to his initial position. His concept of Nature is a differentiated one, with a hierarchy of levels of being in which God occupies the highest level, yet even to say this would not express the difference between deity and the creatures. In one passage, Eriugena writes: 'Among the divisions of the created universe I certainly would not place it, but for placing it within the divisions of that universe which is comprehended by the term "universal Nature" I have not one but many reasons. For by that name "Nature" is usually signified not only the created universe but also that which creates it.'[10] He goes on to state clearly the difference between the divine Nature which 'through itself by itself in itself' is essence, life, wisdom and power, and the created nature which has being and life only by partipation.[11] Again, God is not a part of Nature but 'the causal Beginning of all those things, and the essential Middle which fulfils them, and the End in which they are consummated'.[12] Yet with equal firmness he claims that God is 'inseparable from every universe that he has created',[13] and even that 'God is all things everywhere'.[14] But even this last statement, when seen in the context of Eriugena's full and very subtle teaching about the relation of God to the world, need not bear a pantheistic interpretation. Still, it is clear that for him God and the world are not two separate realities but, however different they are, belong together in a whole.

We can now go back for a moment to clarify that rather puzzling expression used by Eriugena when he said that Nature is the whole realm of the things that are and the things that are not. What about those things that are not? They are said to be the things that cannot be apprehended by either intellect or sense, and within the hierarchy of Nature we can now see what they are. Surprisingly, God himself is the principal case of that which is not. Since he is the creator of the things that are, he is not himself one of them. He does not exist, as human beings or trees or angels exist, and his mode of being is altogether different. God is beyond being, as we shall see. At the opposite end of the scale, the merely potential fall below the level of being. Matter, if it could be found in an unformed state, would belong here, but one would also include, for instance, human beings who do not yet exist but will exist in the future, or anything else which does not exist but has the potentiality for coming into being.

Let us now consider in more detail some of those elements in Eriugena's teaching which stress the otherness and transcendence of God, sometimes in extreme ways.

Since we have begun from the thought that God is the creator of all things, so that he must be in some sense their Cause, it would seem that we could at least affirm his existence, even if we could not say much more about him. Yet even to affirm his existence would require qualification, for we have already seen that there are grounds for counting God among the things that are not. It is laid down as a general rule that any property which has an opposite cannot properly be predicated of God,[15] and this doctrine is extended to being or existence, even if one may question whether being is a property or predicate.

At this point Eriugena is heavily dependent on Dionysius the Areopagite, and in fact his teaching is little more than a recapitulation of that of his predecessor. We are reminded by Eriugena that there are two ways in theology, the cataphatic and the apophatic. 'These two,' he says, 'which seem to be the contraries of one another, are in no way mutually opposed when they are applied to the divine nature, but in every way and at every point are in harmony with each other.'[16] For instance, according to the cataphatic mode, we say 'God is wise', but we do not mean that he is *properly* wise, that is to say, wise in the ordinary signification of the world as used in human intercourse. In the apophatic mode, we say, 'God is not wise', but this does not imply any inconsistency or incoherence with what has already been asserted, for the word 'wise' is now being used in its proper sense, and that was not the case with the cataphatic assertion. But the dialectic now proceeds to a third assertion which combines the cataphatic and the apophatic, namely, that God is *more than* wise. What is the meaning of this 'more than' (*plus quam*)? Eriugena insists that this third proposition, in spite of its affirmative form, is in fact negative, for we do not know what that 'more than' means – for instance, what it would mean to be 'more than wise'? This is part of the divine incomprehensibility.

At this point, however, a critic might say that to declare that God is more than wise must be an empty or meaningless statement. In view of the explanation given on the relation between cataphatic and apophatic, he might agree that there is no incoherence or contradiction involved in these two modes, but when the conclusion is reached that God is more than wise or more than good or whatever it might be, and we are told that this too belongs to the apophatic way of speaking, then it might seem that we have not reached any conclusion and that the purported conclusion is an empty form of words. But I do not think that this objection holds up. Accusations of meaninglessness usually rest on insufficient care or insufficient effort on the part of the person who brings the accusation in trying to understand what the proposition or statement means. In the present case, it may freely be acknowledged that it is beyond human comprehension to form a clear concept of what divine wisdom or divine goodness would be. But on the basis of our own experience of finite wisdom or finite goodness and of the defects which attend these, we are at least being pointed in a definite direction when we hear expressions like 'more than wise' or 'more than good', so that these are by no means empty – indeed, I think we would have to say that they have more affirmative content than Eriugena is willing to allow, though as he develops his concept of God, he tends himself to import more content into it.

Let us now see how this dialectic works itself out in the all-important matter of what we mean by God's 'being' or 'existence'. God is said, in the kind of language which Eriugena has taken over from Dionysius, to be 'superessential'. As Eriugena summarizes it, the divine nature is essence, affirmation; it is non-essence, negation; it is superessential, affirmation and negation together. But, he tells us, this superessential 'is fully negative in meaning . . . For it says that it is not essence but more than essence, but what that is which is more than essence, it does not reveal. For it says that God is not one of the things that are, but that he is more than the things that are, but what that "is" is, it in no way defines' (*illud autem esse quid sit nullo modo diffinit*).[17] Rather similarly, we find him saying: 'The divine is incomprehensible to all reason and all intellect, and therefore when we predicate being of him we do not say that he is; for being is from him, but he is not himself being (*ex ipso enim esse, sed non ipsum esse*). For above this being after some manner there is more than being (*aliquo modo superesse*).'[18] In a different place, he declares that 'only this definition can be predicated of God, that he is "He who is more than being" (*Qui plus quam esse est*)'.[19] This is surely a subtler and more adequate name for God than Thomas Aquinas' famous 'He who is' (*Qui est*).[20] But again one must say that there is more content to Eriugena's definition than he himself is sometimes willing to admit, or than would be admitted by sceptics who might criticize his language as empty. For we do know something like different modes or degrees of being, and are able to recognize that the expression 'more than being' points in one direction rather than in another, though its content is not to be fully grasped conceptually. A stone exists simply by lying around in the world. A human being exists in a far more active way by taking responsibility for his life and his world. By extrapolation, we can attach some meaning to the idea of modes of existence above the human level.

It is interesting to note that Eriugena derives at least the sketch of a trinitarian doctrine of God from the mere idea of his being and thus, in the manner of dialectical theists in general, found the notion of the triune God in natural rather than revealed theology. He speaks of God 'subsisting in a threefold way' (*ter subsistens*). From the fact that things exist in the world, we can affirm of their creator that he is, albeit in the analogical mode of predication already explained; from the marvellous order of things, that he is wise; and from their motion, he is found to be life.[21] It is clear that this natural theology of the threefold subsistence of God is much closer to Christian trinitarian doctrine than was the triad of Plotinus. For in the idea of 'more than being' we can recognize the Father as the ultimate Source; in wisdom the Word, by or through whom all things were made; while the universal life which is said to spread through everything is identified by Eriugena with both the World-soul of some philosophers and the Holy Spirit of Christian theologians.[22]

Erigiuena works systematically through the ten categories of Aristotle, showing that, as these are applicable to finite things, none of them may be properly applied to God. Yet, as we have already seen in the case of being or substance (οὐσία), something, however inadequate, may be gathered about God, so it is in the case of the other categories: God is more than place, more than time, more than motion, and so on. 'He is defined by nothing, but defines all things.'[23] As an example of Eriugena's speculative construction, we may consider what he has to say about God and motion; the choice of this category has the further advantage that it helps us to see the relation of God as described in the first division of Nature, 'that which creates and is not created', with God as described in the fourth division, 'that which neither creates nor is created'.

Since motion has an opposite, namely, rest, Eriugena's dialectic demands that both motion and rest must be predicated of God, so we find him duly saying of God that he is 'motion at rest and rest in motion'. This does not mean that God moves in relation to anything else. The paradox is explained to mean that God moves 'from himself in himself towards himself' (*a se ipso in se ipso ad se ipsum*).[24] This is another way of describing God's fundamental character as creator, and likewise another way of expressing his threefold mode of being. The hidden essence comes forth into an intelligible world, then the things of that world return to their source. 'The motion of the supreme and threefold and only true Goodness, which in itself is immutable, and the multiplication of its simplicity, and its unexhausted diffusion from itself, is the cause of all things, indeed *is* all things.'[25] So the end is all things gathered together in God, and when that has come about, God would be 'that which neither creates nor is created'. But we would be mistaken if we supposed that this end is something that will be attained at some future time. Just as God's creativity had no beginning in time, so it will have no temporal end. The creating and the perfecting go on eternally. Though Eriugena teaches that the end will be the return of all things into the Cause from which they proceeded, he can also say that this is already the case. Sin prevents us from seeing this, and when sin is removed, the vision of the truth is clear.[26]

I have expounded at some length those parts of Eriugena's teaching in which he stresses the transcendence of God, and we have seen that he makes the difference between God and the creatures so absolute that it would seem that we could know virtually nothing of God at all. Thus he writes: 'For even the Cause of all things, which is God, is only known to be from the things created by him, but by no inference from creatures can we understand what he is.'[27] This would seem to reduce natural theology to an absolute minimum – we can know of God from the creatures simply that he exists, and even this word 'exists' is being used in a metaphorical sense. Yet we have also seen that in spite of his own negations, Eriugena seems to be able to make a number of assertions about God, and however guarded these may be, they surely claim some kind of knowledge of who or what God is. We have heard that he is more than being, more than motion, more than time, and so forth. It cannot plausibly be maintained that these are purely negative descriptions – they at least point towards some affirmation. Again, he was able to deduce that God subsists in a threefold way, as essence, wisdom and life, and to sketch out the form of the triune God. It will not therefore surprise us to find that in a later part of his work he seems to give a larger role to natural theology. He asks: 'By what means then can we inquire into and investigate the trinity in unity and unity in trinity of the divine Goodness so as to have some likely belief of it (*verisimile credamus*) by which we may adore it, unless, under its guidance and precept, "Seek and you shall find", we begin our ascent to it by employing as steps examples from the Nature which has been created by it?'[28] Here it seems to be acknowledged that there is at least enough reflection of the divine creator in his works that from them we can gain such knowledge of God as could claim verisimilitude – and what more could we ask than that, for do we get beyond verisimilitude even in our knowledge of created Nature itself?

Here we have to take note of a very important point in Eriugena's teaching, though it seems hard to reconcile it with his own starting point. That starting point, it will be remembered, was the fourfold division of Nature, and the first of these divisions, identified with God, was 'that which creates but is not created'. But very soon he qualifies this in a quite fundamental way by saying that in a sense God is also created, or better expressed, creates himself in his works. For God, willing, acting, being are all one and the same, so that he is in that which he makes. The divine Nature, 'although it creates all things and cannot be created by anything, is in an admirable manner created in all things which take their being from it'.[29] Is this startling doctrine that God is making himself in the things that he makes a contradiction of the definition of him as 'that which creates and is not created', or is it still another way of speaking of God that has a legitimate place within the logic of God-language, just as we found to be the case with the fourth division of Nature, 'that which neither creates nor is created'? I think that what Eriugena is proposing here is something like the conception of the 'consequent nature' of God in the philosophy of Whitehead, and that both of these thinkers are striving for an understanding of God that will express both his otherness and his involvement in the world-process. But let us look more closely at what Eriugena has to say.

In response to the question of a student who asks him what Dionysius meant by the name of 'Nothing', Eriugena makes the following reply:

I should believe that by that name is signified the ineffable and incomprehensible and inaccessible brilliance of the divine Goodness which is unknown to all intellects, whether human or angelic, for it is superessential and supernatural; which, while it is contemplated in itself neither is nor was nor shall be, for it is understood to be in none of the things that exist because it surpasses all things, but when, by a certain ineffable descent into the things that are, it is beheld by the mind's eye, it alone is found to be in all things, and it is and was and shall be. Therefore, so long as it is understood to be incomprehensible by reason of its transcendence (*per excellentiam*), it is not unreasonably called 'nothing', but when it begins to appear in its theophanies, it is said to proceed, as it were, out of nothing into something, and that which is properly thought of as beyond all essence is also properly known in all essence, and therefore every visible and invisible creature can be called a 'theophany', that is, a divine apparition.[30]

It is remarkable that in this passage Eriugena goes so far as to say that the divine essence is *properly* known in all essence. It would seem that his doctrine of theophanies is quite an important qualification of the negative theology.

What, then, is a theophany? Eriugena seems to have borrowed the term from Maximus the Confessor, and he took it to mean an active self-communication of God in and through the things of the world. That is to say, a theophany is not just some passive trace that God has left in his works, and from which we might infer his existence. Rather, God through his divine word has descended into the creation and there he communicates himself to those beings who are able to mount up to meet him, though this ascent towards God, sometimes called 'deification', is itself enabled by the divine grace and love. 'It is from God, then', writes Eriugena, 'that the theophanies happen through grace in the angelic nature and in human nature when it has been illuminated, purified and perfected, as a consequence of the descent of the divine Wisdom and of the ascent of the human and angelic understanding.'[31] The whole of Nature, then, is or at least is able to become the vehicle of theophanies, and since these arise through God's actual self-communication, the borderline between natural and revealed theology is a tenuous one. All beings in the created order, from the highest to the lowest, may be the occasion of a theophany. Clearly, however, a special place belongs to those beings that are intelligent and spiritual, angels and human beings. We may leave the angels aside (they figure much less prominently in Eriugena than they do in Dionysius) and concentrate our attention on the human being. He is the recipient of the theophanies, it is in him that the theophanies take place, and he himself is a theophany, that is to say, a manifestation on the finite level of the divine being.

In a rather striking metaphor (though it had been used by some earlier writers) Eriugena calls the human being a 'workshop' (*officina*). 'Man,' he says, 'is not inappropriately called the "work-shop" of all creatures, since in him the universal creature is contained. For he understands like an angel, reasons like a man, is sentient like an animal, has life like a plant and subsists in body and soul. There is no creature that he is without.'[32] Here we come again on the idea of man as the microcosm, summing up in himself the whole of creation. But we are asking about man as the exemplary theophany. Is there a sense in which he manifests God as well as the 'universal creature'?

Two replies may be made to this question. The first is a reminder that God makes himself in the creatures and manifests himself in them, so that to the extent that the human being reflects in himself the wealth of created being, he is also reflecting what we may conveniently call the 'consequent' nature of God, that is to say, God as he has made himself in the creation, put himself into the creation and expressed himself in it. But there is a further answer. These physical bodies of ours, Eriugena believed, are not an original or essential constituent of human nature. Sin has corrupted them. He does not teach that human beings were originally bodiless, but that the unfallen human body was a celestial or spiritual body. Incidentally, he also taught that these original human bodies were without sexual differentiation! This teaching obviously borders on some kind of gnosticism. It is not very important in Eriugena's system, but I mention it because it leads him to look for the essential nature of man in his spiritual being. It is as a spiritual being that man is made in the image of God, and because he is made in that image, he is also a potential theophany of God. There are two ways of expressing the manner in which the human being mirrors the divine Nature. He is 'an intellectual idea eternally made in the mind of God',[33] that is to say, he is the realization of one of the primordial creative ideas in God's mind. More directly, however, he reflects the triune being of God, and here Eriugena's argument may remind us of similar passages in Augustine. The trinity in the human soul is variously expressed. It is essence, power and operation, and also intellect, reason and sense,[34] but these are equated by Eriugena and held to reflect the divine trinity. The pious seeker after God is held to have in his own soul a mirror (*speculum*) in which the triune God is manifested.[35] It is from this image that the truth of which it is an image must be sought.[36] But we are also warned, as true dialectic requires, that this knowledge of God will always remain metaphorical.

That last sentence reminds us of the dialectical character of all Eriugena's thought. Though he regards the human person as a mirror from which we can learn something of the divine being, this does not infringe the otherness of God; Eriugena's understanding of God is indeed, in the words of one of his most acute interpreters, 'purified of anthropomorphism'.[37] On the other hand, he is not asking us to take some cold impersonal Absolute for God – that would be as one-sided a caricature of his views as we have seen the accusation of pantheism to be. Consider, for instance, what he says about love: 'Love is a bond or chain by which the totality of all things is bound together in ineffable friendship and indissoluble unity . . . Rightly therefore is God called love since he is the Cause of all love and is diffused through all things and gathers all things together in one and involves them in himself in an ineffable return, and brings to an end in himself the motions of love of the whole creation.'[38] There is nothing anthropomorphic about this conception, but surely this is a God to whom human beings can make a response of love. Alongside the speculative ideas of the *Periphyseon*, one has to set such writings of Eriugena as his *Homily on the Prologue to the Gospel of John* and his *Commentary on the Gospel of John*; one then sees how these same speculative ideas are much more compatible with traditional religious beliefs about God than might have been expected.

There are, however, two serious weaknesses in Eriugena's system, and I think they are connected. One is his treatment of evil; the other is his undervaluation of time and the temporal order. These weaknesses seem to be almost endemic in metaphysical systems of this type, and both of them can be almost exactly paralleled in modern writers such as F. H. Bradley.

Evil is not taken seriously enough by Eriugena, any more than it was by Plotinus. It is appearance, not reality. 'The cloud of fleshly thoughts and the darkness of variegated fantasies'[39] prevent us from seeing the reality. It is significant that the sins he mentions belong to the flesh, and there is nothing about sins of the spirit. It is assumed that if we could rise above the flesh, we would see things in their wholeness, and the distortions arising from our unclear vision would be resolved.

But this unsatisfactory treatment of evil leads back to a way of understanding time. When Eriugena talks about the divine Nature creating through its word and the primal ideas, and how it then diffuses itself through the universe and finally brings all things back to itself, this seems to be a great creative and salvific movement in time and history, until God is all and in all. But this too is appearance. The ideal reality is static and already perfect, for those who have eyes to see it. It is surely ironical that in his discussion of the prologue to John's Gospel, Eriugena praises John above Peter, for while the latter recognized the historical Christ, John had penetrated to the truth of the eternal Word in the bosom of the Father before all ages![40] In contrast to Augustine, Eriugena would seem to be implying here that the Platonists had something more important to say about the Word than the Christians. What need is there for a historical incarnation if the ebb and flow of history go on for ever, while the unseen reality remains unchanged and unaffected? History may be more devalued here than even in Plotinus.

But are these weaknesses in Eriugena's system insuperable? Let us suppose he had taken more seriously his own bold speculation that God is not only the creator but, in some sense, is actually creating himself in the history of the universe. Then evil, too, has to be taken more seriously, and the struggle to overcome it. The idea of a striving and perhaps even of a suffering God becomes a possibility, a God who has really ventured himself and engaged himself in the vicissitudes of history. So perhaps Eriugena's thought already contained the resources for its own renewal and development.

VIII

Renaissance: Cusanus

Cusanus, the Latin name for a native of Cusa or Kues in western Germany, is one of the designations – the briefest one – applied to the most famous son of that somewhat obscure town. His original name was Nicholas Krebs, and the name by which he is probably best known is Nicholas of Cusa. I have chosen him as representative of dialectical theism in the time of the Renaissance, for his life spanned the years 1401–1464, when the new learning was on the rise all over Europe. Although a churchman and eventually a cardinal, and although much involved in ecclesiastical affairs, Nicholas was also a philosopher and was deeply interested in mathematics and science. Historical labels are inexact, but it does seem to me that Nicholas belongs to the Renaissance rather than to the Middle Ages, at least, in those matters with which our own inquiry is specially concerned. We shall see that while he owed much to Dionysius and other earlier thinkers in the neo-Platonist tradition, he introduced new ideas which point forward to Leibniz and even to Hegel. I would agree with the judgment of Frederick Copleston who writes: 'Although one can emphasize the traditional elements in his philosophy and push him back, as it were, into the Middle Ages, one can equally well emphasize the forward-looking elements of his thought and associate him with the beginnings of "modern philosophy".'[1]

It is, of course, true that in his writings[2] Nicholas of Cusa takes up most of the themes already discussed in Dionysius and Eriugena. But he does not just repeat the teaching of these earlier thinkers but carries it all further. I want to mention two ways in which this happens, and I think I am drawing attention to genuine developments, not just exaggerating minor points.

First, there is quite a considerable sharpening of the dialectic of

God-language. Dionysius and Eriugena were indeed not themselves lacking in sharpness, and it was already clear that dialectic
takes difference seriously and does not seek an obscuring compromise. But Nicholas of Cusa, while accepting this teaching, gives
new emphasis to the clash of contraries in his famous doctrine of
the coincidence of opposites (*coincidentia oppositorum*). Let me express
the difference in the following way. For Dionysius and Eriugena,
the dialectic takes the form:

Affirmation – God is A.
Negation – God is non-A.
Resolution – God is above or beyond (*hyper* or *super*) A.

For Nicholas of Cusa, on the other hand, the form is as follows:

Affirmation – God is A.
Counter-affirmation – God is B (where B is, in logical terms, the
    contrary rather than the contradictory of A).
Resolution – God is, in an incomprehensible way, both A and B.

'God embraces everything, even contradictions.'[3] Perhaps Dionysius and Eriugena could have said that, too, but they do not say it
with quite the thorough-goingness of Nicholas when he asserts the
coincidence of opposites. This has been called 'copulative' theology.

Perhaps one might suggest a parallel at this point in the relation
of Hegel and Kierkegaard. These two were much closer than is
often recognized. Both were dialecticians and interpreted the world
in terms of the clash of opposites. Rightly or wrongly, Hegel has
been accused of resolving the clash too easily by his teaching that
the opposites are taken up and reconciled in a new synthesis.
Kierkegaard – and again I take the precaution of saying 'rightly or
wrongly'– has been charged with the opposite mistake of leaving the
contradictions standing as unresolved paradoxes. Niels Thulstrup
has suggested that the difference between the two philosophers
lies in the fact that Hegel subordinated the individual to the world-
process with the result that unity triumphs over diversity, whereas
for Kierkegaard the category of the individual and his freedom is
primary, so that the diversity cannot be ironed out.[4] Could it have
been that the rising individualism of the Renaissance made Nicholas
of Cusa more aware of the clash of opposites than his predecessors
had been?

But the second point of difference between Nicholas and the
earlier thinkers prevents us from carrying the parallel with Kierke-

gaard too far. Nicholas was too much of a rationalist ever to have been content with the mere assertion of a paradox. He says to one of his students: 'I shall speak and converse with you, but only on the following condition, namely, that unless you are compelled by reason, you will reject as unimportant everything you hear from me.'[5] In another passage addressed to God, the belief is expressed that even God does not impose anything that would go against the freedom and rationality of the individual: 'Thou dost draw us unto thee by every possible means whereby a free and rational creature may be drawn.'[6] Thus, although he affirms the incomprehensible coincidence of opposites in the divine being, Nicholas goes to great lengths in looking for analogies that will persuade us that such a coincidence of opposites is not an impossibility or an absurdity. What is distinctive in his thought at this point is that he turns to mathematics for his analogies. It is true, of course, that from Plato onwards philosophers have interested themselves in mathematics, but for the Renaissance philosopher mathematics had taken on new importance. As we shall see, what specially fascinated Nicholas of Cusa was the logic of infinity. It would be more than two hundred years before the publication of Spinoza's *Ethica ordine geometrico demonstrata*, but already some parts of Cusanus' work look like a *Theologia ordine geometrico demonstrata*. I should add at once, however, that Nicholas would not have claimed to be offering a demonstration. He prized reason, but was also aware of its limitations. Even in the natural sciences, we attain only approximations to the truth, and the case is even more difficult in philosophy and theology. We proceed by comparisons, analogies and models that are always at a remove from the realities. He tells us that the approximation of the mind to truth is like inscribing a polygon in a circle – one can keep on adding sides and so the polygon will keep getting closer to coinciding with the circle, but it will never fully coincide.[7]

Nevertheless, Nicholas does speak of 'the powerful aid of mathematics in the apprehension of various truths relating to God'.[8] His argument is that since mathematics deals with entities that are intelligible, it possesses a certainty that cannot be attained when one is studying entities that are sensible. Perhaps he also had in mind Dionysius' point that unlike symbols have the advantage that they are in no danger of being confused with the reality they represent, and will not therefore become established as idols. Nicholas does himself mention the danger of idolatry if God is represented under attributes derived from the created order, without the appropriate negations.[9] At any rate, it is hard to imagine that a straight line could be set up as an idol!

But before we go on to a detailed examination of the way in which Cusanus makes use of his mathematical analogies, we have to look more closely at his attempt to combine a strong emphasis on the incomprehensibility of God as the coincidence of opposites with his claim to be satisfying the reason of his readers. This means that we have to consider what is signified by the title of Nicholas' most famous work, *Of Learned Ignorance (De docta ignorantia)*. He uses the expression in more than one sense. When it first occurs, Nicholas explains it much in the same manner as Socrates explained the saying of the oracle that no one was wiser than he, namely, that at least he was aware of his own ignorance.[10] So we find Nicholas declaring, 'A person will be the more learned, the more he has become aware that he is ignorant.'[11] This remark would seem to do no more than commend a properly critical caution, which is itself part of rationality. Elsewhere, however, Nicholas seems to go much further. He says: 'Amid so many diverse wonderful things, we are taught by learned ignorance that we cannot know any reason for any of the works of God, we can only wonder at how great the Lord is, of whose greatness there is no end.'[12] This seems a much more sceptical position, with reason reduced to impotence in the face of the surrounding reality. Furthermore, the remedy which Nicholas suggests must sound like a counsel of despair: 'Our ignorance cries, "Find yourself in him, and since everything in him is himself, nothing can then be lacking to you." '[13] But if God is himself the incomprehensible *coincidentia oppositorum*, how can he be the way to understanding finite things? Nicholas' answer, I suppose, is that beyond discursive reason and even beyond intuitive intellection there is mystical illumination, bestowed by God himself on the soul that seeks him. But since not everybody knows this illumination and since it cannot in any case be put into language, I do not think that Cusanus has given us a clear or satisfying account of learned ignorance or of how he combines, as he certainly wishes to do, a recognition of the divine incomprehensibility with the use of rational argument on behalf of his philosophical theology.

However, the fact that Cusanus fails to give us a clear and convincing account of what he means by 'learned ignorance' does not mean that the idea itself is untenable. There have been many other philosophers, some of them working quite recently, who have faced the same type of problem and who have given much better solutions than Cusanus. Quite unintentionally, they provide a way of escape for the embattled Nicholas. Let us consider the view put forward by my own teacher, C. A. Campbell. The philosopher, he pointed out, has a commitment to reason, and must criticize every proposed theory in the light of reason. Even if there are religious insights granted by revelation and not reached by argument, they must be submitted to rational scrutiny. He pointed out further that those who claim mystical experiences or interior revelations themselves argue for the validity of their position, thereby tacitly admitting the competence of reason to judge even in such questions. But at this point, Campbell makes an important distinction. While holding that reason must be the judge in claims to truth, he says: 'The philosopher is not committed by his occupational loyalty to reason to the position that God can be known only if he can be apprehended as an "object" of reason. A philosopher might come (and some philosophers have come) to the considered conclusion that reality is suprarational, that it is not in its ultimate nature amenable to conceptual understanding.'[14] This is in fact Campbell's own position, and he explicitly dissociates himself from the panlogism of Hegel and other philosophers who have upheld the omnicompetence of reason. Clearly, Campbell's position is close to that of Cusanus and other neo-Platonists in this particular matter. And Campbell, I think, shows much more convincingly than Cusanus that belief in a supra-rational or incomprehensible deity is entirely compatible with the exercise of reason in support of that belief. This, I think, gives a defensible sense of 'learned ignorance', beyond the Socratic sense. But this can become clearer only as we work our way further through Cusanus' ideas.

Let us consider now how Nicholas used mathematical analogies to throw what light can be thrown on the mystery of God. He introduces the subject with a discussion on the meaning of the 'maximum'. He tells us: 'I call the "maximum" that than which nothing greater can exist.'[15] The word 'maximum' is, of course, in its proper sense, expressive of quantity, and Nicholas makes use of the logic of quantity in his argument. But he understands this analogically as pointing beyond itself to the infinite being of God. So he tells us that in his usage 'maximum and minimum are taken as terms that are absolutely transcendent in meaning (*transcendentes absolute significationis termini*); they are above all restriction to quantity of mass or energy and embrace all things in their absolute simplicity'.[16] So when one speaks of the 'maximum', or, better, of the 'absolute maximum', one has in mind God, though God as embracing all things. The absolute maximum is not a maximum in relation to anything else; it is the All and includes everything so that there is nothing else beside it. This implies also that it is a unity, for nothing stands over against it; and it is necessity, for nothing would exist without it. Since the absolute maximum is, as we have seen, not a maximum in relation to anything else or comparable to anything else, expressions like 'greater than' and 'less than' can have no meaning when we speak of it. Thus it makes no difference whether we speak of the absolute maximum or the absolute minimum, for these two coincide. The absolute quantity is no more a maximum than it is a minimum. Such oppositions exist only for finite objects, and they alone are measurable and comparable to one another. In the infinite, distinctions disappear. Degrees of more or less cannot subsist in the infinite, for each part of the infinite is itself infinite. 'In an infinite number, if one could attain to it, two would not be less than a hundred, just as an inifinite line made up of an infinite number of lines each two feet long would be no smaller than an infinite line made up of an infinite number of lines each four feet long.'[17] Here, then, we have our first illustration of the coincidence of opposites. God is the greatest and God is the least, or rather, in God these opposites are united, for his unity too is not a quantitative unity but a transcendent unity. Admittedly, we cannot understand what this unity that embraces opposites is, any more than we can grasp the nature of infinite numbers. Yet one can say that the absolute maximum is intelligible in the sense that there is logic that leads to it as a necessity of thought. So Nicholas is able to claim that 'the absolute maximum is intelligible without our being able to comprehend it and nameable without our being able to name it (*incomprehensibiliter intelligibile et innominabiliter nominabile*)'.[18] This powerful paradox is, presumably, the learned ignorance.

Cusanus follows up this initial discussion of the absolute maximum with several chapters on the properties of geometrical figures, from which he attempts to gain further light on the mystery of the divine being. Here it will be enough to give a summary of some of the more interesting points.[19]

If we think of a circle, then we see that the larger we make it, the less is the curvature of its circumference. Curvature, according to Cusanus, is a mark of finitude. As the size of the circle increases, the curvature decreases, and at the maximum it would be reduced to zero. When that point had been reached (if one can entertain the possibility) the circumference would have become a straight line, and would now coincide with the diameter. But, claims Cusanus, 'the infinite is in act everything that the finite is in potency'. So the line contains potentially the circle, and it is not difficult to show that one could also derive from it a triangle and even a sphere. 'If these figures are potentially in the finite line, and if the infinite line is in act all that the finite is in potency, it follows that the infinite is triangle, circle and sphere.' He then proceeds to show that this is the case.

The sensible imagination cannot comprehend how a line can be a triangle, but this is not a difficult problem for the intelligence. Any two sides of a triangle, when added together, cannot be less than the third side. If then that third side is infinite, so are the others. But we have seen that there can be only one infinite, and no infinite can have parts that are greater or less than each other. So the three infinite sides all coincide in a single infinite line. So we seem driven to conclude that an infinite triangle cannot have a plurality of sides. But a triangle *must* have three sides, by the very definition of 'triangle'. So we must say that the one infinite line is three, and the three are one. The allusion to the triunity of God is obvious, but we shall come back to this point later. Meanwhile, we note that Nicholas goes on to show how, from that infinite line which is also an infinite triangle, there may be generated the infinite circle, and then the infinite sphere, but we shall not follow the steps of his reasoning in detail.

Nicholas claims to draw 'very profound doctrines' from the foregoing considerations. These concern first, the relation of God to the creatures, and second, the triune constitution of God himself.

On the first point, it is held that there is an analogy between the relation of the infinite line to the geometrical figures and the relation of God to the creatures. The straight line which generates the triangle, circle and sphere, symbolizes the absolute simplicity and infinite unity of the maximum: simplicity, because nothing could be simpler than a straight line; unity, because, as will be remembered, Nicholas has made the subtle point that whereas the triangle and the other figures are potentially derivable from any straight line, they are actually there in the *infinite* straight line, which means that they are generated without any disruption of the unity of the maximum. This ultimate unity is, of course, of the greatest import-ance to Nicholas of Cusa, just as it was to his neo-Platonist predecessors. 'Deity is infinite unity. God himself said, "Hear, O Israel, your God is one . . ." Nothing could be said more truly.'[20] So the absolute maximum is the reason for all things, it is in all things as they are in it, it indeed is all things. Whether this last point implies pantheism will be considered when we come to what Nicholas says about the universe of finite beings.

Meanwhile we turn to the second point that arises out of his mathematical reasonings, namely, their implications for an understanding of the triune God. For Nicholas, the doctrine of a trinity is not a special revelation but part of natural or rational theology. He had already at an earlier stage taken up the belief of Pythagoras that unity is trinity and advanced some rather artificial arguments in support.[21] He now strengthens his case by the use of mathematical analogies. I deliberately spoke, however, of 'a trinity' rather than 'the Trinity', for it is not easy to see how Cusanus' teaching at this point relates to the Christian doctrine of the Trinity or, for that matter, to the Plotinian triad. Indeed, it is not easy at this point to get a consistent trinitarian doctrine from Cusanus at all.

The first trinitarian statement runs as follows: 'As the maximum line is no more a line than it is a triangle, circle or sphere, but is truly all of these uncompounded, so in the same way the absolute maximum is like the linear maximum, and we may call it "essence" (*essentia*). It is like the triangular maximum, and we may call it "trinity". It is like the circular maximum, and we may call it "unity". It is like the spherical maximum, and we may call it "actual existence" (*actualis existentia*).'[22] Here we have four terms – essence, trinity, unity and actual existence. The essence, corresponding to the maximum line from which the several figures are generated, is presumably the one substance of the triune God. But what are we to make of the remaining designations – trinity, unity and actual existence? Certainly it is not obvious that they correspond to the three persons of the Christian Trinity. Cusanus does in fact go on to further explanations, though these become increasingly complicated as he proceeds, and one must wonder whether the analogies are really doing their work of utilizing the better known to throw light on the unknown. From the triangle, he argues that one may not go on from trinity to quaternity or any higher number, for the triangle is the simplest polygon that there is, all polygons with a larger number of sides can be reduced to triangles, and we have already seen that when one is considering infinity, the maximum and the minimum coincide.[23] With the infinite circle, matters become more difficult. In such a circle, the centre, the diameter and the circumference all coincide. 'You see how the maximum in its perfection and entirety is within everything, simple and indivisible, because it is the infinite centre; and outside everything, surrounding everything, because it is the infinite circumference; and penetrating everything, because it is the infinite diameter. It is the beginning of everything, because it is the centre; the end of everything, because it is the circumference; the middle of everything, because it is the diameter.'[24] With the sphere, we move into three dimensions, and one might have expected Cusanus to draw some interesting trinitarian teaching from this. But he is content to see the sphere, as the most perfect of all figures, summing up his teaching that God is the reason for everything, the beginning, the middle and the end, the ultimate reality on which all actual existence depends.[25]

Though Cusanus has confidently claimed that his method of inquiry could throw light 'on an infinite number of theological matters now obscure', we can already see that this claim is an exaggerated one. At the most, he has shown that it is legitimate to expect that God-language must have a logic of its own, that it is not nonsense to talk of a coincidence of opposites in God, and that in particular there are analogies which allow us to glimpse something of the meaning of triune being. Yet even to be able to claim this much depends on what answers we give to two difficult questions.

The first of these questions relates to the validity of Nicholas' mathematical example. Let us agree that there is a logic of infinity that differs from the logic of finite quantities, and that is frankly paradoxical. One plus one equals two, but infinity plus infinity still equals infinity. What seems questionable is whether one can extend this logic in the detailed ways employed by Nicholas when he tries to describe the properties of the infinite triangle or the infinite circle. So perhaps we have to reduce Nicholas' claim still further and say that it amounts only to the point that since we consider it legitimate to admit paradox in the mathematics of infinity, it is reasonable to admit it also in speculations about the infinite God.

But now one must raise the further question, whether it is possible to use mathematical properties as analogies that can be applied to the being of God. Mathematical entities are the most abstract that can be conceived. God, however, would seem to possess the most concrete being that can be conceived. The universality of God is quite different from the universality of mathematical entities. The first is the universality of a being which is omnipresent and all-embracing but which is at the same time supremely 'beingful', if one may use that expression. The second type of universality is that of the highest abstraction, attained when all concrete characteristics have been removed and one is left with pure quantity or extension. If this is so, can one claim that there is enough in common between the ideas of infinity applicable in these two very different areas of being to make analogical reasoning from the one to the other legitimate? We are told explicitly by Cusanus that the expression 'absolute maximum', used in relation to God, does not have quantitive but transcendent significance.[26] So a further question mark has to be placed against Cusanus' claim to be drawing profound theological truths from his mathematical exercises.

In any case, one may wonder whether, in his anxiety to avoid anthropomorphism or any picture of God that could be turned into an idol, Nicholas has not gone to the opposite extremes, and presented a God so remote and impersonal that he could hardly be an object of worship or the goal of the religious quest. Although we are told that the 'absolute maximum' is not a quantitative expression, its associations are certainly quantitative. Similar objections, perhaps even more severe, can be brought against some of the other ways in which Nicholas speaks of God. In a late writing, he argues that 'not-other' (*non aliud*) is the appropriate name for God, that this name is a 'precious symbolism' in which God 'shines forth to those who are searching', and that it expresses 'that which for many years I sought by the coincidence of opposites'.[27] I suspect, however, that many readers (and I would be among them) will think that 'not-other' is a regression rather than an advance in the quest for some knowledge of God. The argument by which Cusanus seeks to establish the case for naming God as 'not-other' seems to me quite sophistical and unconvincing. The argument goes on the assumption that definition is the ideal form of knowledge. A definition states the essence of what is defined, that is to say, it shows it to be 'not-other' than . . . 'The definition which defines itself and all things is the definition which every mind seeks. If anyone sees that "definition is not-other than definition" is most true, he also sees that "not-other" is the definition of definition.' But since it is God who defines all things and determines their essences, he is that 'definition which defines itself and all things', and consequently he is appropriately named 'not-other'.[28] One cannot deny the ingenuity of Nicholas' reasoning as he proceeds to unpack the meanings of 'not-other', yet he is constantly in danger of losing himself in sophistry and speculation, and that is why I have said that the treatise in which he expresses these views is a decline from rather than an advance on his earlier work, *Of Learned Ignorance*.

But to get a balanced view of Cusanus' teaching on God, one must also go to his spiritual writings, especially *The Vision of God*. In this writing, he takes his departure from a symbolism that contrasts sharply with the impersonality and abstractness of the absolute maximum and the not-other. The symbolism this time is frankly anthropomorphic – the picture of an omnivoyant face, the eyes of which, through the skill of the artist, seem to be looking directly at any observer of the picture, no matter where he is standing, and to follow him as he moves about. This analogy, it seems to me, in spite of its anthropomorphism, better expresses the coincidence in God of universality and concreteness than such analogies as absolute maximum and not-other. For 'absolute sight', as Nicholas calls it, or, as one might also translate it, 'sight free from limitation', is also sight directed to particulars. If one made the complaint that God as absolute maximum or as not-other is a faceless God, this alternative model gives to God a face; but because it is the omnivoyant face, this is a face that no finite observer can fully see, though where he is, it is directed towards him. So Nicholas can say that this is the 'face of faces'. He tells us: 'In all faces is seen the face of faces, veiled and in a riddle; but unveiled it is not seen, until above all faces one enters into a secret and mystic silence where there is no knowledge or concept of a face.'[29] At this point, the anthropomorphic associations of the face are transcended in the vision of the absolute face. I have said that this analogy of the omnivoyant face unites the polarities of universality and concreteness in a way not found in Nicholas' more speculative analogies, and we do in fact find him returning to his theme of the coincidence of opposites. God dwells 'within the wall of paradise, and this wall is that coincidence where later is one with earlier, where the end is one with the beginning, where alpha and omega are the same'.[30] Just as the universality or infinity of God does not swallow up concreteness and particularity, so, as well as being eternal, he seems to be also in some sense in time: 'Thou, from eternity, hast seen and read, together and once and for all, all written books, and those that can be written, regardless of time; and, in addition, thou dost read these same books one after another with all who read them.'[31]

It is intersting to note here that although Nicholas visualizes God's vision as taking in the future as well as the past, this is not to say that the future is already determined. It remains open as possibility. God has seen and read all books that *have actually* been written, and also those that *can conceivably* come to be written, though in fact this may never happen.

We must now leave Nicholas' teaching about God and consider what he says about the universe and human beings. The universe is represented as a kind of infinite counterpart to God. God, as we have seen, is the absolute maximum, while the universe is a restricted or contracted maximum (*maximum contractum*) which has come into being through emanation (*emanatio*).[32] God is in all things and all things in God, or, to put it in another way, all things are an unfolding (*explicatio*) of God, while he in turn is an enfolding (*complicatio*) of all things. Sometimes Nicholas uses language about the relation of God to the universe that provokes the usual charge of pantheism that is regularly brought against thinkers in this tradition. But the accusation fails here, as it does with Plotinus, Dionysius and the rest. It is incompatible with the strong emphasis on the incomprehensibility and transcendence of God found in Nicholas, and it fails to note his distinction between the absolute maximum and the restricted maximum. In his *Apology*, he explicitly says that although all things are in God as that which is caused is in its cause, it does not follow that the cause and the caused are the same; or, in other words, the universe is in God and stands in intimate relation to him, but it does not exhaust his being.[33] This is the doctrine which later became known as panentheism, not pantheism.

Nevertheless, the universe mirrors some of the divine character. For instance, it manifests a profound unity. 'Because it is clear that God is in all things as all things are in him, and because we see that God is in all things by the mediation, so to speak, of the universe, it appears that everything is in everything, no matter what is no matter what.'[34] Everything is what it is because of everything else, and implies everything else – the doctrine of internal relations, as philosophers of a later time were to call it. This is an organic universe, in which everything affects everything else and is in turn affected. An example given by Nicholas is the human foot, which has its significance only in relation to the entire human organism and all the parts of that organism. He quotes with approval Plato's view that the world is an animal, and he believes too in a World-soul, though this is simply God.[35] The universe mirrors God not only in respect of unity but also as trinity. All things are threefold, constituted of form, matter and the nexus between them.[36]

There are gradations of beings within the universe, and a special place belongs to the human being. 'It is human nature (*humana natura*) that is raised above all the works of God, and, being made a little lower than the angels, comprises both intellectual and sensible natures; embracing all things in itself, it has been called very reasonably by the ancients the microcosm or miniature world (*microcosmos aut parvus mundus*).'[37] Since human nature embraces within itself all levels of being in the universe, then if it could be raised to union with God, all things would be brought to their perfection in it. And, according to Cusanus, humanity does have this potentiality for union with the maximum. He applies his analogy of the polygon inscribed in a circle, in a new way. The polygon is now human nature and the circle the divine nature. 'If the polygon were to become the maximum, than which no greater can be, it would not subsist as a finite angular figure in itself, but would now be inseparable even in intellect from the eternal circular figure.'[38] At that point, of course, one would have come to the union of God and man. Nicholas identifies this moment with the incarnation of the divine Logos in Jesus Christ, and so passes from natural or philosophical theology into revealed theology. But we should notice that the idea of incarnation, as distinct from its historical actualization in Jesus Christ, is for Nicholas, like the doctrine of the Trinity, an implication of his natural theology. I do not think, either, that one could say that his natural theology had been constructed in order to lead up to this point, for in its major ideas, that natural theology is a refinement of the pre-Christian system of Plotinus. It suggests rather that dialectical theism leads the mind in the direction of a doctrine of incarnation, and this is confirmed when we reflect how many of the world's religions have moved in the same way. Incarnation may be, as Kierkegaard said, the absolute paradox, but it is a paradox implicit in the dialectical unfolding of the religious belief in God.

IX

Enlightenment: Leibniz

With Gottfried Wilhelm Leibniz (1646–1716) we come fully into the world of modern philosophy. It is true that his elaborate and highly idiosyncratic metaphysic might at first sight seem to come out of an altogether different age, yet when we examine it, we find that in many respects it anticipates Whitehead, though in others it reaches back to Plotinus. Like Whitehead, Leibniz was a mathematician, and is usually credited with the invention of the infinitesimal calculus, independently of Newton though some years later than him. As in the case of Nicholas of Cusa, the mathematical interests have a considerable influence on Leibniz's general philosophy. But Leibniz had also a lifelong interest in religion. He is said to have been drawn to philosophy by a desire to investigate the elusive notion of substance, with a view to fostering reconciliation between Catholics and Protestants, divided over the question of transubstantiation. It is an irony that when this profoundly theistic and Christian philosopher died, no priest or minister of religion could be found to officiate at his funeral, apparently on the grounds that he had been a very infrequent churchgoer!

In the preface to the major work which he published during his lifetime, *Essais de théodicée*,[1] Leibniz remarks: 'There are two famous labyrinths where our reason very often goes astray.'[2] The first of these labyrinths consists of a complex of questions that affect everyone; questions about the government of the universe, especially how the omnipotence and foreknowledge of God can be reconciled with the presence of evil in the world and the exercise of human freedom. The second labyrinth is a tangle of technical questions about continuity, indivisibility and infinity, underlying which are questions about the nature of substance and matter. This group of questions is said to be of concern to professional philosophers rather than to the mass of people, but since these are the ultimate questions, the answers given to them are bound to affect the answers given to questions that are more obviously of common concern. We shall in fact begin by entering the second labyrinth and considering Leibniz' metaphysic.

We can see the problem as the ancient opposition between the one and the many. At an early stage, Leibniz became dissatisfied with the metaphysic of Descartes, which was very prevalent at that time. He was dissatisfied on the one hand with the dualism of Descartes, who recognized two fundamental substances, mind or thinking substance (*res cogitans*) and matter or extended substance (*res extensa*); and he was further dissatisfied by the definition of matter in terms of extension alone, for there must be *something* extended for matter to have the fundamental characteristic of impenetrability. What then were the alternatives to the Cartesian system? There were two of which Leibniz took cognizance – atomism and monism. Atomism, however, would mean sheer pluralism. We have to remember that in the seventeenth century atoms were still supposed to be hard solid particles, impenetrable and indivisible. Out of such atoms, Leibniz believed, there could not have arisen a unified cosmos. At the opposite extreme was the monism of Spinoza. There is only one substance, both thinking and extended, God or nature, and the multiplicity of entities which make up the world are simply modifications or adjectives of that one substance. This abstract monism was as little acceptable to Leibniz as atomistic pluralism. His own solution is a dialectical synthesis of these two opposing views, and this means an organic view of the universe, which is not just the sum of its constituent parts but is in a sense present in each part, so that the nature of each part is determined by its place and function in the whole. Since dead inert material atoms could never give rise to a true universe organically ordered, they cannot be the ultimate stuff of the world. 'There is no chaos in the inward nature of things, and there is organism everywhere in a matter whose disposition proceeds from God.'[3]

In Leibniz' view, the atoms (understood in the sense of indivisible units) which make up the universe are of an entirely different kind from those visualized by the old-fashioned materialists. These Leibnizian atoms, which he called 'monads', are said to be 'simple substances' (where 'simple' means 'without parts'), yet substances which are able to enter into compounds. These monads are not, of course, material. Each one is a centre of primordial energy (*vis primitiva*). This energy or capacity for action is spiritual rather than material, yet Leibniz makes it clear that monads are always embodied in matter. Thus he not only brings together atomism and monism, but also transcends the Cartesian dualism. There are no disembodied souls, but equally there is no matter that is entirely soulless. Each monad is entirely self-contained and impenetrable to every other. It has 'no windows', in his famous phrase.[4] Yet in an organic universe, each monad stands in some relation to every other. It would seem to be the function of matter to provide the network through which the monads can belong together within the system. So each monad is said to mirror the whole universe. Latta claims that 'an omniscient being could see the reality and history of the whole universe within the lowest monad'.[5]

Mention in this sentence of 'the lowest monad' indicates that in this philosophy there is a hierarchy of beings. There are in fact three levels of monads, though these are not sharply marked off from one another. We consider them in order, beginning with the lowest level.

The lowest level of monads consists of those which form what we generally call 'inorganic' substances, though for Leibniz, as we have seen, organism is everywhere, so that there is nothing that is sheerly inorganic. A lump of rock, for instance, is not just a piece of solid, inert matter, or even a collection of solid, inert atoms. Although Leibniz was writing long before the development of modern atomic theory, he was already fascinated by the problem of the microstructure of things, and, to some extent, this is what he is trying to express in his theory of monads. These units of energy are the ultimate stuff of the universe, and each of them has in itself form, order and organic pattern. Each of them mirrors in itself the whole universe; it is constituted by its relation to the rest of the universe and in turn makes its contribution, however small, to the constitution of everything else. As I have pointed out, the basic problem of Leibniz' metaphysic is the ancient one of the dialectic between the one and the many. 'The universe is all of one piece,' he writes. 'The least movement extends its effect there to any distance whatsoever, even though this effect becomes less perceptible in proportion to the distance.'[6] Presumably any object in the world like a lump of rock, to go back to our example, is constituted by a large number of monads – we could suppose that there is one to every organic particle of which that lump of rock is made up, whether it be atom, molecule or crystal, or even perhaps sub-atomic particle. And wherever there is this organic form, there is the rudiment of mind. This explains why Leibniz considers his monads to be spiritual rather than physical and why, in opposition to the dualism of Descartes, he will not allow pure matter or pure mind, but holds that all matter has some element of 'soul', so that its workings need the concept of organism and are not explicable in merely mechanical terms, as Descartes had believed even about animals and the human body, while on the other hand all mind is associated with matter. Leibniz teaches that amid the many monads which constitute anything there is a 'dominant' monad which gives to that thing its general character and determines the direction of its development. Obviously, however, this would be more apparent at higher levels, for instance, in the life of plants. Our lump of rock has a low level of unity and is commonly regarded as 'inorganic', which means simply that no monad belonging to it has sufficient dominance to establish the kind of unity that we observe at higher levels. It should be noted too that no monad can contain another. Each is an 'atom' in the old-fashioned sense of a simple, indivisible entity. Each is therefore claimed to be indestructible, though it may change and develop, and it may move from one composite of monads to another.

Monads, as we have seen, are said to be spiritual and to have the rudiments of mind. This does not for a moment mean that they are conscious. The rudiments of mind are form, order, organism, and only at the higher levels of being do these attain consciousness and self-consciousness. Yet their presence even in so-called 'inorganic' matter is evidence that even there the rudiments of the mental are present, hence the inherent absurdity of any genuine materialism. Admittedly, Leibniz' language – like that of Whitehead at a later time – can be misleading, and might suggest a kind of 'panpsychism' or universal presence of mind which gets exaggerated into the idea that there is some universal consciousness permeating all things. The language, I say, can be misleading, for Leibniz attributes to all monads, even those on the lowest level, the two functions of perception and appetition. Although the monads have 'no windows', this means only that no one of them can enter another. Each of them also 'mirrors' the universe, because within the organic universe it affects and is affected by everything else. Perception need not be conscious, and indeed it is so only in the highest monads. Unconscious perception, as Leibniz understands it, is simply being open to the effects of other entities, and in some way registering these effects. It could be perhaps compared to what Whitehead calls a 'prehension'. Leibniz, like many other philosophers, was dissatisfied with the empiricists' account of perception, which stressed the passive reception of impressions from without impinging on the *tabula rasa* of the mind. But the mind, too, is active in constructing its picture of the world. This active element is expressed by the term 'appetition' in Leibniz. Everything, he believed, has a tendency to strive towards the realization of its own potentiality for being; it strives to develop its own perfection as that thing which it is. Again, this is the language of conscious existence, and it has to be carefully interpreted when we project it back on to the level of unconscious entities. When we ascribe appetition to the monads belonging to a lump of granite, we do not mean that this lump of granite is consciously striving to become something, but that it has, in an Aristotelian term used by Leibniz, an 'entelechy', a condition in which it fully and clearly manifests 'granitehood', the characteristics that belong to this particular kind of rock.

Most of these conceptions gain both in clarity and plausibility when we move to higher levels of monads. In plants and animals, the notion of a dominant monad becomes much clearer, for although these organisms are made up of a multitude of living cells, each of which is itself a tiny organism, the plant or animal as a whole has a unity transcending the lesser unities of its several parts, so that these lesser unities contribute to the unity of the whole biological organism. The behaviour of a plant can likewise give us a clearer idea of unconscious perception. For instance, a plant will grow towards the light, not only in some sense 'perceiving' it, but also responding to it. Animals, in turn, have elaborate and often highly sensitive organs for perceiving events in the environment. An eagle has powers of vision and a dog has sensitivity to smell far beyond what a human being can perceive, yet we may suppose that the perceptions of an eagle or a dog fall far short of human perception in respect of richness of informative content, for this demands powers of interpretation and understanding which are more highly developed in the human being than in the animal.

Just as perception can be unconscious or compatible with a low level of consciousness, so can appetition. A plant presumably shows us appetition at an unconscious level. From the seed onward, it is already growing – we might even, in a more Leibnizian way, say 'thrusting' – towards the full-grown plant, even overcoming hindrances in the way. An acorn embraces in itself the entelechy of the mature oak. It might, of course, be objected that we need not introduce such an obscure and quasi-metaphysical idea as that of 'entelechy' to account for such behaviour. Is it not sufficient to say that the recipe for oakhood is already encoded in the molecular structure of the cells of the acorn? Here, I think, we have to remind ourselves of the uses and abuses of reductionism.[7] From the point of view of empirical science, reductionism is an indispensable tool in the search for manageable 'explanations'. But such reductive explanations are always partial and abstract. There remains the unanswered problem of why the primitive constituents of the universe have the possibility and the tendency to evolve into living organisms. Reductionism is the attempt to explain the higher in terms of the lower, but it is never an exhaustive explanation, because there are some characteristics of the higher that cannot be brought within the categories applicable to the lower; for instance, organism cannot be fully grasped within the categories of mechanism. The alternative is to seek to explain the lower in terms of the higher, that is to say, to look for analogies between the higher activities which we know in human existence and the behaviour of animals, plants and even inanimate matter. We can see *something like* appetition or striving even in plants, and still more in animals, where we can speak of instinct, urge and even desire. These, moreover, are not simply 'blind', for the appetition is now in some measure co-ordinated with perception. However, I am not saying that the procedure of explaining the lower by analogy with the higher is, *in isolation*, any more satisfactory than reductionism, since it could easily lead to animism or anthropomorphism. Both ways of explaining have their use and their rightful place in the search for fuller understanding.

The third level of monads is seen in human beings, and in any other rational, self-conscious, finite beings that may be found in the universe. Here, perception is accompanied by understanding, reason and reflection, so that we not only perceive the phenomena that present themselves at any given moment, we also perceive something of their interconnectedness and even of their necessity. Appetition has also advanced to a higher level and is expressed in the rational will. Again, the 'entelechy' of the human being, if one may still use the expression, is no longer only a pattern realizing itself in biological growth but an idealized conception of humanity, to be realized by intellectual exploration, moral effort and spiritual aspiration. Leibniz well understood, of course, that the human being carries with him on to his level of being something of the primitive perceptions and appetitions characteristic of the lower levels. Perception remains always to some extent confused, and never reaches a clear and distinct view of the universe, while appetition is never the action of the pure rational will, but continues to be diverted by passion and irrational desire.

What remains somewhat obscure in Leibniz's monadology is the precise nature of matter and its relation to the monads. The monads are alone real in the full sense, and we have seen that they are simple, spiritual, indivisible energies, and so not extended in space. But nevertheless every monad has its body or embodiment. This is what is immediately perceived by the monad, and through it the entire universe is represented. The body then appears to be necessary to the monad, yet it is phenomenal rather than real. It seems to be a kind of precipitate or organ formed by the pure spiritual energy of the monad.

The self-conscious, rational human being is the highest in the hierarchy of finite or created monads. But above him is the culmination of the hierarchy in God. Here we may notice that Leibniz offers two arguments for the reality of God, and they express again the dialectical nature of his thinking, for one is *a priori* and the other *a posteriori*. They are based on two principles which Leibniz regarded as fundamental to his reasoning, one of them rationalist and one of them empiricist, the principles of contradiction and sufficient reason.

In virtue of the principle of contradiction, 'we judge *false* that which involves a contradiction, and *true* that which is opposed or contradictory to the false'.[8] On this *a priori* principle, Leibniz bases a form of the ontological proof of the existence of God. His argument is quite different from the one found in either Anselm or Descartes. They believed that the idea of a perfect being carries within itself the affirmation of the existence of that being. Leibniz, however, makes the point that perhaps the idea of a perfect being is self-contradictory, like, say, the idea of the greatest possible number. The first step must be to show that the idea of God is possible and free from contradiction. Leibniz believes that he can show that God is possible, as the absolute simple being on which all others depend. Then God's reality follows from his possibility, 'for all real possibility includes a tendency to existence, and there can be nothing to hinder this tendency in a being supposed to be perfect'.[9] We may be doubtful whether this argument succeeds, or whether Leibniz, with all his subtlety, has purged the ontological proof of its sophistries.

We turn then to Leibniz' second fundamental principle, that of sufficient reason. According to this, 'we hold that there can be no fact, real or existing, no statement true, unless there be a sufficient reason why it should be so and not otherwise, although these reasons usually cannot be known by us'.[10] This principle seems to presuppose a universe in which things do not happen just by chance, and since I think that all of us live from day to day on that assumption, we can hardly quarrel with it. Leibniz goes on to use the principle to establish the reality of God, in a manner reminiscent of the third of the five ways of Aquinas. There are innumerable contingent facts dispersed throughout the universe. There must be a sufficient reason for these, and this must be something which is not contingent, but a necessary being, namely, God. The argument as stated in this form raises the same problem as we noted in the case of Aquinas: Is this necessary being a being of the same order as the contingent beings dependent upon it? If so, why do we stop the series at that point, rather than looking for a more ultimate being? On the other hand, if we say this necessary being is of a different order, perhaps not a 'being' at all, the argument seems to lose its force, for the kind of connection we are demanding is found only among the beings which make up the world. Admittedly the argument from contingent to necessary being is a strong one and cannot be easily set aside. Some objections to it, such as Findlay's point that there can be only logical, not existential necessity,[11] have been abandoned, while new formulations of the argument, such as Mascall's,[12] have shown that it still possesses considerable force. Elsewhere Leibniz states the argument in a negative form which seems to me to have certain advantages over the form which I have outlined above, and we shall come to this other form very shortly.

Meanwhile, however, we must notice an ambiguity which enters into Leibniz' conception of God. On the one hand, he can speak of God as the supreme monad, the dominant monad of the universe. As such, God too possesses perception and appetition, though in a perfect manner which, presumably, would as far transcend our human experience of these activities as perception and appetition in a piece of rock fall below our level. Yet he can also speak of God as having created the finite monads, and we have seen that God possesses necessary being and imparts contingent being to the entities within the world. These ways of speaking suggest that God transcends the world of monads and is of a different order of being. There is an inconsistency here, and while it would be going too far to say that it is a deliberate inconsistency, nevertheless it seems to be inevitable in Leibniz' system and to express something important in his thinking about God. Leibniz makes it clear more than once that he is opposed to the monarchical idea of God as he is conceived in popular versions of classical theism. 'Our end,' states Leibniz quite clearly, 'is to banish from men the false ideas that represent God to them as an absolute prince employing a despotic power, unfitted to be loved and unworthy of being loved'.[13] He insists too that the moral law cannot be made to rest simply on the decree of God.[14] By speaking of God therefore as both beyond the community of monads and as the principal member of that community, he is recognizing both the uniquely transcendent being of God and his involvement in the world.

There is another point to be noted about the relation of God to the world in Leibniz' thought, and it further qualifies the divine transcendence. God is the creator of the finite monads, but he does not create them simply by decree. Leibniz introduces a peculiar word. 'God alone is the primary unity or original simple substance, of which all created or derivative monads are products, and have their birth, so to speak, through continual fulgurations of the divinity from moment to moment, limited by the receptivity of the created being, of whose essence it is to have limits.'[15] The Latin word *fulgur* means a 'flash of lightning', so that when the created monads are said to be 'fulgurations' of the divine being, the mode of production would seem to be closer to emanation than to making. The very word 'fulguration' may remind us of one of the terms used by Plotinus to express the idea of emanation, namely, ἔκλαμψις, or 'radiation'.[16]

We may attend at this point to some interesting remarks of Latta:

The relation of God to the other monads is the crux of Leibniz' philosophy. He wishes to maintain both the individuality of the monads and their essential unity with God. Thus he seems to take 'fulguration' as a middle term between creation and emanation. 'Creation' would mean too complete a severance between God and the other monads; 'emanation' would mean too complete an identity between them. 'Fulguration' means that the monad is not absolutely created out of nothing nor, on the other hand, merely a mode or an absolutely necessary product of the divine nature, but that it is a possibility tending to realize itself . . . ready to spring or 'flash' into being at the will of God.[17]

The position is further complicated by the fact that monads cannot include one another so that God, in so far as he is supreme monad, cannot indwell finite monads as a world-soul. Furthermore, though all monads have bodies, God is explicitly said to be an exception. But it is through their bodies that the monads perceive one another, so one has to wonder how God is in communication with his creation. There do seem to be inconsistencies here, though these may be inevitable in any account of God that is dialectical and acknowledges that in him there is something like a *coincidentia oppositorum*. Leibniz might have got some help at this point from the mystics, but he does not seem to have been interested in them. The obvious link would be with Nicholas of Cusa, but Leibniz, in all his voluminous writings, seems to have mentioned Nicholas only once, and then he was referring to his mathematics, not his philosophy![18] Leibniz does admit that there are 'truths above reason', but apparently only in the sense that there are some matters about which we never learn *enough*, not that we might come across a reality which, by its very nature, transcended the grasp of reason.[19]

Let me come now to that negative form of the argument for God's existence from the principle of sufficient reason. In a writing called *Principes de la nature et de la grace*, from the same year as *La monadologie*, Leibniz poses the famous question, 'Why does something exist, rather than nothing?'[20] He says that this is the first question we are bound to ask, once we have accepted the principle that 'nothing takes place without sufficient reason'. It is a matter for wonder that anything at all should exist. The theologian Tillich wrote about the 'shock of non-being', but far more potent is the shock of being. None of the things that we observe has any necessity in its existence. It might not have been at all, or it might have existed differently. The fact that there is something rather than nothing (admittedly, an unsatisfactory way of expressing it) argues that there is a source of being which is not contingent but necessary. If there were no such source of being, then there would be nothing at all. But what then is this 'source of being'? It can hardly be another being of the same order as those whose existence it is supposed to explain, for then we could ask why *this* being should be. Even the description of it as a *necessary* being is not adequate. Mystics have spoken of that which is 'beyond being' (Dionysius) or 'more than being'

(Eriugena), and we have tried to interpret these expressions.[21] A philosopher of recent times has declared: 'God is not the necessary being. He is the original unnecessary, the ultimate sheer fact. And in face of this, we are petrified with an astonishment tinged with awe'[22] – what I have called the 'shock of being'. This transcendent mystery which gives being cannot itself be another being or a supermonad or anything of the sort. It is strictly incomprehensible, but we have to posit it because, after all, there is something and not nothing.

But do we have to posit it? Is Leibniz' question a proper one? I have already acknowledged that it was badly formulated. To ask 'Why does something exist?' is too vague – as Munitz has pointed out, it is like asking 'Does it fly?'[23] Until one has done something to clarify the 'something' and the 'it' in these questions, they cannot be understood. Munitz' own first move is to ask, 'Why does the world exist?' Of course, this question might be challenged too, on the grounds that the world itself is 'the ultimate sheer fact'. But to many people the physical universe does not appear to have ultimacy and is as contingent as any of its constituent items. Munitz thinks this question about the 'why' of the world is 'an ineradicable feature of the human response to the world and can neither be removed nor reduced to anything else'.[24] According to Heidegger, who has revived Leibniz' question, 'each of us is grazed at least once, perhaps more than once, by the hidden power of this question, even if he is not aware of what is happening to him'.[25] Heidegger has in his own way clarified and given a focus to Leibniz' question.[26]

We have been thinking of the relation of God or the ultimate reality to the universe of monads in general, but special interest belongs to his relation to that highest rank of created monads which constitute the self-conscious minds of human beings. Leibniz makes two important points in this connection. The first is that the creation of human beings was in some sense necessary to God. He would not be truly God without rational minds (*esprits*) to acknowledge and respond to his deity – and perhaps the world would not be strictly world without rational minds to ask about its 'why'. 'God would have no glory were not his greatness and his goodness known and admired by spirits.'[27] Perhaps one should not say that finite spirits are necessary to God, but there is a sense (on this view) in which they complete God and enhance his being as God. Certainly, this view of Leibniz sharply contradicts those theologians who have taught that God is so utterly complete and self-sufficient that the creation makes no difference to him. I have already criticized this theological prejudice as tending to acosmism, and perhaps even to inhumanity.[28] A second point about the human being in Leibniz' philosophy is that he mirrors God. We have seen that even the lowest monad mirrors, however obscurely, the whole universe. But whereas monads mirror the universe, 'minds are also images of the deity or author of nature himself, capable of knowing the system of the universe and, to some extent, of imitating it through their own inventions'.[29] So Leibniz can also say that each human being or spirit is like a 'little god' in its own world. Whatever the distance between God and the human creature, there is also some analogy, for the human being has an aspiration towards the infinite. Thus man is not only a microcosm, summing up in himself the levels of being in the universe, he has also an analogy of being with God. If this is accepted, then, as I have argued elsewhere, it makes possible an anthropological argument for the existence of God.

It seems to me that Leibniz made considerable difficulties for himself by his insistence that the monads have 'no windows' and cannot interpenetrate one another. This also implies that God and the world are effectively isolated from one another. Each monad simply unfolds the possibilities that belonged to it from the beginning. God cannot intervene in the world, and, since he has no body, it is hard to see how he could perceive the world or have any knowledge of it at all. Yet he is also said to be the principal monad and the governor of that system of monads of which the world is constituted and which is ideally the kingdom of God. Leibniz attempts to solve the difficulty by his principle of pre-established harmony. He accepts that God does not intervene, because there is no need for him to do so. Everything has been arranged in advance, so that the monads unfold in harmony with one another, and likewise there is a pre-established harmony between each monad as a centre of spiritual energy and its body. Already in creating the universe, God had given to it this harmony, so that all the parts work together with each other and with the whole. In this respect at least, Leibniz seems close to the deism of the Enlightenment. God set the universe going in the beginning, but it is now a self-regulating organism, and he takes no direct part in its continuing evolution. It is as if, to use the language of our own time rather than that of Leibniz, God had 'programmed' the universe and it now runs accordingly.

Does this mean that the entire course of universal history is determined in advance? Not quite, for God could foresee not only what would in fact happen, but also all the possibilities that might happen. So there is room for human freedom, yet this could never finally frustrate the divine purpose. 'The infinity of possibles, however great it may be, is no greater than the wisdom of God.'[30]

But if God, the perfect being, is the source of the world, and if it runs its course according to that perfect harmony which he has established from all eternity, why is there evil in the world? Leibniz offers several answers to this question. First, he claims that the good exceeds the evil: 'In the universe, not only does the good exceed the evil, but also the evil serves to augment the good . . . I make bold to say that we shall find, on unbiased scrutiny of the facts that, taking all in all, human life is in general tolerable.'[31] Again, he does not think that the world was made solely for human convenience, and our judgments may be all too human: 'We find in the universe some things that are not pleasing to us, but let us be aware that it is not made for us alone.'[32] Furthermore, we see only glimpses of the universal process, but God sees the process in its entirety: 'God sees in each portion of the universe the whole universe, owing to the perfect connection of things . . . If we could understand the structure and economy of the universe, we should find it is made and directed as the wisest and most virtuous could wish it.'[33] Finally, the greatest evils arise from the misdeeds of the human race, not from the arrangements of the world: 'One single Caligula, one Nero, has caused more evil than an earthquake.'[34] (It is a remarkable irony that these words were written half a century before the Lisbon earthquake of 1759, often supposed to have been a major cause of the decline of eighteenth century optimism!)

The arguments I have quoted so far are palliatives. Leibniz boldly tells us that 'my fundamental assumption is that God has chosen the best of all possible worlds'.[35] This famous expression, 'the best of all possible worlds', is not so brashly optimistic as it is sometimes taken to be. It implies that there were constraints operating on God, so that the best of all possible worlds might still be very far from a perfect world. Finitude itself implies imperfection before there is any question of sin; for instance, the finite creature cannot know everything, and therefore makes mistakes.[36] If God had made the creature perfect, it would no longer have been a creature but a second God, which is contradictory.[37] But God chooses what is best on the whole and even, 'by a wonderful art', turns human errors to good.[38]

This teaching of Leibniz was satirized by Voltaire, whose hero, Candide, eventually settles down to 'cultivate his garden'.[39] The implication is that one should get on with the practical tasks of life, and leave metaphysical speculation alone. But to this one might reply that anyone who cultivates a garden does so with the implicit hope in his heart that what he is doing is worthwhile and will bring forth appropriate results. In spite of all the complaints they make, human beings live *as if* this world does have value and is worthy of hope and trust. This is what Leibniz makes explicit in his *Théodicée*, as against those whom he terms 'malcontents', the apocalyptists and the utopians. There is perhaps an echo here of the Almighty's challenge to Job, to take over the running of the universe and make a better job of it.

Leibniz ends his book with an allegory. Pallas Athene, goddess of wisdom, conducts the high priest, Theodorus, through a building which rises in the form of a pyramid. 'You see here the palace of the fates, where I keep watch and ward. Here are representations not only of that which happens, but also of that which is possible. Jupiter, having surveyed them before the beginning of the existing world, classified the possibilities into worlds, and chose the best of all.' She then conducts the priest through one hall after another. Each hall represents a world, a different possible arrangement of events. Each is more beautiful than the one before it. At last they come to the topmost room in the apex of the pyramid. It is so beautiful that Theodorus falls into a swoon and has to be revived by the goddess. This is the real true world, the one which Jupiter has chosen as the best of all the possibilities, the one where our humanity must and can unfold itself.[40]

X

Nineteenth Century: Hegel

Georg Wilhelm Friedrich Hegel (1770–1831) is an obvious candidate for our selection of representative figures in the history of dialectical theism, for dialectic was of the very essence of his philosophy and he had a lifelong interest in theology and the philosophy of religion. Admittedly, as we have already noted,[1] there has been much controversy over Hegel's contribution to religious thought, and while there were many who hailed him as the great champion of theism and even of Christianity (and this is how he himself wished to be understood) there were others who regarded him as a pantheist or even an atheist. Perhaps in recent decades most students of religion have been less familiar with Hegel's own work than with Kierkegaard's polemic against him as the philosopher who had betrayed Christianity or reduced it to a mere appendage of his philosophical system. For a long time, Hegel has been out of favour, and perhaps especially so among theologians. But it may be the case that his stock is reviving, and clearly some contemporary German theologians, notably Moltmann and Pannenberg, are quite deeply indebted to him. Even so, most people today are likely to be put off by the sheer complexity and intricacy of his all-embracing system. He is perhaps the most difficult to understand of all the great German philosophers, not even excepting Heidegger. But it is not just the difficulty, it is the sheer ambitiousness of the great philosophical structure that puts us off. With Hegel, the development of European philosophy seems to come to a point where it collapses under its own weight, so that it can be succeeded only by new ventures that will be by comparison modest and fragmentary, and perhaps inevitably more sceptical.

Concerning Hegel's profound and serious concern with religion and the philosophy of religion, I do not think there can be any question. Two distinguished interpreters of his thought from recent years, however they may differ on other matters, are agreed about this. J. N. Findlay claims that 'Hegel developed his ideas, not so much in reaction to the opinions of philosophers, as in deep ponderings on the meaning of the Christian religion', and that he 'certainly approached his Absolute through religion'.[2] Likewise, Charles Taylor testifies about Hegel: 'The fact that his conception of the Christian religion underwent profound changes and yet remained central to his basic views right through to the mature system shows that this orientation was not the result of a passing influence.'[3] What proved to be the 'passing influence' was the theological instruction he had received at Tübingen and which Hegel found so inadequate that he was driven in search of a more satisfying interpretation of religion. But the very fact that he looked for such an interpretation and was not simply put off, as were so many of his contemporaries, is a clear indication of his conviction of the importance of religion for the human spirit and explains the prominence which he gave to the subject in his writings.[4]

Hegel's early writings, unpublished in his lifetime, are in fact mainly devoted to questions of theology and philosophy of religion. Even at this stage we can see emerging the dialectical nature of his thinking – the clash of opposites and the attempt to find a resolution. Hegel already appears as a rationalist, a child of the Enlightenment opposed to every kind of superstition and demanding that even religion must be justified by reason. Yet he is also aware that no narrow rationalism can fully represent the richness of the human spirit, and that a place must be found too for sensibility, imagination and feeling.

Of these early writings, *The Positivity of the Christian Religion* was composed when Hegel was about twenty-five. It comes from his most rationalistic phase, and presents a view of Christianity very much like the one we find in Kant's *Religion within the Limits of Reason Alone*. By 'positivity', Hegel means everything that constitutes Christianity as a concrete historical religion – its organs of authority, institutional structure, cultus, creeds, ministry, doctrine and so on. 'Jesus', he declares, 'was the teacher of a purely moral religion, not a positive one,'[5] and like most rationalists of that period, Hegel seems quite unaware of how biased his judgment is, and how little it could be supported from rational historical research. It was the disciples of Jesus, he argued, who transformed Christianity into a positive religion. Even its moral teaching was made to depend on a heternomous authority. In its original form it had been a kind of natural religion, the essence of any true religion, concerned with human duties and the pursuit of the good. In its positive form, it had been diverted from these original goals. Furthermore, in bringing along its Old Testament background, Christianity in its positive messianic form had imposed an alien tradition on the German people. Here we glimpse Hegel's nationalism and even a hint of anti-Semitism. 'Christianity', he complained, 'has emptied Valhalla, felled the sacred groves, extirpated the national imagery as a shameful superstition . . . and given us instead the imagery of a nation whose climate, laws, culture and interests are strange to us and whose history has no connection whatever with our own.'[6] So the first element chronologically in Hegel's philosophy of religion was a strong rationalist bias, and even in the subsequent dialectical working out of his ideas, the weight, as we shall see, remains on the rationalist side. Nevertheless, he was soon to move beyond the rationalistic moralistic view of Kant.

The revised understanding of religion is found in Hegel's *The Spirit of Christianity and Its Fate*, written some three or four years after *The Positivity of the Christian Religion*. It is now made clear that spiritual truth is not to be grasped by intellect alone, and that it has what nowadays we would call an 'existential' dimension. In a passage like the following, one can recognize some kinship with the view expressed fifty years later by Hegel's arch-critic, Kierkegaard, namely, that the deepest truths cannot be objectively formulated but must be grasped and appropriated in inwardness.[7] Hegel writes:

Nowhere more than in the communication of the divine is it necessary for the recipient to grasp the communication with the depth of his own spirit. Nowhere is it less possible to learn, to assimilate passively, because everything expressed about the divine in the language of reflection is *eo ipso* contradictory; and the passive spiritless assimilation of such an expression not only leaves the deeper spirit empty, but also distracts the intellect which assimilates it and for which it is a contradiction. This always objective language hence attains sense and weight only in the spirit of the reader and to an extent which differs with the degree to which the relationships of life and the opposition of life and death have come into his consciousness.[8]

Something like a genuine dialectic has emerged here. We have left behind the one-sided formalism of Kant, the narrow rationalism of the Enlightenment, and likewise the Old Testament conception of God as transcendent lawgiver. Christianity is seen as a synthesis of these ideas with love and with a mystical relationship to God in which the intellectual contradictions are overcome. One could speak also of a new sense of the divine immanence, more Greek than Hebrew. So Hegel can claim that spirit can be known only by spirit. 'The relation of spirit to spirit is a feeling of harmony, is their unification. How could heterogeneity be unified? Faith in the divine is only possible if in the believer himself there is a divine element which rediscovers itself, its own nature, in that on which it believes, even if it be unconscious that what it has found *is* its own nature.'[9]

Although I made a comparison a few sentences back between Hegel and Kierkegaard, it might seem that when Hegel talks of a feeling of harmony, of a quasi-mystical relation of unity between the human and the divine, and even of a kinship between the human and the divine spirit, the comparison is more with Schleiermacher than with Kierkegaard. It is, of course, worth remembering that in the very years when Hegel was writing *The Spirit of Christianity and Its Fate*, Schleiermacher was busy on his famous work, *On Religion: Speeches to Its Cultured Despisers*, published in 1799. The Romantic rediscovery of feeling and the revolt against the Enlightenment were very much in the air, and one could say quite correctly that Hegel's work was a dialectical synthesis between the rationalism of Kant and the aestheticism of Schleiermacher, between the religion of the Enlightenment and that of Romanticism. But to put it simply like that would not do justice to the complexities of Hegel's thought. He clearly does want to make room for feeling, and he could on occasion write very appreciatively of the importance of feeling in human experience, especially religious experience. But the defect of feeling, as Hegel saw it, is that it does not get beyond the immediacy of the given. Unless we are content to swim in vagueness and subjectivism, we have to go on from feeling to show the reasonableness of religion and its solid intellectual supports. When I first introduced the topic of dialectic,[10] I pointed out that one should not suppose that in any actual dialectical opposition, the conflicting factors have equal weight. So while it is true to say that in Hegel there is a dialectical synthesis of the interpretations of religion offered by Kant and Schleiermacher, that is to say, of intellect and feeling, the greater weight undoubtedly lies with intellect. Thus when Hegel refers to Scheleiermacher, he usually does so in critical terms and may even seem to be doing less justice to the place of feeling in religion than is required by some of his own more balanced statements. So we find him mentioning a view 'which makes great pretensions and has gained widespread acceptance and conviction at the present time' (these words were written in 1807) . . . 'The Absolute, on this view, is not to be grasped in conceptual form, but felt, intuited; it is not its conception, but the feeling of it and intuition of it that are to have the say and find expression.'[11] As I have mentioned, feeling is for Hegel only the beginning of the knowledge of God, and it has to be developed in conceptual form.

Before we leave the early theological writings, we may take note of another dialectic which emerges there and becomes very important for Hegel's mature thought – the opposition between the universal and the particular. Everything that is fragmentary and isolated needs to be completed in a larger whole, and this is true of the isolated human individual. Deeper even than original sin is an original sense of unity and belonging. 'When the trespasser feels the disruption of his own life or knows himself as disrupted, then the working of his fate commences, and this feeling of a life disrupted must become a longing for what has been lost. The deficiency is recognized as a part of himself, as what was to have been in him and is not.'[12] The opposite of this is the person who wants to be an isolated self-sufficient individual. As an example of such a person, Hegel chooses Abraham, for whom he has a very low regard. Abraham is said to have snapped the bonds of communal life and love by leaving his original home in Mesopotamia. Thereafter he lived as a self-sufficient man among foreigners whom he kept at arm's length. He regarded the whole world as his opposite. 'Abraham wanted *not* to love, wanted to be free by not loving.'[13] Hegel links his isolation with his transcendent monotheism. This negative estimate of Abraham contrasts very sharply with the praise which he receives from Kierkegaard in *Fear and Trembling*. To Kierkegaard, Abraham is a hero precisely because he is an individualist and has the temerity to set aside conventional morality. For Kierkegaard, it is the individual human being who is the concrete reality, and society an abstraction. To do Hegel justice, one must say that his aim is to unite dialectically the universal and the individual, but with him the weight was so much on the side of universality that one can sympathize with Kierkegaard's protest, even if it was exaggerated. But it is surely Hegel who has the deeper insight at this point. He expressed it at a much later point in his career when he declared: 'It is the character of the person to supersede its isolation, its separateness. In friendship and love, I give up my abstract personality and win thereby concrete personality. The truth of personality is just this – to win it through this submerging and being submerged in the other.'[14]

As we have seen, the theological views expressed in the early writings are already pointing forward to the mature system, and it is to it that we must now turn for a fuller understanding of Hegel's teaching on God and religion. The most comprehensive view of the system is presented in *The Phenomenology of Mind*, and this great work itself, I would say, is built on the basis of three ideas which sometimes overlap one another and spread into every part of Hegel's philosophy. These three fundamental ideas are spirit, dialectic and notion.

Spirit (*Geist*) is, for Hegel, the ultimate reality. But although Hegel is usually regarded as an idealist, there is no suggestion that matter is unreal. However, as we already saw in discussing Plotinus,[15] matter simply *cannot* be the ultimate reality, unless one surreptitiously imports some of the characteristics of spirit into it. The essence of spirit is dynamic form, the creativity which constructs an ordered universe out of matter. In Hegel's own language, 'Spirit is alone reality. It is the inner being of the world, that which essentially is, and is *per se*; it assumes objective, determinate form and enters into relation with itself – it is externality (otherness), and exists for self; yet in this determination and in its otherness, it is still one with itself – it is self-contained and self-complete, in itself and for itself at once.'[16] Thus spirit goes out from itself, yet remains within itself in a complex relationship of itself to itself. As subject, it knows itself as reflected in the object, while the object in turn knows spirit as the original subject. In this complex movement of spirit, we can recognize in Hegel something comparable to the *exitus* and *reditus* of the neo-Platonists. In this process, spirit and matter, God and world, are not separate but correlative. 'Nature is by no means something fixed and finished for itself, which could also exist without spirit; rather does it first reach its aim and truth in spirit. Just so, spirit on its part is not something abstractly beyond nature, but exists truly and shows itself to be spirit in so far as it contains nature subjugated to itself.'[17]

The world-process whereby spirit unfolds and realizes itself in material nature and in history is a dialectical one, characterized by the clash of opposites which are then reconciled in a higher synthesis. The dialectic is strikingly described by Hegel in the following terms: 'the ultimate nature of life, the soul of the world, the universal lifeblood, which courses everywhere and whose flow is neither disturbed nor checked by any obtruding distinction, but is itself every distinction that arises, as well as that into which all distinctions are resolved; pulsating within itself but ever motionless, shaken to its depths, but still at rest.'[18] It is clear from this that for Hegel dialectic is not just a characteristic of thought, but belongs to the course of reality itself. This suggests in turn that thought and reality are closely related or even virtually identical, as indeed we might expect if spirit is both the formative reality of the world and that which knows itself in and through the world-process.

So this brings us to the third point, the notion (*Begriff*). Hegel makes a distinction, which is important for his philosophy of religion, between 'idea' (*Vorstellung*), which might also be rendered in English as 'representation' or even 'image', and 'notion'. We could say that the notion goes beyond simple representation and is a thinking of something in depth or in several dimensions. The notion grasps something not just as it immediately presents itself, but as it has come to be in the course of its dialectical development. It is a thinking of all the moments of that development collapsed into a simultaneity. 'The bud disappears when the blossom breaks through, and we might say that the former is refuted by the latter; in the same way, when the fruit comes, the blossom may be explained to be a false form of the plant's existence, for the fruit appears as its true nature in place of the blossom. These stages are not merely differentiated; they supplant one another, as being incompatible with one another. But the ceaseless activity of their own inherent nature makes them at the same time moments of an organic unity, where they not merely do not contradict one another, but where one is as necessary as the other.'[19] To grasp the notion is to think all these moments in their equal necessity. To give another of Hegel's examples of the difference between idea and notion: 'When we want to see an oak, with all its vigour of trunk, its spreading branches and mass of foliage, we are not satisfied to be shown an acorn instead.'[20] The absolute notion would be the whole reality thinking and knowing itself in all its moments.

Let us now see how these three fundamental ideas of spirit, dialectic and notion contribute to Hegel's philosophical theology, and ask what kind of theism emerges – or perhaps I should say, whether the resultant view can properly be called theistic. It does seem clear that Hegel does not present us with a case of classical theism. There is no pure self-sufficient absolute Spirit transcendent of the world-process, and only such a Spirit would be 'God' in the sense of classical theism. Though Hegel speaks of the absolute Spirit as the first and foremost moment in the world-process, 'Spirit absolutely self-contained', he acknowledges that this is an abstraction, because from eternity this absolute Spirit has been 'in the process of realizing its constitutive notion' and is 'passing over into a form in which it exists for another'.[21] So the transcendent self-subsistent and self-sufficient God is simply a hypothesis, posited at the 'beginning' of an eternal process which had therefore no beginning. Absolute Spirit needs the finite spirits in and through which it knows itself and eventually returns to itself. However, this must not be interpreted in an atheistic way, as if the absolute Spirit has been completely dissipated into the finite spirits. It is true that Hegel quotes the solemn words of Luther's Good Friday hymn, 'God is dead', but this is not to be understood as atheism. He is indeed acknowledging that from eternity the absolute Spirit has been going out into the finite, but it has not exhausted itself in this process. The stream has never dried up, as it were: the absolute Spirit knows itself in the finite spirits as well as through them, it is both for itself and in itself. 'Spirit is the being which is in the process of retaining identity with itself in its otherness.'[22] If spirit can never be isolated or frozen as a self-sufficient God at the beginning, neither is it simply the sum of the finite spirits existing at any moment of the process. Still less can spirit be identified only with the result, the return to the source, as if God came into being only at the end of the process. We have another case of an opposition in which the two sides are not of equal rank. Hegel's language is often unclear, but I think it does come through that God is the unity which synthesizes spirit and nature, that in this synthesis spirit rises above nature, and that God is the governing principle of the whole process.[23]

So we do not look for God as the supposed undisturbed absolute spirit at the beginning, nor do we lose him among the multitude of finite spirits on the way. He is the governing reality extending through and embracing the whole process of *exitus* and *reditus*, the dynamic spiritual form which makes it what it is. He is at once the beginning, the middle and the end, much more like the triune God of Christianity than the monarchical God of some strictly monotheistic system. Hegel himself makes clear the parallel with the Christian Trinity. The first moment is absolute being, spirit absolutely self-contained. But this absolute spirit has already from eternity determined to sacrifice itself (compare Christian language about the 'lamb slain from the foundation of the world'). So spirit goes out into the realm of finite existence, where the actual historical sacrifice and reconciliation take place. Finally, spirit which has thus abased itself returns to its origin and is now fully manifested and unfolded as spirit. In these three moments, it is not difficult to recognize the Father, the Son and the Holy Spirit.[24] God is not to be identified with any one of these moments, but is all three in their unity.

I think that this idea of God which emerges in the philosophy of Hegel may be justly claimed as an example of dialectical theism. Here is a God who is above time, who indeed gives birth to time as the medium for the unfolding of spirit. Yet he is also a God within time, for it is in history that the actualization of the possibilities of spirit take place. It is not true to assert that in the Hegelian system time is an illusion or that history is devalued. On the contrary, time and history are necessary to God for the exploration of the riches of spirit. It is true that from eternity God has sacrificed himself, just as in Barth's Christian theology God from eternity has elected Jesus Christ and the human race in Jesus Christ. But in both cases, it is only in history that the concrete events of incarnation and sacrifice take place. However, I think it may be conceded that in the dialectical opposition between the universal and the concrete, Hegel gives more weight to the universal. Thus what he calls 'absolute religion' is rather like a natural theology in which the doctrines of Christian revealed theology have been universalized. 'The incarnation of divine being,' he declares, 'is the simple content of absolute religion.'[25]

There is a sense in which religion is the highest reach of the finite spirit and sums up in itself all the moments of spirit. Yet it is not quite the highest. Higher still is absolute philosophy. Although we have seen that in the dialectic of Hegel there is an attempt to synthesize the rationalism of Kant and the aestheticism of Schleiermacher, we have also seen that the bias is towards rationalism. Certainly, he moved far from an abstract rationalism, and complained about the emptiness of a merely philosophical faith, which he called 'nothing but a sapless abstract', and he warned that 'it ought never to be confused or identified with the spiritual fullness of Christian faith'.[26] But he seems reluctant to say what is this spiritual fullness which goes beyond the intellect. He tends to identify it with feeling, and to regard feeling in turn as an immediate awareness which is only the beginning of knowledge. So he tells us that 'the immediate consciousness of God goes no further than to tell us *that* he is: to tell us *what* he is would be an act of cognition, involving mediation'.[27] Religion remains in the realm of the idea (*Vorstellung*), in the sense of 'representation' or 'image', an immediate and therefore partial view of something in one of its moments. Philosophy pushes on to the notion (*Begriff*), the sum of the moments in their necessary unity. For instance, religion represents God as Father, Son and Holy Spirit, philosophy goes beyond this to grasp the dialectical unfolding of spirit. There is justice in Pfleiderer's criticism:

> Hegel's theory of religion leant too much to the side of the intellect, as Schleiermacher's had leant too much to the side of feeling. The errors of both thinkers arose out of their character and mode of thought, and were further confirmed by the opposition in which they were engaged against prevailing errors. As Schleiermacher's pietist sentiment was repelled by the barren cleverness of the Enlightenment, so the vagueness of Romanticist subjectivism raised a feeling of opposition in Hegel's solid thinking, which always cared only for the thing itself, for the kernel of the thing. All the value and dignity of religion, to which he was with his whole soul devoted, seemed to him to be in danger, if its whole significance should be placed in the subjective form of feeling, and the objective reasonableness of its contents, its truth, overlooked.[28]

We could put the criticism in a different way by saying that Hegel recognized a form of feeling or intuition that lies this side of the intellect, but did not entertain the possibility that there may be valid intuitions that reach beyond reason. Likewise, he does not seem to admit that the representational or imaginative language of religion, with its rich symbolism and mythology, though it lacks the precision of a conceptual or notional grasp, may nevertheless have the power of pointing beyond that which is conceptually graspable.

But Hegel will not have it so. There is an interesting passage in which he compares mysticism and speculation, and claims that they are very much the same. Mysticism cannot be taken to mean that the highest reality must remain veiled in incomprehensibility. That highest reality does indeed lie beyond the reach of an abstract rationalism – the 'understanding', in Hegel's terminology – but it can be both reached and comprehended by the speculative reason, so that this speculative use of reason is the true mysticism. It probably is true that for some types of people, metaphysical speculation is not far from mystical contemplation. The English philosopher F. H. Bradley was apparently such a person,[29] but although Bradley stood in the broad Hegelian tradition, he radically departed from the teaching of the master in holding that reality is suprarational.

C. A. Campbell, who shares Bradley's radical doctrine of suprarationalism, believes that Hegel has still much to teach to later generations of philosophers, but thinks that we cannot go along with him in his panlogism. A philosopher is committed to rational investigation of reality, but he is not committed 'to the position that God can be known only if he can be apprehended as an "object" of reason'.[30] He might come to the conclusion (as did Campbell himself) that reality is supra-rational and is ultimately not amenable to the conceptual grasp. He might believe, for instance, that while reason can grasp the nature of beings and the relations among them, it cannot grasp the nature of being as such. Hegel does in fact say that God, 'far from being a being, even the highest, is simply Being (*das Sein*)'.[31] But such is his confidence in reason that he thinks that it can penetrate even the mystery of being and that this mystery will reveal itself to speculative philosophy. Thought, it is claimed, 'is the highest and, in strict accuracy, the sole mode of apprehending the eternal and absolute'.[32]

There are two important doctrines which appear to be entailed by Hegel's panlogism. Both of them have consequences for his view of God and religion, and call for consideration.

The first is his well-known teaching that the real is the rational, and the rational is the real.[33] What does this mean? At first sight, this might seem to be Hegel's version of the view of Leibniz that this is the best of all possible worlds.[34] If indeed, as Hegel asserts many times and in many ways, reason and its dialectical process constitute the very soul of the world, then this would certainly seem to imply that the real is the rational. But clearly this could be taken in one or other of two senses. It might suggest that the real is coming to be in the historical process, and that only when the reality has been fully conformed to reason and is fully expressive of reason could one assert that the real is the rational. It is precisely when something has been brought to coincide with its own concept that truth has been attained. Taken in this somewhat idealist sense, many people who are not Hegelians might be prepared to agree that the real is the rational, or that the highest reaches of truth and reality have been attained when all things as they are conform to the ideal of reason. But it is probably the case that Hegel intended his dictum in a stronger sense. We have seen that he rejects the idea that God comes at the end of the process. God is in the whole process, which, strictly speaking, has neither beginning nor end. W. Wallace translates Hegel's dictum: 'What is reasonable (*vernünftig*) is actual (*wirklich*), what is actual is reasonable'. This stronger reading of the doctrine declares that things as they are are reasonable – 'whatever is, is right'. This view is not only close to Leibniz' teaching about 'the best of all possible worlds', but reflects back all the way to Plotinus' teaching that if we could only see things in their true nature and relations, we would realize that 'even as things are, all is well'.[35]

To some minds, this will seem like an affront, and a refusal to face the evil and irrationality that abound in the world. But then the question arises, 'Could the world be any different from what it is?' Even Leibniz' teaching about the best of all possible worlds suggests that the world we know is contingent, and that there are other possibilities, though this is the best possibility of all. Even today, we hear people speculating about other possible universes that would be quite different from the one we know. It is sometimes said, for instance, that since only a universe that brought forth cognitive beings, such as the human being, could be known, there may be an infinite number of universes in which there are no cognitive beings, and which are therefore unknown. But such a supposition seems to me to be embroiled in so many metaphysical and epistemological problems that it is hard to see how it could make any sense to entertain it. Our business is to apply our minds to the only universe we know, not to universes (if they could be called 'universes') which are *in principle* unknowable. It is this real world with which Hegel is concerned, and he believed that everything that happens in it takes place by an inner rational necessity. At any given moment, therefore, the actual is the reasonable, in the sense that it is a necessary point that has been reached in the total unfolding of spirit, so that it would have its justification within the sum of moments, of which it is only one.

Is Hegel then a determinist, with no room for freedom in his system? I do not think this follows. His difficulty at this point is not essentially different from that of the Marxist who believes in the inevitable processes of dialectical materialism or of the Christian who believes in a divine providence that overrules all things. I said that there are two important doctrines that follow from Hegel's panlogism, and it is time for us to look at the second, for it helps to resolve some of the problems raised by the first. This second doctrine is that of the 'cunning of reason'. The world-process is, so to speak, programmed in such a way that whatever these finite agents do is made to serve a higher end than they themselves visualized. 'God lets men do as they please with their particular passions and interests, but the result is the accomplishment of – not their plans, but his, and these differ decidely from the ends primarily sought by those whom he employs. The good, the absolutely good, is eternally accomplishing itself in the world; and the result is that it needs not wait upon us, but is already by implication, as well as in full actuality, accomplished.'[36] It is this vision of the self-accomplishing and accomplished good that is truth and reality, while our preoccupation with evil is an obscuring illusion. We are not deprived of freedom, but our true freedom is to co-operate in the work of spirit.

This vision of the divine spirit and of the absolute good actualizing itself and this summons to the human being to identify himself with the adventure of spirit is religion, and Hegel sums up the meaning of religion in noble words:

Religion is for our consciousness that region in which all the enigmas of the world are solved, all the contradictions of deeper-reaching thought have their meaning unveiled, and where the voice of the heart's pain is silenced – the region of eternal truth, of eternal rest, of eternal peace. Speaking generally, it is through thought, concrete thought, or, to put it more definitely, it is by reason of his being spirit that man is man; and from man as spirit proceed all the many developments of the sciences and arts, the interests of political life, and all those conditions which have reference to man's freedom and will. But all these manifold forms of human relations, activities and pleasures, and all the ways in which these are intertwined; all that has worth and dignity for man, all wherein he seeks his happiness, his glory and his pride, finds its ultimate centre in religion, in the thought, the consciousness and the feeling of God. Thus God is the beginning of all things and the end of all things.[37]

Yet, noble though these words are and impressive the system to which they belong, we may still retain the lingering suspicion, shortly to be brought to expression by Kierkegaard, that it had all been made too rational, too coherent, too transparent, and that the mystery of God and his dealings with the world, like some unconquered Himalayan peak, still soars above the reaches of human thought.

XI

Twentieth Century (1): Whitehead

Among Anglo-Saxon philosophers of recent times, Alfred North Whitehead (1861–1947) is among the very few who have taken metaphysics seriously. In the earlier part of his career, he gained distinction as a logician, mathematician and physicist, but then went on to become a professor of philosophy and the creator of a comprehensive theory of reality.[1] Whitehead was opposed to any attempt to restrict philosophy to an analytic or positivist role. He believed that the great ages of the human race have been those in which there has reigned 'some profound cosmological outlook', and that in the absence of 'a co-ordinating philosophy of life', there ensues 'decadence, boredom and the slackening of effort'.[2] This seems a bold assertion, and in fact Whitehead makes many broad generalizations about the mental and spiritual history of the human race, which need to be critically examined. He was, however, convinced that philosophy has a constructive as well as an analytic task, and that this constructive task consists in providing a system of general ideas in terms of which our experience can be interpreted as a whole. To quote his own words: 'Speculative philosophy is the endeavour to frame a coherent, logical, necessary system of general ideas in terms of which every element of our experience can be interpreted. By this notion of "interpretation" I mean that everything of which we are conscious, as enjoyed, perceived, willed or thought, shall have the character of a particular instance of the general scheme.'[3] Of course, a speculative philosophy is not simply plucked out of the air. It may very well begin with an act of imagination or a flash of intuition (as do also many scientific discoveries) but it goes on to relate the speculative element to knowledge of detailed fact and the discipline of exact logic.

Whitehead's philosophy is not easy to understand, and in the course of expounding it, he found it necessary to deploy a large number of technical terms. In this chapter, I can hope to set forth only the broad outlines, with special attention to his doctrine of God and God's relation to the world. I think it will soon become clear that Whitehead's teaching on these questions presents us with another example of dialectical theism, and that he stands in continuity with the other thinkers considered in this part of the book. In many respects, he is close to Leibniz. But perhaps Whitehead, working in an age that had become hostile to metaphysics, was more aware than his predecessors of the questionable nature of metaphysical speculation. How does one evaluate a speculative system of this sort? Clearly, it is too vast in its scope and has too many ramifications and even ragged edges to be susceptible to the kind of verification or falsification that may be applied in the case of a single proposition or a limited and well-defined hypothesis. Whitehead suggests two main criteria. One is fruitfulness – the ideas of the system, however they may have been derived, prove their worth in lighting up new areas of inquiry. The other is coherence; speculation must be controlled by logic, and Whitehead calls coherence 'the great preservative of sanity'.[4] But to these two criteria one should add the third point that Whitehead remained modest about the achievement of any metaphysic. No metaphysic attains to completeness, none is free from some imbalance or hidden incoherence. 'There remains', he writes, 'the final reflection, how shallow, puny and imperfect are efforts to sound the depths in the nature of things. In philosophical discussion, the merest hint of dogmatic certainty as to finality of statement is an exhibition of folly.'[5]

Whitehead calls his system a 'philosophy of organism', and this description already tells us quite a lot about it. It suggests a comprehensive unity embracing a diversity of things each of which derives its character from the whole as well as contributing to the whole. A philosophy of organism, which Whitehead acknowledges to have originated with Leibniz,[6] is, he believes, the type of philosophy to which we are directed by the findings of the natural sciences. Nowadays it is not only biology that requires the concept of organism. Physics has departed from the view that things are made up of hard impenetrable material particles, and the atom has come to be understood as an intricate pattern of energy, requiring a minimum of time as well as of space for its existence. The fundamental unit of nature is not the solid particle but the event.[7]

So Whitehead believed that his philosophy of organism offers an alternative to popular scientific materialism, an alternative which is more in accordance with the concepts of contemporary science. He comes back repeatedly to the criticism of materialism and related philosophies. His basic criticism is as old as Plotinus,[8] but, I believe, remains valid: if you begin with dead, inert, mindless, unorganized matter, then you will never have anything else. If ontological reductionism is carried through consistently, it brings us into an *aporia*. In Whitehead's words, 'The aboriginal stuff or material from which a materialistic philosophy starts, is incapable of evolution.'[9] Form, order, direction, the 'mental' element, in the very broad sense of that term, are not accidental in the world but belong to its original givenness. 'It is not the case', claims Whitehead, 'that there is an actual world because there is an order in nature. If there were no order, there would be no world. Also, since there is a world, we know that there is an order. The ordering entity is a necessary element in the metaphysical situation presented by the actual world.'[10]

But if Whitehead rejects materialism, he is equally forthright in his rejection of its traditional rival, idealism. He gives as his main reason for this rejection the fact that 'this idealistic school, as hitherto developed, has been too much divorced from the scientific outlook'.[11] But there is a broader reason for the rejection, namely, that idealism, like materialism, is one-sided. Materialism and idealism are alike abstractions, and to the extent that they have presented abstractions from the whole of experience as if these abstractions were in fact the whole, they are guilty of what Whitehead called the 'fallacy of misplaced concreteness'.[12] We could put this objection in another way that would link it with the philosophies already discussed in earlier chapters by saying that the materialist and the idealist[13] both fail to be sufficiently dialectical in their thinking. The dialectical character of Whitehead's own thought is exhibited in the following passage:

The universe is dual because, in the fullest sense, it is both transient and eternal. The universe is dual because each final actuality is both physical and mental. The universe is dual because each actuality requires abstract character. The universe is dual because each occasion unites its formal immediacy with objective otherness. The universe is *many* because it is wholly and completely to be analysed into many final actualities – or, in Cartesian language, into many *res verae*. The universe is *one*, because of the universal immanence. There is thus a dualism in this contrast between the unity and the multiplicity. Throughout the universe there reigns the union of opposites, which is the ground of dualism.[14]

In this passage, Whitehead has been somewhat careless in his use of the terms 'duality' and 'dualism'. His own philosophy acknowledges duality in the universe, but a duality that is embraced within a unity. Everything that exists combines within itself polar opposites; for instance, a mental pole and a physical pole. But Whitehead rejects any dualism, if that means the setting up of these polar opposites as if they were independent metaphysical ultimates. He is against what he calls the 'bifurcation of nature', whether it takes the form of Descartes' dualism of *res cogitans* and *res extensa*, or Locke's separation of primary and secondary qualities. He declares himself against any attempt 'to bifurcate nature into two divisions, namely, into the nature apprehended in awareness and the nature which is the cause of this awareness'.[15] Nature embraces both the mental and the physical, and either of these by itself is an abstraction from the whole in its rich concreteness. 'For natural philosophy,' he maintains, 'everything perceived is in nature. We may not pick and choose. For us, the red glow of the sunset should be as much part of nature as are the molecules and electric waves by which men of science would explain the phenomenon.'[16] From this it follows, too, that we learn about sunsets from poets and painters as well as from scientists.[17]

In the light of the passages just quoted, I think it would be fair to say that Whitehead's philosophy is a species of naturalism. But it is certainly not a reductionist form of naturalism. It implies a rich concept of nature, one which includes spirit as well as matter, value as well as fact, beauty as well as size and shape, though I doubt if Whitehead would have gone as far as Eriugena in expanding the concept of nature to include even God. But certainly he did include man in nature, so that in this philosophy one could say that nothing human is alien to nature. At this point, his philosophy differs sharply from those forms of existentialism (such as Sartre's) in which man is so strongly contrasted with nature that there is virtually a dualism. Whitehead writes: 'It is a false dichotomy to think of nature *and* man. Mankind is that factor *in* nature which exhibits in its most intense form the plasticity of nature.'[18] In speaking of the 'plasticity' of nature, Whitehead is asserting that there is a measure of openness in the world and the possibility of novelty. In an organic universe, the world-process is not like that of a rigidly determined mechanical system. Although each actual occasion gathers up the effects of all those that have preceded it, there is room for novelty. In the case of a predominantly physical entity, such as a molecule, the room for novelty may be negligible, whereas in the case of a human being, endowed with conscious mind and will, personal freedom has emerged. That is why the human being is said to exemplify in a paradigmatic way the plasticity of nature.

Is Whitehead's attempt to set the human being firmly *within* nature a downgrading of personal existence? It would be if he proceeded in a reductionist way, trying to explain the higher in terms of the lower, perhaps maintaining that personal existence is 'nothing but' an epiphenomenal by-product of material processes. But this is far from his intention. Rather, he works the other way round, explaining the lower in terms of the higher. We have noted already Whitehead's belief that a world could not evolve out of a formless material matrix. So he boldly posits that even in a molecule or an atom, perhaps even in an electron or any other sub-atomic event, there is a mental as well as a physical pole. This doctrine of the omnipresence of mind (if one may so speak) is sometimes called 'panpsychism'. It has been severely criticized as something like a reversion to primitive animism. However, such criticisms do not hold. When Whitehead claims that every actual entity has its mental pole, he is not saying that molecules and trees have a conscious life like ours. It is a mistake to equate mind with consciousness, for only in human beings and higher animals does mind attain the conscious level. Of course, it is at this level that we experience what is most distinctive in mind. But could mental activity, as we know it at the higher levels, ever have come into being, did not the potentiality for it already exist at the most elemental levels of the universe? Wherever there is order, pattern, organism, form, there is the rudiment of mind, though it may be far below the level of consciousness. The argument here seems to depend on something very close to Leibniz' 'principle of sufficient reason',[19] and, in my view, that is one of the strongest principles in philosophy. In fact, Whitehead's teaching in this part of his philosophy is strongly reminiscent of Leibniz. In at least one place, Whitehead uses the term 'monad' as an equivalent to 'actual entity/occasion'.[20] It will be remembered, too, that the monads of Leibniz were dynamic, spiritual entities, but most of them far below the level of consciousness. One important difference, however, is that whereas the monads were enduring, indeed, immortal entities, the actual occasions of Whitehead come into being and then perish, and apparently endure for only a fraction of a second. Each one is itself changeless for as long as it lasts, and change occurs in the transitions from one occasion to another. These concepts of Whitehead are not merely speculative, for they obviously derive from quantum theory in physics, and have here been generalized in a metaphysical way.

The problem that arises from Whitehead's inclusion of the human being *within* nature is not so much that personal being is reduced or devalued as rather that there is a danger of projecting personal qualities upon inanimate nature. This danger is increased by Whitehead's use of terms like 'experience' and 'feeling' in relation to inanimate objects. But the general term which he uses for relations between actual entities is a neutral one – 'prehension'. 'Actual entities involve each other by reason of their prehensions of each other. There are thus real individual facts of the togetherness of actual entities, which are real, individual and particular, in the same sense in which actual entities and prehensions are real, individual and particular.'[21] Elsewhere he explains that he uses the word 'prehension' in the sense of 'uncognitive apprehension', or, more precisely, 'apprehension which may or may not be cognitive'.[22] What would be meant by an apprehension that is not cognitive? Presumably it could mean taking account of something, in the sense of responding to it without necessarily being aware of it. For instance, the earth in its movements responds to the sun's gravity; it could be said to take account of the sun. Even scientists find it hard to get away from some anthropomorphisms, but certainly do not intend to give them their full value. Incidentally, there is quite a close parallel between Whitehead's pair of terms, 'prehension' and 'apprehension', and Leibniz' pair, 'perception' and 'apperception'. The monads perceive one another, but this may not be conscious perception. When Leibniz wishes to specify that the perception is conscious, he speaks of 'apperception'.[23]

The notion of 'prehension' is absolutely foundational to Whitehead's philosophy. For him there are no 'atomic facts' in the universe, that is to say, facts which would remain unchanged if they could be lifted out of the context of related facts. In this matter, Whitehead follows the idealists rather than the realists. He has a doctrine of internal relation just as strong as what we find in Hegel. Everything is what it is in virtue of its relations to everything else. We usually think of a thing as located at a particular place, but this is the fallacy of 'simple location', abandoned, according to Whitehead, by modern physics. 'There is,' he says, 'a focal region which in common speech, is where the thing is. But its influence streams away from it with finite velocity throughout the utmost recesses of space and time.'[24] Elsewhere he says: 'Nature is conceived as a complex of prehensive unifications. Space and time exhibit the general scheme of interlocked relations of these prehensions. You cannot tear any one of them out of its context. Yet each one of them has all the reality that attaches to the whole complex. Conversely, the totality has the same reality as each prehension; for each prehension unifies the modalities to be ascribed, from its standpoint, to every part of the whole. A prehension is a process of unifying.'[25] In view of these statements, it will not surprise us to find him saying in another place something that we find also in Plotinus, Nicholas of Cusa, Leibniz and others in the same tradition: 'Each unit has in its nature a reference to every other member of the community, so that each unit is a microcosm representing in itself the entire all-inclusive universe.'[26]

Actual entities belong to the minute structure of the universe. How about the macroscopic world of ordinary experience? The objects that we encounter in daily life are made up of many actual occasions, distributed through time and space. Such objects are said to comprise a 'society' of actual entities. The degree of unity exhibited in such a society is variable. In a lump of metal, for instance, the unity is of low grade, and this would be called a 'corpuscular society'. In an animal or a human being, the degree of unity is very high. In such cases there emerges a 'dominant occasion', like the 'dominant monad' of Leibniz. This dominant occasion is the centre of direction for the whole society of occasions which make up the organism in question. Where there is a dominant occasion, the mental pole has achieved the level of consciousness. It must be said, however, that Whitehead's concept of the self remains obscure. He can indeed use the traditional term 'soul' to describe the dominant occasion in the human person. This 'soul' is itself a society, that is to say, it is the succession of occasions contiguous in time, each prehending those that have preceded it.

Some commentators have believed that in spite of his use of the term 'soul', Whitehead's understanding of the self is similar to Hume's – there is no abiding self, only an ever-changing stream of successive experiences. To compare him with Hume may be going too far, but, as one critic, George F. Thomas, has pointed out, personality is not one of Whitehead's basic categories, and is in fact said to be a 'derivative notion'.[27] While I did say earlier that Whitehead is more in danger of projecting human qualities on nature than of reducing the human mind to an epiphenomenon of matter, one may have to make an exception in this matter of the 'soul'. The notion of the soul as a society of occasions rapidly succeeding one another seems to me to come ultimately from quantum physics, and to be quite inappropriate for an understanding of the human reality.

For eight years I taught alongside an eminent process theologian, Daniel Day Williams. He looked to Whitehead for his categories of theological explanation, while I looked to Heidegger, and we used sometimes to compare the merits and demerits of the use in theology of these two philosophers. I had to concede that Whitehead provided a much more adequate theology of nature, but Williams in turn admitted that Heidegger had the more profound understanding of the human person. It is a serious weakness in Whitehead's philosophy that his teaching about the human being is so inadequate and is perhaps entirely on the wrong tracks. Still, as he himself once said, 'No one man, no limited society of men, and no one epoch can think of everything at once.'[28] Any philosophy will prove inadequate at one point or another, and although Whitehead no more than any other philosopher succeeded in thinking of everything at once, we can congratulate him on having compassed so many things.

Having prepared the ground by considering the main features of Whitehead's metaphysics, we can now turn to that which is of special interest to us as natural theologians – the doctrine of God with which he completes his system. Like Leibniz, Whitehead expresses his distaste for any view of God which stresses chiefly his power and rule.[29] But we may find that he reacts so strongly against a one-sidedly monarchical view of God that he ends up by himself being one-sided in an opposite direction.

Thus, although in most theistic philosophies God is the author and creator of all that is, this is not the case in Whitehead. The ultimate appears to be an obscure agency called 'creativity'.[30] He speaks of 'the creativity which drives the world',[31] and by it he seems to mean that pulsating flow of energy which continuously brings each actual occasion into existence after its predecessor. God's role in Whitehead seems to be rather like that of the Demiurge in Plato's *Timaeus*; that is to say, he gives to the world form, order and direction, but not existence. According to John Cobb, 'Whitehead's argument for the existence of God, in so far as there is an argument at all, is primarily the traditional one from the order of the universe to a ground of order.'[32] Obviously, there is order in the world; we have seen that Whitehead holds that there can be an actual world only if there is already an order of nature.[33] But does this entitle us to speak of God? We do find Whitehead saying: 'Faith in reason is the trust that the ultimate natures of things lie together in a harmony which excludes mere arbitrariness. The faith in the order of nature which has made possible the growth of science is a particular example of a deeper faith.'[34] This 'deeper faith' might not be faith in a God who transcends the world and imposes order upon it, but the argument could support faith in an immanent God within the process, a principle of rationality and direction which has shaped the world that we know. Perhaps it is something like this that Whitehead has in mind when he speaks in semi-mythological language of the divine Eros. 'We must conceive the divine Eros as the active entertainment of all ideals, with the urge to their finite realization, each in its due season. Thus a process must be inherent in God's nature, whereby his infinity is acquiring realization'.[35]

In the passage just quoted, there appear to be two ways of thinking about God. One way sees him as involved in the world-process, realizing goals and ideals in that process, perhaps even realizing himself in it. The other way sees him as 'the entertainment of all ideals', a kind of ideal harmony already in some sense complete and drawing the world towards itself as its goal.

The twofold nature of God adumbrated here is given much more precision and detail in Whitehead's writings. It is already present in his recognition that God is an actual entity.[36] Every actual entity, as we have seen, has both a mental and a physical pole, and this would have to be true of God, as of any other actual entity. Whether it was consistent on Whitehead's part to include God among the actual entities is a question – we remember the problems that arose for Leibniz from his attempt to include God among the monads, albeit as the supreme monad. Whitehead has to make it clear that God is unique among the actual entities. For instance, whereas ordinary actual entities are constantly coming into being and passing out of being, God is everlasting. Again, while it is true that every actual entity prehends every other, God's experience seems to be uniquely inclusive, so that he enjoys (or suffers) the experiences of all the finite actual entities.

The two sides of God's nature are called by Whitehead the 'primordial nature' and the 'consequent nature', though it must be remembered that these are inseparable. Either by itself is an abstraction, and when we speak of 'God', we mean both natures together in their polar unity. The primordial nature is said to be 'free, complete, primordial, eternal, actually deficient and unconscious'. The consequent nature is 'determined, incomplete, consequent, everlasting, fully actual and conscious'.[37] There are obviously many difficulties and obscurities in these descriptions.

First of all, it is interesting to note the terminology of 'primordial' and 'consequent'. This implies that the mental or conceptual pole has a certain priority in the being of God, and this in turn implies that it would be wrong to consider Whitehead as a pantheist or to suggest that he teaches only a God evolving in and with the universe. In his primordial nature, God already contains all possibilities. In Whitehead's language, he includes all 'eternal objects', these understood as the possible forms of being, rather like the ideas of Plato. They are in themselves eternal and unchangeable, but they enter into the world-process and become actualized in concrete occasions. Since God contains all possibilities, he is on his primordial side complete. God's contribution to the creative process is to select for each occasion its 'subjective aim'. Again the language is anthropomorphic. It means something like the 'entelechy' of Leibniz, that is to say, the form in which the particular entity would attain the fullest level of being possible for it. In Whitehead's language, this is again expressed anthropomorphically as the 'satisfaction' of that entity. In the case of higher beings, such as the human person, the subjective aim (which might be a moral or spiritual ideal) would be consciously pursued. The fact that God selects for every entity its subjective aim is not to be interpreted as determinism, but it is a form of providence which the finite entities will not always fulfil. Inanimate objects will not always attain their satisfaction because of the imperfections that necessarily belong to the finite, and human agents will not attain their satisfaction because God does not compel them. He acts by attraction, and the ideal set before them is a 'lure' to which they are free to respond or from which they may turn away. Whitehead believes that in each case the subjective aim chosen by God is the best possible for the occasion – a doctrine which recalls the teaching of Leibniz about the best of all possible worlds, though both philosophers would be grossly misunderstood if these doctrines were interpreted as some kind of brash optimism. The very fact of finitude means that even the best-laid schemes of God will often go wrong.

While I think this is a fair explanation of Whitehead's view of the activity of God on his primordial side, it leaves difficulties about some of the adjectives which he used about God. How can God in his selection of possibilities be both 'free' and 'unconscious'? Does not free selection entail consciousness? Again, how much are we to read into the expression 'actually deficient'? Does it mean simply that God has not actualized his purposes in space and time? Or does it mean that God, on his primordial side, is not quite real or not yet real? I do not think it can mean the second of these, for Whitehead, as we have seen, always insists that there must be form, order, ideas, before there can be an actual world. But does this mean that the ultimate reality is ideal, and that in spite of his protests, Whitehead has idealist tendencies?[38] This might not be surprising in one who admired Plato so much.

But now we must look at the other side of God, his consequent nature, always remembering that the two sides are inseparable. By virtue of his consequent nature, God is involved in the world and its history. He is the principle of concretion by which actual entities attain their satisfaction; he is involved in the 'creative advance of the world';[39] in a sense he is making himself in and with the world – as Eriugena had also taught.[40] That explains why, in his consequent nature, God is said to be incomplete. He is drawing the world on to the complete ideality of his primordial nature. In this process, God is receiving and suffering as well as acting. We have seen that in some sense he takes up into himself the experiences of all actual occasions and transmutes them in his own experience. Could we say that in his consequent nature he is the dominant occasion of the world, even the soul of the world? – though I do not think that Whitehead uses these expressions. Of course, we have again to remind ourselves that this does not reduce God to a world-soul, for he remains at the same time in his primordial nature, and presumably enjoys a measure of transcendence in virtue of that primordial nature. God, we are told, 'does not create the world, he saves it; he saves the world as it passes into the immediacy of his own life'.[41]

Though we shall have to criticize rather severely some elements in Whitehead's concept of God, it seems to me that its great strength lies in its dialectical recognition of the dipolar nature of God – that he is both beyond time and in time, transcendent of the world and immanent in it, active and yet the recipient of action and even enduring suffering. These features of Whitehead's teaching go far to meeting the objections that may be brought against classical theism. They present a God who is not only more credible but more worshipful, and they also safeguard the relative worth and dignity of the world. In classical theism, the relation between God and the world was quite asymmetrical, but in Whitehead's scheme, elements of symmetry are introduced.

Nevertheless, while his teaching may be applauded as a needed corrective to one-sided distortions in classical theism, Whitehead has gone so far in his reaction that one is finally left wondering whether his God is really deserving of the name of God. I think we can accept his stricture that the human race has usually fashioned God in the image of an imperial ruler, and that even Christianity habitually forgets the crucified Jesus as the manifestation of God to go a-whoring once more after the pre-Christian deities of power – indeed, I have myself written elsewhere of the humility of God and complained about our apparently ineradicable tendency to turn God into a despot.[42] Yet these truths have to be held dialectically, and the humility of God would be unimportant were God not also the ultimate reality. Whitehead uttered a great truth in his famous phrase about God as 'the great companion – the fellow sufferer who understands'.[43] This is both a metaphysical and a spiritual truth, and it can hardly be denied that it has been obscured, if not actually denied, by the classical teaching about God. But a God who could only suffer helplessly with his finite fellow beings would simply not be 'God', in the sense understood by those who use the word.

I am not saying that Whitehead's God is *only* a suffering God, for apparently he transmutes the world's suffering and leads the universe towards an ultimate harmony in which suffering and evils of all kinds will be resolved. But we come back to the problem that Whitehead's God is not ultimate – he is one actual entity among many, admittedly unique, yet co-ordinate with the world so that 'it is as true to say that God creates the world as that the world creates God'.[44] This is one of several 'antitheses' emphasizing the symmetry of God and the world, for instance, the world is immanent in God and God is immanent in the world, God transcends the world and the world transcends God, and so on. We are told that 'God and the world are the contrasted opposites in terms of which Creativity achieves its supreme task of transforming disjoined multiplicity into concrescent unity.'[45] This sentence seems to me to place more than ever a question mark against what Whitehead calls 'God'. Is not Creativity (which Whitehead capitalizes) the true God or the God beyond God, superior both to 'God' and the world? And what are we to make of this personal language ascribed to Creativity, as 'achieving its supreme task'? Admittedly, the language may be figurative, for Whitehead, as we have seen, lacks a developed concept of personality, and he does not ascribe personality to God in explicit terms, though to speak of God as 'suffering' would seem to imply that there is some personal element in God. But the point I am making is that Creativity achieving its supreme task seems to have a good claim to be considered the true God in Whitehead's metaphysics.

It is tempting to suggest that Whitehead's conception of God would have been much more persuasive had he incorporated the ultimate creativity into the divine being. That would have made his God really ultimate, and also closer to the belief of most religious people that God is the creator of the world. But it would also mean that Whitehead's dipolar God would need to be transformed into a triune God. The first member of the trinity or triad would be what he calls 'Creativity', the ultimate category and mysterious source of everything, the sheer fact of being, beyond our understanding or questioning, rather like The One of Plotinus. The second member of the triad would be what Whitehead calls the 'primordial nature' of God, that repository of the eternal ideas which determine the possibilities for the world and give to it its pattern and direction. Clearly, this second member looks like the Logos or Nous of philosophies derived from Plato. Finally, the third member would be Whitehead's 'consequent nature' of God, the indwelling Spirit or Psyche or World-soul, striving within the cosmos for the realization of its ideal possibilities.

But it is not my business to try to reconstruct the philosophy of Whitehead, or to try to fit it into the structure of theology – he has already plenty of admirers in the United States engaged in such tasks. My own discussion of Whitehead, like my discussions of other philosophers in this book, has been undertaken only for the purpose of exploring one of the possible forms of dialectical theism in the hope of profiting both from its insights and its failures. We have found, I think, examples of both.

XII

Twentieth Century (2): Heidegger

At the beginning of this historical interlude in which I have been reviewing the philosophies of some representatives of what I have been calling 'dialectical theism', I felt it incumbent on me to offer some defence of the choice of Plotinus as the first representative figure, for some would question whether he was a theist at all. Even more do I feel obliged to defend the choice of my last representative, Martin Heidegger.[1] Some people have regarded him as an atheist, even a nihilist. Such judgments could come only from those who have the most superficial acquaintance with his teaching. Certainly, Heidegger could not be described as a theist in the mould of classical theism. But still less could he be called an atheist. John R. Williams, in a study of Heidegger's philosophy of religion, suggests that ' "panentheism" accords well with the elements in Heidegger's thought that are relevant to religion'.[2] Although I have not myself made much use of the term 'panentheism', I have acknowledged its kinship with what I call 'dialectical theism',[3] and I think it may be claimed that however the contours may have changed, there remains a discernible resemblance between the thought of Heidegger and that of most of the earlier thinkers we have considered, all the way back to Plotinus.

It is surely not an accident that no recent philosopher has exercised such an influence on the theology of the twentieth century as has Heidegger. Bultmann, Tillich and Rahner, to name only three of the most eminent names, are among the many theologians deeply in Heidegger's debt. One could hardly understand these thinkers in any depth without knowing the Heideggerian background to some of their ideas.

But here is the irony of the situation. It is not very difficult to point to what theologians have owed to Heidegger, but what is much more difficult is to say with any confidence just what Heidegger himself thought of theology and of religion generally. Clearly, for instance, he must have influenced the way in which some very important Christian theologians have thought of God. But did Heidegger himself have any concept of God? Is there any place for God in his philosophy?

Of course, we may remember that in his youth Heidegger spent some time in a Jesuit seminary. Many years later, he frankly declared: 'Without my theological origin, I would never have attained to the way of thinking.'[4] It should be noted that in much of his writing Heidegger prefers to speak of 'thinking' and 'thinkers' rather than of 'philosophy' and 'philosophers', so in the sentence quoted, he is acknowledging that his theological beginnings were an essential step on the way to philosophy. But over against this, one has to set the fact that during most of his career he kept theology at a distance, and several times declared that the tasks of the theologian and of the philosopher are quite different. In another writing, not much later than the one in which he confesses the indebtedness of his thinking to theology, he takes a very different stance and says: 'Someone who has experienced theology in his own roots, both the theology of the Christian faith and philosophical theology, would today prefer to remain silent about God, when he is speaking as a thinker.'[5] Admittedly, the reason for this silence might be that the name of God has been so much abused and misunderstood. When Heidegger died in 1976, his former student, the philosopher Hans-Georg Gadamer, gave a memorial lecture with the title 'An Invocation to the Vanished God'.[6] In it he declared: 'It was Christianity that provoked and kept alive this man's thought; it was the ancient transcendence and not modern secularity that spoke through him.' Later in the lecture he asked why someone who was as deeply stirred by theological questions as he believed Heidegger had been, had not himself become a theologian but had, on the contrary, deliberately avoided direct involvement in theology. 'Because', Gadamer answerd, 'he was a thinker, it was thinking that was at work in him. He felt no empowerment (*Ermächtigung*) to speak of God. But what would be needed to speak of God, and that it would not do to speak of him as the sciences speak of their objects, that was the question that stirred him and showed him the path of thinking.'

Gadamer's remarks do not remove the ambiguity in Heidegger's relation to theology. Throughout Heidegger's writings, early and late, there are many scattered allusions to the themes of God, religion and theology.[7] Many of the allusions are brief, some are obscure, and they are not all easily harmonized. But there are more than enough to show us that Gadamer was correct in seeing in Heidegger a man deeply interested in theological questions, even if he did not think that a philosopher ought to be drawn wholly into them. It was surely again no accident that after Heidegger's death the popular German magazine *Der Spiegel* featured a commemorative article based on an interview that Heidegger had given ten years earlier, on condition that it would be published only posthumously, and the title chosen for the article was 'Only a God Can Save Us',[8] an expression which Heidegger uses in the course of the interview and which is said to have been on his lips several times in his later years.[9] But the expression is vague enough. What did he mean by this indefinite phrase, 'a God'? What God? Probably not the God of traditional Christian theism, but if not, then what? We must examine his works in hope of finding an answer.

At the age of eighteen Heidegger read a treatise by Brentano on the various meanings of 'being' in Aristotle, and it was this that set the direction of his own philosophy. He conceived the task of philosophy to be an inquiry into the meaning of being, and his first major work, *Sein und Zeit* (1927), was an ambitious attempt to lay the foundations for a general ontology or science of being. One might suppose that a philosophy of being would raise the question of God, but this does not happen in *Sein und Zeit*, which concentrates on the analysis of human existence as the *locus* in which the question of being is raised. Nevertheless, the book does make some mentions of theology. Quite near the beginning, there is a densely packed passage which runs as follows: 'Theology is seeking a more primordial interpretation of man's being towards God, prescribed by the meaning of faith itself and remaining within it. It is slowly beginning to understand once more Luther's insight, that the "foundation" on which its system of dogma rests has not arisen from an investigation in which faith is primary, and that conceptually this foundation not only is inadequate for the problematic of theology, but conceals and distorts it.'[10] The remark occurs in a discussion of what constitutes progress in a science. Heidegger holds that it is not the accumulation of information that counts as progress, but the capacity of a science to undergo a revolution in its basic concepts. He then gives examples of fundamental changes that were even then taking place in mathematics, physics, biology, the historical sciences and, finally, theology. When we remember that the words were being written in 1926 and that Heidegger was at that time teaching in the University of Marburg where he had among his colleagues both Bultmann and Tillich, then it is not difficult to identify the profound theological changes to which he is referring. Barth, Gogarten, Tillich, Bultmann and other theologians of what was still the younger generation were asserting the independence of their subject, recapturing the insights of the Reformers, going back to the New Testament sources and, generally speaking, finding the foundations of theology within faith itself. In particular, they were discarding the old natural theology and the metaphysics that went along with it, in the belief that these were alien importations and damaging to the true task of theology.

Heidegger knew the work of these men and was sympathetic to it, but the full implications of what he was saying can hardly be grasped from the brief passage I have quoted. Fortunately we have from the year 1927 a lecture entitled 'Phenomenology and Theology'.[11] This gives a much fuller account of Heidegger's thoughts on theology at that time, but because of his reticence on matters theological, this lecture was held back from publication for forty years. Heidegger stresses as strongly as he can the difference between philosophy and theology. Philosophy, we are told, has to do with the question of being, but theology is a special or positive science, and this means that it deals not with being, but with a special area of beings. 'Theology', says Heidegger, 'is a positive science, and as such absolutely different from philosophy.' A positive science (also called an 'ontic' science) deals with a region or specific area of beings or objects. 'Ontology, or the science of being, on the other hand, demands a fundamental shift of view: from the beings to being'. So Heidegger makes the extraordinary assertion that 'theology, as a positive science, is closer to chemistry and mathematics than to philosophy'. Its closest neighbour, however, is said to be history. 'Theology, as the science of faith, that is to say, of an intrinsically historical mode of being, is to the very core a historical science.' There is not much encouragement here for philosophical theology!

There are a few other mentions of theology in *Sein und Zeit*, and they vary between hostility and a kind of patronizing friendliness. Thus, while Heidegger approves of the theologians who seek to reconstruct their subject on a foundation drawn from faith itself, he is equally approving of efforts to purge philosophy of any theological influences. He speaks of 'residues of Christian theology which have not as yet been radically extruded from philosophy'.[12] He cites as an example the idea that there are 'eternal truths' – an idea which he rejects in favour of a more dynamic, existential understanding of truth as the event of uncovering. On the other hand, we find him acknowledging that certain ideas that are of importance for his own philosophy have their origins in Christian theology. So he observes that 'transcendence', understood as the human being's reaching out beyond itself, has its roots in the Bible,[13] and he declares it to be 'no accident' that the phenomenon of anxiety, so important for his own early philosophy, has been studied chiefly by Christian thinkers.[14] Finally we should not omit a footnote in which Heidegger criticizes the traditional understanding of God's eternity which, he thinks, has been derived from our common understanding of the permanence of objects within the world. This would be inappropriate if applied to God. If we are to think of his eternity at all, then it must be on the analogy of our human temporality. God's eternity would then be understood 'only as a more primordial temporality which is "infinite" '.[15] Though this is no more than a hint, it is one of the very few constructive remarks that Heidegger makes about God, and we shall return to it at a later point.

A year after the publication of *Sein und Zeit*, Heidegger was called to the chair of philosophy at Freiburg. His inaugural lecture was entitled *Was Ist Metaphysik?* and there are about it a number of features which suggest a religious or mystical interest on Heidegger's part and which are reminiscent of ideas to be met in Plotinus, Dionysius, Eriugena and other thinkers in that tradition. Heidegger claimed that the way to understand the nature of metaphysics is to take up a definite metaphysical question. The question he proposes to discuss is the question of nothing. In a university, the positive sciences, as we have seen, all deal with some particular area of beings. When these positive sciences have divided up among them the total realm of beings that we encounter in the world, it might seem that there is nothing left for the philosopher. Exactly so, says Heidegger. Philosophy is left with nothing as its subject-matter. But this is not to be understood as nihilism. On the contrary, what is counted as nothing by those who are interested only in the beings that make up the world is said to be 'beinger' (*seiender*) or more beingful than any being. The nothing is disregarded in our concern with things because it is no thing, no object, no particular being. It is no part of the objective phenomena studied by the sciences, yet it is what makes these phenomena possible. The ancients held that *ex nihilo nihil fit*, but Heidegger claims on the contrary that *ex nihilo omne ens qua ens fit*.[16] For this nothing is being. It is not any particular being or anything that can be objectified – indeed, it is 'wholly other' to the beings, and it is interesting that here we find Heidegger using an expression about being that Barth and Otto used about God. The comparison with Otto is apt, for we also find Heidegger saying that before the mystery of being, we experience the sense of awe (*Scheu*). The lecture ends with the question of Leibniz: 'Why are there beings at all, rather than just nothing?'[17] Although the lecture deals with metaphysics, it already contains the seeds of what Heidegger was later to call the overcoming of metaphysics. Twenty years after giving his inaugural lecture, he composed an introduction to it and called it *Der Rückgang in den Grund der Metaphysik*.[18] He quotes from a writing of Descartes, who had compared the whole of philosophy to a tree, of which the roots are metaphysics, the trunk physics, and the branches which come out of the trunk the other special sciences. But Heidegger wants to push the inquiry further back. 'We are asking', he says, 'what is the ground in which the tree of philosophy has taken hold?' The trouble about metaphysics is that it has never got beyond the roots of the tree and has never inquired about the ground in which the tree is planted. It is at this point that Heidegger distinguishes between traditional philosophy or metaphysics and a more original thinking about being. He writes: 'A thinking which thinks of the truth of being can no longer be satisfied with metaphysics, though its thinking is not opposed to metaphysics. To continue the metaphor, it does not tear up the roots of philosophy. But it digs and ploughs the ground for philosophy. Metaphysics remains the origin of philosophy, but it does not attain the origin of thinking. Metaphysics is overcome in the thinking of the truth of being.' Metaphysics, Heidegger thinks, has never got beyond the being of beings; it has not attained to the thinking of being as 'wholly other' than the beings. Traditional metaphysical theology falls under the same condemnation. That is why, as we have already seen, Heidegger declares it to be an ontical science, at an immeasurable remove from the original thinking of being. Metaphysics and theology – Heidegger lumps the two together as 'onto-theology', always a pejorative expression with him – take one of two forms. Either they trace back the beings to some common underlying substance, or else they trace them to some supreme, divine being. They do not attain to original thinking.

Heidegger's ambivalent attitude to theology and his belief that it is a completely different kind of study from philosophy is further exposed in his *Einführung in die Metaphysik*. This book opens with the question which ends the lecture *Was Ist Metaphysik?*, 'Why are there beings at all, rather than just nothing?' According to Heidegger, this is the basic question for philosophy, understood as the science of being. But, he claims, it is not a question for theology and is not even seen to be a question by the theologian. The latter thinks he already knows the answer to the question of why there are beings rather than nothing. 'Everything that is, except God himself, has been created by him. God himself, the uncreated creator, "is".'[19] Now, such an answer is said to miss the point of the question, understood at the philosophical level. The question, philosophically understood, is an ontological question which asks about the relation, or perhaps one should rather say, the difference, between being and the beings. The Christian doctrine of creation has misunderstood the question as an ontical one, so it traces back everything that is, except God, to something else that is, namely God. It follows the mistaken way of traditional metaphysics in trying to account for the existence of beings by deriving them from another being, though admittedly a supreme or divine being.

This is what Heidegger calls 'onto-theology', a confused mixture of metaphysics and theology. Its confusion lies in failing to differentiate being from the beings; indeed, it assimilates being to the beings. But, says Heidegger, 'we think of being rigorously only when we think of it in its difference from the beings, and of beings in their difference with being.'[20] Indeed, as he had already maintained in his Freiburg lecture, one must think of being as 'wholly other' to the beings. Thus, from the point of view of the positive sciences which concern themselves with beings, with what is objectively real, and nothing else, being must be counted as nothing, for it is not a being and, strictly speaking, one cannot say that being 'is'.

But while he is critical of onto-theology as confusing the issue if it is allowed to influence philosophical inquiry, Heidegger immediately goes on to offer some defence of theology within its own field as an exposition of faith – presumably the type of theology practised by Barth and others and claiming to be free of metaphysical elements. 'There is,' writes Heidegger, 'a thinking and questioning elaboration of the world of Christian experience, that is to say, of faith. That is theology. Only epochs which no longer believe fully in the true greatness of the task of theology arrive at the disastrous notion that philosophy can help to provide a refurbished theology, if not a substitute for theology, that will satisfy the needs and tastes of the time. For the original Christian faith, philosophy is foolishness.'[21]

In the passage just discussed, Heidegger seems to be saying, much as Hegel did before him, that theology is inferior to philosophy, and speaks out of faith and cannot raise the radical question of being, for it does not rise to the level of a truly philosophical conceptual thinking. Yet, on the other hand, he acknowledges that from the theological point of view, philosophy is mere foolishness. Perhaps that is because philosophy's quest for conceptual clarity cannot capture the concrete content of faith. So we find Heidegger saying in another place: '*Causa sui* is the right name for the God of philosophy. But man can neither pray nor sacrifice to this God. Before the *causa sui* man can neither fall to his knees in awe, nor can he play music and dance before this God. The godless thinking which must abandon the God of philosophy, God as *causa sui*, is thus perhaps closer to the divine God.'[22] In this we seem to hear an echo of Pascal's famous contrast between the God of philosophy and the God of Abraham, Isaac and Jacob.[23] And like both Pascal and Kierkegaard, Heidegger thinks rather poorly of attempts to prove the reality of God – a God who first of all needed someone to prove his existence would be somewhat less than divine.[24]

But when one considers Heidegger's remarks on the relations of theology and philosophy, and his strictures on onto-theology, the question must be raised whether he has not permitted himself to generalize in an inadmissible way about the immensely diversified fabric of Christian theology and even so-called 'natural' theology. Has all traditional theology been of the onto-theological variety? Have all Christian thinkers thought of God as another being in addition to the beings of the world, as something else that 'is' in addition to all the things that are? Have those who have used metaphysical language about God really been talking about some other God from the God of faith, so that one cannot kneel in awe before such a God? It seems to me that as soon as we ask such questions, we see at once that they must be answered in the negative. Eric Mascall, for instance, is a philosophical theologian who tells us that the way to the conception of God as the *ens causa sui* or necessary being is tied in with the 'capacity for wondering contemplation'.[25] The metaphysician F. H. Bradley claimed that 'with certain persons, the intellectual effort to understand the universe is a principal way of experiencing the deity' – and he did not mean just an abstract concept of God but an experience which 'both chastens and transports us'.[26] Heidegger himself associates the feeling of awe with the intuition of that 'nothing' which is wholly other than the beings, yet more 'beingful' than any of them. The boundary between a philosophy of being and what Heidegger is pleased to call 'onto-theology' is not nearly as clear-cut as he would like us to believe.

Has not the very use of an expression such as *ens causa sui* already transcended the meaning of *ens*, so that the reality it designates cannot belong within the realm of *entia*, for the qualification *causa sui* seems to indicate that here we are dealing with something that is 'wholly other' to what we commonly call *ens*? Admittedly, Christian theology has been confused on the point and some of its language has been inadequately analysed and has been used without proper care. But theologians themselves have been in varying degrees aware of the inadequacies of their language. Some have been aware of the tension between the God of faith and the apparently abstract God of philosophy, while some have used for God in relation to created things precisely the expression which Heidegger has used to differentiate being from the beings – the 'wholly other'. The mystical tradition, as we have already met it in Dionysius, Eriugena and others, has been especially conscious of the difference between God and the beings and of the consequent limitations of their language about God – language which often resembles that of Heidegger himself. Though human language almost inevitably objectifies God, his reality lies beyond the objectification. In a conversation with Heidegger, a Japanese interlocutor says to him: 'For us, the void (*das Leere*) is the highest name for what you like to express by the word "being".'[27] Admittedly, this remark is made from the standpoint of Buddhism, but many Christian mystics, including John Eckhart who has obvious links with Heidegger, could have said the same. They were aware that God is not to be found among the beings; he is nothing from that point of view, and their theology was no onto-theology.

It is not only among explicitly mystical writers but in a much broader stream of Christian theology that there struggles to find expression a way of speaking about God that will respect the unique difference that lies between him and the beings which make up the world. Perhaps Tillich has been most explicit in identifying God with being in something like Heidegger's sense, but he has not been alone in this, and especially since Nietzsche's proclamation of the death of God and the decline of the old monarchical concept, many theologians have been searching for an understanding of God that would be neither onto-theological nor a simple reversion to the unphilosophical language of the Bible. But even the older tradition is not to be dismissed as onto-theology. In an earlier chapter, we examined some aspects of the classical theism of Thomas Aquinas. It is true that in the five ways of proving that there is a God, Thomas uses language suggesting that God is a being (*ens*), even if a highly distinctive being. Yet when one considers what must be implied in notions like 'first cause', 'prime mover', 'necessary being' and so on, one sees that these cannot be additional items of the same order as causes, movers, beings, such as we know them. Rather, each is the ground and condition of all the items that we reckon causes, movers, beings. Though the language is not entirely clear and may even be misleading, what we have here is not an attempt to derive some entities from another supreme entity, but to indicate the ground of all entities, and this cannot itself be an entity. When Thomas says that *Qui est* or 'He who is' is the most appropriate name for God, this might seem to be a clear proof that he thinks of God as a being or entity – and, indeed, I have earlier indicated a preference for Eriugena's title for God, *Qui plus quam esse est*.[28] But Thomas also says that the name *Qui est* is appropriate, 'because it does not signify any particular form but rather being itself (*esse ipsum*)'.[29] God is therefore the same as being itself. Here the word 'being' (*esse*) is understood in an active verbal sense, not as a substantive (*ens*).

I think one has to say very firmly that Heidegger must not be allowed to lay down what it is permissible for theologians to say, or to decide unilaterally where the boundary between theology and philosophy is to be drawn. The affinities may be much stronger than he acknowledged, though clearly he did not want to be drawn into theological discussions himself. In this connection, I may mention that in 1964 I was invited to a conference set up by the late Carl Michalson at Drew University for theologians troubled by the problems of God-language and especially by the problems of whether one can find a way of speaking about God that does not objectify him. Heidegger was invited to this conference, since it was thought that he might have some sympathy with its aims. Although he did not attend, he sent a paper on 'The Problem of a Non-objectifying Speaking and Thinking in Today's Theology'.[30] In general terms, Heidegger acknowledged the objectifying tendency of language and lamented that in modern times everything seems to be represented as an object for control and manipulation. As against that tendency, he declares his belief that what is most proper to language is 'a saying of that which reveals itself in manifold ways to human beings'. But typically he declined to draw any implications for theology. He reiterates his view that theology must confine itself within the area of faith, and that it is in this context that theologians will have to work out their own problems of language. This reticence on Heidegger's part may be thought somewhat inconsistent with his repeated criticisms of onto-theology!

So far, our results are somewhat negative. We have seen that although Heidegger often refers in one context or another to the questions of God and theology, he wants to stand off from these questions. But perhaps we can press the matter further. Is there anything in Heidegger's philosophy that might properly be called 'God', even if he himself avoids God-language? One of his many distinguished former students, Karl Löwith, has declared that Heidegger's philosophy 'is in its very essence a theology without God'.[31] But a theology without God or without some holy reality corresponding to God is a self-contradiction. If, in spite of all he has said, there is a theology in the philosophy of Heidegger, then there must be an idea of God or of a surrogate for God.

Is being a candidate for the role of God in Heidegger's philosophy? That would mean he had a doctrine of God very similar to the one taught by Tillich, who probably derived his concept of being from Heidegger in the first place. It is in his *Brief über den Humanismus* that Heidegger uses the most exalted language about being in its relation to human beings, though we have already noted that as early as the lecture *Was Ist Metaphysik?* being (which is also nothing) has a numinous, awe-inspiring character. Now, in the *Brief über den Humanismus*, we are told that 'before he speaks, man must let himself be addressed by being'.[32] He is the recipient of being's self-communication, the being among all the beings that can respond to the wonder and mystery of being. It is true that Heidegger explicitly says that being is not God, but in the very next sentence, he makes it clear that by 'God' he understands a supreme being in the onto-theological or metaphysical sense. On the other hand, he explicitly dissociates himself from atheism, and especially from the atheism of Sartre. The latter had quoted a sentence from *Sein und Zeit* which says that only as long as a human understanding of being is possible, 'is there' being, and Sartre had taken this to mean that man himself is the ultimate and that being is an idea produced by human subjectivity. Heidegger claims that this is a misinterpretation of his thought. In German, the phrase ' "there is" Being' is written ' "*es gibt*" *Sein*', and although the words '*es gibt*' are used in everyday German in the weak sense of 'there is' – Sartre, in fact, had translated them into French as '*il y a*' – they mean literally 'it gives'. Heidegger insists that he meant these words to be taken in their literal sense as denoting an act of giving, and in the original text they do indeed appear in inverted commas to show that they have a special sense. We may ask then: 'Who or what gives?' Heidegger's answer is that being gives itself and communicates itself to human beings. Thus, in contrast to Sartre's existentialism, which is also an atheistic humanism with man as his own ultimate, Heidegger is able to declare: 'Man is not the lord of beings. Man is the shepherd of being.'[33] At this point we seem to have come very close to the identification of being with God or God with being. But for Heidegger the word 'God' is so closely tied to the onto-theological idea of the supreme being that he explicitly denies, as we have seen, that being is God. Again, although he dissociates himself from atheism, he leaves the question of God open. Nothing, he tells us, is decided about God. One would have to move beyond the traditional metaphysical question about God's existence or non-existence. Now Heidegger tells us in cryptic terms: 'Only from the truth of being can the essence of the holy be thought. Only from the essence of the holy is the essence of divinity to be thought. Only in the light of the essence of divinity can it be thought or said what the word "God" is to signify.'[34]

Can we venture an exposition of the three sentences just quoted? The 'truth of being' means the uncovering of being, and according to the lecture *Was Ist Metaphysik?* this uncovering takes place when, in the mood of anxiety, and in awareness of his own finitude, the human being finds that all particular beings, including his own, lose their definition and are enveloped in a unity in which their separateness is lost – a unity which from one point of view is nothing but from another, being, and which has obvious resemblances to the experiences of some mystics. Incidentally, although Heidegger speaks of the mood of anxiety, Ricoeur points out that this is the reverse side of the sense of belonging, and that the whole experience can be given a more affirmative interpretation, as the sharp lines of demarcation between individual beings disappear in the intuition in and through them of the all-embracing being to which they belong. This uncovering of being is also, as we have seen, the occasion for awe and makes it possible to think the essence of the holy. From this point, Heidegger claims, one may go on to seek the meaning of 'God'.

As I have said earlier, Heidegger is not a theist in the classical sense. But the description he gives of the passage from the truth of being to the question of God puts him in the succession of those 'dialectical theists', mainly mystics, whom we have considered in earlier chapters. There are clear parallels between Heidegger and thinkers, both ancient and modern, who would claim to be theists and even Christians. Being is to God as the thearchy is to the persons of the Trinity in Dionysius or as *deitas* is to *deus* in Eckhart or as *Transcendenz* is to the cipher of the personal God in Jaspers. I do not mean that there are exact parallels here, but there are certainly strong family resemblances.

One of the most striking is Heidegger's depiction of being as the union of opposites, like God in the thought of Nicholas of Cusa. 'Being is both utterly void and most abundant, most universal and most unique, most intelligible and most resistant to every concept, most in use and yet to come, most reliable and most abyssal, most forgotten and most recalling, most said and most reticent.'[35] So being appears absurd, but in truth it is suprarational. 'Perhaps being itself does not trouble itself about the contradictions of our thought.'[36]

Heidegger's relation to the mystical tradition is further evidenced by what he teaches about thinking.[37] He takes over from the mystics the term *Gelassenheit*, which might be translated as 'collectedness', 'serenity' or 'imperturbability'. This collectedness is attained by meditation, a kind of thinking that is open and receptive. This kind of thinking is seen by Heidegger as the goal to which philosophy leads. It is said to be close to the reflection of the poet. On the other hand, Heidegger contrasts it with the 'calculative' thinking of the scientist and technician, and with the assured faith of the theologian. Scientists and theologians, he claims, do not think. At this point again, Heidegger must be accused of prejudice. Many scientists are not merely calculative in their thinking, but imaginative and creative, while theologians do not merely repeat the propositions of faith.

Heidegger's thinking is also a waiting. At the very beginning of *Sein und Zeit*, he had claimed that time is the horizon for an understanding of being. He has always considered being in dynamic, historical, temporal terms, and we have seen too that he speaks of God in terms of a primordial temporality.[38] Being is not timeless; it includes becoming and has a history. But Heidegger maintains that in the Western world, from the time of the Greeks onward, there has taken place a forgetting of being in the course of an increasing preoccupation with the beings, culminating in the technological era. He writes: 'In the beginning of Western thinking, being is thought, but not the "It gives" as such. The latter withdraws in favour of the gift which It gives.'[39] Here we come back to the understanding of being as a primordial act of giving (introduced almost casually in *Sein und Zeit*). The act is forgotten through preoccupation with what is given. Yet I doubt if Heidegger would attach any blame to this forgetting. He seems to suggest rather that being withdraws itself, and it may be the fate of a whole historical epoch to have forgotten being. 'What is history-like in the history of being,' he says, 'is obviously determined by the way in which being takes place and by this alone . . . this means, the way in which it gives being.'[40]

This notion of the absence and then the possible return of being is another echo of the mystic's experience of God. It also reflects the poetry of Hölderlin, whom Heidegger greatly admired. Hölderlin gave expression to the sense of alienation that was mounting in the nineteenth century, and his language was definitely religious, though perhaps as much pagan as Christian. The gods have departed; they have not ceased to exist, but they are absent. Still, the very perception of the absence of the gods is a tacit acknowledgment of them and of their possible return. But Heidegger does not believe that any effort on our part can bring about that return. 'Whether God lives or remains dead is not determined by the religiousness of man, and still less by the theological aspirations of philosophy and science. Whether God is God is determined from and within the constellation of being.'[41] There is an unmistakable touch of fatalism in this. But Heidegger is not a pessimist. In the article mentioned earlier entitled 'Only a God Can Save Us', he declares that he is neither a pessimist nor an optimist. Even the experience of the absence of God is a liberation from complete fallenness into preoccupation with the beings. But we cannot think God into the present, we can only prepare either for his appearing or his continuing absence, but we can hope for a new advent.[42]

Mention of this dynamic and even mildly eschatological element in Heidegger's thinking about God and being directs our attention to still another concept that appears in his later writings – the event (*das Ereignis*). John R. Williams believes that it is the event rather than being that comes closest to 'God' in Heidegger's thought. What then is 'the event'? It seems to be the 'It gives', whereby being communicates itself to man and, in a sense, entrusts itself to him. This event is the ultimate idea in Heidegger's philosophy. He writes: 'There is nothing else to which one could trace back the event or in terms of which it could be explained. The event is not the result of something else but an act of giving that reaches out and imparts like an "It gives", something which even being needs to attain its own character as presence.'[43] These sentences seem to support Williams' contention that 'the event is the ultimate concept in Heidegger's philosophy', and likewise the idea that God or being is a verb rather than a noun, an event rather than a substance. But I would be reluctant to agree with Williams when he says that the event is 'beyond being'. It is certainly beyond the beings, but in Heidegger being too is beyond the beings, wholly other to them and transcendent of them. I would say myself that the event is an event within being, or perhaps the event of being or even the event which constitutes being and reveals that the essence of being is giving. If the truth of being is finally uncovered as the 'It gives', then surely this ultimate giving, this original event of donation, deserves the name of 'God'.

Part Three

Dialectical Theism and Its Implications

XIII

A Dialectical Concept of God

Near the beginning of this search for deity, I set out the bare outlines of a concept of God. At that stage we could be only very tentative and provisional. But it was necessary to provide a minimal idea of what we mean by 'God', otherwise we would not know how or where to look. Though we do not search for an understanding of anything if it is already within our grasp, we could not even begin our search unless we had some idea of what is being sought. So we began on a pretty low key. We looked up a couple of standard dictionaries to find out what educated people think they mean when they use the word 'God'. We took a cursory glance at the history of the word, both in its religious and its philosophical uses. We noted the tensions that sometimes arise between the God of religion and the God of philosophy, and the unfortunate tendency of the human mind to be one-sided in its thinking about God. This in turn suggested that we look for a more dialectical concept. An examination of classical theism reinforced our distrust of one-sidedness, which can be justly blamed for some of the incoherences and implausibilities attaching to the classical idea of God and leading in the past two centuries to a decline in belief in God. But when we considered the main rivals to theism, namely atheism and pantheism, we found them to be even less persuasive than classical theism. So we were directed towards a more consciously dialectical form of theism – a view close to what is sometimes called 'panentheism', though we found that term confusing and not particularly helpful. We then proceeded to investigate through certain representative figures the long and rich tradition of dialectical theism which has persisted in the West from Plotinus down to the present and has constituted a neglected alternative to classical theism and its atheistic and pantheistic rivals. We are now in a position to develop a concept of God which will be much fuller than the tentative one from which we set out. I shall present this concept in a series of dialectical oppositions within God. These oppositions are not destructive contradictions or even sheer paradoxes of the 'take it or leave it' variety. So far as possible, I must show that in every opposition, each side has its right and each side can and must be asserted. But I draw attention to the modifying expression, 'so far as possible', for there must be limitations to any finite being's understanding of God. A 'God' understood and neatly packaged in philosophical concepts would not be God.

The first dialectical contrast is between being and nothing. God is being and God is nothing. In applying the language of 'being' to God, I am, of course, taking up a very ancient tradition. Aquinas claimed that the most proper name of God is 'He who is',[1] but the use of the language of 'being' for God goes back long before him to patristic and classical writers. Some of them, in turn, such as Philo, believed that their philosophical concept of God in terms of being had a religious justification in the name which God is said to have made known to Moses: 'I am who I am', or simply, 'I am'.[2] The language of 'being' has, however, many ambiguities. The parts of the verb 'to be', such as 'am' and 'is' and 'are', are most frequently used as the copula, showing that a predicate is being applied to a subject: 'The sky is blue', 'You are crazy', and so on. But it can also be used absolutely, implying reality or existence. An example would be 'God is', though nowadays this mode of expression is somewhat archaic, and we would be more likely to say, 'There is a God', or 'God exists', or 'God is real'. But even this absolute use of the language of 'being' is variable in meaning, for there are many different ways in which something can exist. Most commonly, when we assert that something exists, we mean that it can be found within the world of space and time. But clearly God does not exist in that sense. He is not an item within the world, so that in the ordinary sense of the word 'exist', God does not exist, he is nothing. Still, it would seem very odd to someone who believed in God as the ultimate reality to be told that he does not exist! As we have noted in the case of some of the mystical writers discussed earlier in the book, when they say that God does not exist or that he is nothing, they mean that his mode of being transcends the kind of being that is exemplified by the existence of objects in space and time. That is why I said that Eriugena's name for God, 'He who is more than being', is more subtle than Aquinas' 'He who is'.[3] When we speak of God as 'being', we do not mean that he exists as a rock or a galaxy or even a human being exists. He is not a being in the ordinary sense of the word. God exists in the sense of the source of all existence. He is, so to speak, existence raised to a higher power, not so much 'being' as 'letting be'. It is significant that the Bible does not begin by saying that God exists, but by claiming that he brings things into existence: 'let there be light', and so on. God precedes all existences by being the condition of their existence, so he is not himself numbered among the existents. That is part of the reason for the elusiveness of God, and explains why any empiricist philosophy, if it remains strictly empirical, has no place for God. Existence, as we understand it in our everyday dealings or as it is defined by empiricism, excludes God. Inevitably, he is nothing.

Why then should we use the language of 'being' about God? Is this not misleading? Here I think we may remind ourselves of the question asked by Leibniz and Heidegger: 'Why are there beings at all, rather than nothing?'[4] Any existent being within the world can, in principle, be shown to derive its existence from other beings within the world. Its existence is contingent on other beings. But the world (or universe) itself cannot be explained in that way. If it is felt that one must seek a reason for the existence of the world, this cannot be another existent but a reality of an entirely different order, a reality which is not an existent but a source of existence.

'Not *how* the world is, is the mystical, but *that* it is', wrote Wittgenstein,[5] and this is another way of expressing the question of Leibniz and Heidegger, which in turn expresses what I have called the 'shock of being', the astonishment that there is indeed a world rather than nothing. Wittgenstein thought the question is unanswerable and should not even be asked – we can only be silent. We cannot frame the idea of a 'superexistent' transcending the existent things of the world, any more than a dog or cat coming into my study can understand what a book is. In each case there is a level of reality beyond the power of comprehension. Yet people do not just remain silent. They stretch language to the uttermost, not to comprehend, but, again in Wittgenstein's term, to 'show' or 'point to' (*zeigt*) the mystery. The religious man uses the word 'God' without claiming to know who or what God is, the philosopher may, like Heidegger, use the word 'being' but can only tell us that being is 'wholly other' to the beings, that it is the ultimate event of 'giving', behind which we cannot go but which we posit as the source of the sheer fact of the givenness of the world, that there is a world and not just nothing. For, as Leibniz somewhat quaintly put it, 'Nothing is simpler and easier than something' (*Car le rien est plus simple et plus facile que quelque chose*).[6] He meant, I suppose, that things do not just come into existence of themselves, and that if there were no creative source, one would naturally expect there to be nothing at all.

The second dialectical opposition in God is that between the one and the many. God is the unity holding all things together and without which there would be chaos. But this is not a barren undifferentiated unity. God is also the fullness of being, and embraces within himself all the richness of being. Being is not to be regarded as an empty abstraction, but as a *plenum*. So the assertion that God is being is at the same time the attribution to him of all affirmative characteristics, though, of course, analogically. Thus, as Augustine says, 'it is the same to God, to be and to be great'.[7] Similarly, it is the same for him to be and to be good, to be and to be just and so on. It could be said, however, that this richness of attributes is not really a plurality in God, and that it is only the limitation of our own minds that leads us to distinguish these aspects of the unitary divine being. This may be so, but there is another way in which an inner differentiation seems to follow from the recognition that God is to be understood as being, for being comprises a number of modes. In discussing God as being, we had in mind principally what may be called the 'primordial' mode of his being – the ineffable and incomprehensible superexistence which does not itself exist but is the creative source and condition of everything that does exist. This is the deepest and most mysterious region of deity, God in his otherness and transcendence. This is the originary act of giving which we cannot understand but to which we can point. We posit this originary event because there is in fact a given – the world or universe. God has come out from the hiddenness of the ultimate mystery to bring into being a cosmos evolving under ordered laws. I call this second mode of divine being the 'expressive' mode, because in it the divine activity has come out into the openness and intelligibility of the cosmos. God has not been content, so to speak, to stay shut up in his impenetrable mystery, but from all eternity there has been an event of giving, whereby he has shared being with that which is other than himself. It is clear that what we have in mind here is close to the traditional Logos or Nous, that rational and intelligent aspect of deity which is also the agent in forming the creation. We must suppose too that although the furthest depths of deity (the primordial being) remain veiled to us, something of the divine nature – and this very word 'nature' (*natura* or φύσις) means originally an 'emerging' or 'arising' – is communicated or revealed in the cosmos, for in some way it must express the reality from which it arises. Inevitably, such revelation is at the same time a veiling, because the ineffable 'event' which precedes and conditions existence is now being expressed under the forms of existence. But there is a third mode of being, what we may call 'unitive' being. The cosmos or nature which has emerged through the creative activity of the Logos seeks to return to its source, not in the sense of being swallowed up once more in the mystery from which it has emerged, but through forming a new and richer unity, a unity which necessarily includes distinctness, and to which our best clue is the intimate personal relation between two human beings. This unitive mode of being invites comparison with the idea of the Spirit of God, immanent in the creation, striving within the creation to bring it to its fulfilment. God is not only Logos or intelligence; we may also ascribe to him something analogous to appetition. While we may suppose that the 'return' to God is operative at all levels of the creation, we are ourselves aware of it at the conscious level in religion, man's quest for God. It is not fanciful to see at the origin of religion something like an ἀνάμνησις; the dim corporate memory of humanity of its origin in God, to which human finitude coupled with the capacity for transcendence, remains as an abiding testimony.

From the very idea of God as ultimate being, coming out into a creation and then returning, we have to think of his unity as differentiated into what, for want of a better term, I have called 'modes'. This suggests once again that the doctrine of a triune God belongs to natural theology. It is significant that the philosophers considered earlier in this book, with one exception, arrived at a trinitarian conception of God, and did so without explicit appeal to Christian dogma. The one exception was, of course, Whitehead, who preferred a binitarian or dipolar view, but I tried to show that his concept of God would gain in depth and plausibility if he were to incorporate into it his ultimate category of creativity and so move from a binitarian to a trinitarian view.[8]

The third dialectical opposition in the concept of God is between his knowability and his incomprehensibility. We have already touched on this problem, when we asked whether one is not reduced to silence before the mystery of God. That question was forced on us by Wittgenstein, who indeed recognized the mystical, as he called it, but believed it to be inexpressible. One can point, but one cannot say anything. 'God', he said, 'does not reveal himself *in* the world.'[9] In a sense, of course, this must be true. God, as the creative reality beyond the realm of existents, cannot be found among the existent entities of the world. But if what we have said about God's expressing himself in the creation has any truth to it, or, again, if God is not simply primordial being but also expressive and unitive being, then he does not confront us as a pure unknown. Obviously, the depth of divine being cannot be known, for he is in some respects wholly other and, I would say, suprarational. If we thought that we had grasped him, then it would not be God that we had grasped. Most of the thinkers whom we have considered were very cautious, almost to the point of agnosticism, in their talk of God – they emphasized the negative way, and recognized that anything else we say is analogical. Only Hegel and Whitehead among our 'representative figures' were thoroughgoing rationalists.

The knowledge of God is indirect and is mediated through images and symbols. But because God has come out from his hiddenness to express himself in and through the creation, the knowledge we have of him, though indirect, is genuine. As I have argued elsewhere,[10] the human being has a special place in the creation, so far as we know it, as the image of God in the finite or as a kind of microcosm, summing up in himself the range of being.

Another point should be noted in this problem of the knowability of God. We do not reach the knowledge of God by a deduction or inference from the world. Rather, it seems to be the case that God is intuited in the world as a presence or as its unity, as indeed I noted very early in this inquiry.[11] I would agree with H. A. Hodges that 'the foundation of theism is not a speculative guess or inference or theory, but an imaginative vision of existence which can be of deep significance for life'.[12] When one ventures to speak of 'intuition' or 'vision', can one claim that these provide knowledge? Some people would deny it, and in any case any pretended intuition or vision would need to be subjected to critical investigation, and be backed up by some metaphysical theory. We shall defer this question until we come to the consideration of mysticism, for the mystic appears to make the largest claims to having a direct vision of God, though usually he is reserved about the content of the vision. For the present, we content ourselves with the claim that God is both incomprehensible and knowable.

The fourth dialectical opposition in God is between his transcendence and his immanence. In some ways, this is the fundamental opposition, and I might have been expected to put it first. However, I reserved that place for the opposition between being and the beings, the ontological difference, as Heidegger calls it. The order in which these oppositions are presented does not matter very much, for each overlaps the other and all are mutually involved and reciprocative.

By 'transcendence', when the term is applied to God, is usually meant his otherness from the world (the ontological difference), his precedence over the world (as its creative source), his surpassing of the merely natural levels of existence (as the ground of the order which manifests itself in nature). However, I have more than once suggested that the divine transcendence might be conceived in a more dynamic way in analogy with human transcendence, namely, as God's capacity to go out from and beyond himself. His 'immanence', on the other hand, refers to his indwelling of the creation, his presence and agency within the things and events of the world.

In acknowledging that God is both transcendent and immanent, it is not meant that one has got to seek some half-way position in which both transcendence and immanence would be weakened. Rather, God is in some respects wholly transcendent, in some respects wholly immanent. Obviously, as the primordial 'It gives' (where 'It gives' is a more evidently dynamic equivalent of the traditional 'I am') God is utterly transcendent and is separated by the ontological difference from the beings. But in the expressive and unitive modes of his being, God is thoroughly immanent in the creation. A commonly used metaphor, which I have employed myself elsewhere,[13] is that of the artist in relation to his art-work. The artist fully transcends his work, which he conceives in his imagination and then gives to it an embodied form, whether it be a painting or a poem or a piece of music. Once it has this form, the art-work has a measure of independence. Yet the artist is now immanent in his work. He has put something of himself into it and, though it is external to him, it can also be considered like an extension of his personal being. William Temple thought that even the analogy of the artist does not sufficiently illustrate the intimacy of God's indwelling of the world, and leaves him too external.[14] But all analogies are imperfect, and it is hard to imagine a better one.

Classical theism emphasized the divine transcendence in a one-sided way, to the neglect of divine immanence. In our earlier discussion of Plotinus, I claimed that his conception of emanation is not entirely incompatible with the biblical understanding of creation, and that to do justice to the divine immanence and the intimacy of the God-world relation, the common metaphor of 'making' as used of God's creation of the world needs to be modified by some recognition of emanation. This is particularly so with the higher levels of creation, and it is significant that in the second of the two biblical accounts of creation, God both makes man of the dust of the ground and then breathes into him the breath of life, thereby, it would seem, imparting something of himself.

No theologian of modern times has been more insistent on the divine transcendence and the distance between God and the creatures than Karl Barth. In fact, he says explicitly that in Christian theology 'all ideas of creation as divine emanation are forcefully excluded; we are not told that the world is the word of God, but that it is by the word of God'.[15] But when he comes to the detailed exegesis of the biblical accounts of creation, it seems to me that even Barth allows for something like emanation, in the case of those higher creatures that are endowed with spirit, particularly the human being. So when he comes to God's words in the first of the two Genesis accounts of creation, 'Let us make man in our own image, after our likeness', he points out that in the case of the human being, the creative word is given a unique formulation: 'In the creation of man, a special formula, "Let us make", is used; the creative fiat is not directed outwards towards the creature to be created, but inwards in the form of the "Let us"; it is a summons to intradivine unanimity of intention and decision.'[16] If this in itself is not entirely clear, it is clarified on the next page where Barth says of man's being made in the divine image that 'there exists a divine and therefore self-grounded prototype to which this being can correspond'.[17] It seems not unreasonable to read these passages as meaning that in the creation of man, God endows him with something that he has summoned out of his own inner nature. Clearer still is a passage dealing with the special role of Israel, and suggesting that from the beginning God had put himself into Israel, so that we could even say that the incarnation was already in process. The passage reads: 'In and with Israel's election God has from the very first offered, surrendered and sacrificed no less than something of himself, in some sense hazarding himself, so that from the very first the existence of Israel includes in itself the existence of the Son of God.'[18] Barth may abhor the word 'emanation', but it seems to me that he comes very close to admitting the reality for which the word stands. 'God', he tells us, 'has said Yes to the Israel created not only by himself but of himself', and he compares the relation of Israel to God to that of Eve to Adam, 'bone of his bones, and flesh of his flesh'.[19]

One further point is important. If we overstress the image of 'making' in our attempt to characterize the unimaginable event of creation out of nothing, we cannot help introducing notions of arbitrariness and externality and even a tendency toward acosmism, as we have seen in our discussion of classical theism. The creation is highly dispensable and God is not affected by its fate.[20] But if God is ultimately that mysterious primordial event of giving to which natural theology has led us, if his very essence is the 'It gives', then we may say that it is his very nature to create, to overflow himself in his generous bestowal of the gift of existence. We are not saying that creation is necessary to God, as if there were some fate that compelled him to create. We are saying that God in the fullness of his being goes out from himself to posit another who is nevertheless derived from himself and so of infinite value and concern to him. Such a God seems to me more in accord with the demands of the religious consciousness than a God who might or might not have created, and whose creation was so external to him that its disappearance would have left him precisely the same as he was when it existed. I would rather say with Nietzsche's Zarathustra as he watched the rising sun: 'Thou great star! Where were thy happiness without those for whom thou shinest?'[21]

The discussion of transcendence and immanence has prepared the way for the fifth dialectical opposition – that between impassibility and passibility. According to classical theism, God is pure act, and in him there is neither passivity nor potency. He acts upon the creation, but this is a purely asymmetrical relation, and there is no way in which the creation can affect God. These statements obviously envisage a transcendent God to whom the creation is quite external, and since we have already seen reason for modifying such a view of the divine transcendence, we must be prepared also to modify the traditional belief in divine impassibility. If we take seriously the belief that God is in a significant degree immanent in his creation and involved in its affairs, then he must be deeply affected by everything that goes on in the world. He must be deeply concerned with the fate of a world into which he has put himself, and the suffering of that world must in some way be also experienced by God. There is surely little to admire or worship in a God who remained untouched by the sufferings of his creatures. Such a God might be a product of philosophical speculation, but he would hardly be the God of religious experience. The God of Israel, for instance, was represented as a loving husband or father, full of steadfast love towards his people, so that they could say that 'in all their affliction, he was afflicted'.[22] If there is any love in God (and his generous creative giving would seem to be the archetype of love), then of necessity there is also vulnerability, for it is impossible to love a person without being grieved by that person's suffering and sin. In creating an existent other than himself, and in granting to that existent a measure of freedom and autonomy, God surrendered any unclouded bliss that might have belonged to him had he remained simply wrapped up in his own perfection. In creating, he consents to know the pain and frustration of the world. All this needs to be strongly asserted against the teaching of divine impassibility presented in traditional theism.

But, as I warned in the course of our discussion of Whitehead,[23] there is a great danger that the reaction against the monarchical God, throned above the conflicts of the world, may be carried to the length where he becomes a puny godling, not so much the source of anything affirmative as the hapless victim of a world that has got completely out of control. Such a being would be no more 'God' than would the unfeeling ruler who remained untouched by the sufferings of the world. A truly dialectical understanding of God does not substitute passibility for impassibility, but claims that God unites these two characteristics in himself. What could this mean? Does it make any sense to acknowledge that God suffers, and then to say that he is also impassible?

I think it does make sense. God is the ultimate reality, the primordial source of everything that is, the originary event of giving. Because of this ultimacy, he cannot be annihilated or overcome. Everything, even the events which grieve him, proceeds eventually from him, so that if God were no more, the world too would be no more. There may be many ways in which the suffering of God differs from the suffering of human beings, but there is one fairly obvious difference. Whereas the suffering of a human being can overwhelm and eventually destroy the person concerned, this cannot happen in the case of God. He can accept the world's pain, and does in fact accept it because he is immanent in the world-process, but he is never overwhelmed by it. He has an infinite capacity for absorbing suffering, and even for transforming it, though we cannot know how this transformation takes place. Christianity speaks of it indirectly, when it sets together the opposing symbols of cross and resurrection, and when it teaches that in the light of resurrection, the cross is transformed from being the instrument of the passion into the symbol of life and salvation. Or perhaps one should rather say, it becomes the symbol of life and salvation without ceasing to be the instrument of the passion. Likewise God is the God who stands in solidarity with his people in their sufferings, but this does not make him any less the God of creation, providence and judgment, but rather helps us to understand what these descriptions mean. God is passible and impassible. Without his passibility, his sharing in our affliction, there could be no bond of sympathy between him and us. Without his impassibility, his power to absorb and overcome and transform, there could be no final faith in God and we would have to join those pessimistic atheists who tell us that the cosmos is fundamentally absurd and meaningless, so that it would have been better if this sorry scheme of things had never come into existence.

The sixth dialectical opposition is between eternity and temporality. In the traditional teaching, God has been said to be above time, eternally the same and immune from change. Our own human experience is so thoroughly temporal that it is hard for us even to attach a meaning to the word 'eternity'. Yet perhaps it is our own temporality that drives us in search of eternity. Temporality implies for us loss, decay, passing away, and we imagine to ourselves the opposite state of affairs where everything that is good is preserved and saved from dissolution. Eternity can hardly mean sheer timelessness. It has been understood rather as a transcending of mere successiveness in the simultaneous enjoyment of past, present and future. In human experience, we are sometimes able to transcend successiveness for short spans of time, and this gives us some clue to what might be the divine experience in which a thousand years are said to be like yesterday.[24]

Without, however, speculating on the form of the divine experience, I think we can say that God, to be worthy of the name of God, must be eternal. Part of his otherness and transcendence is his immunity from the ravages of time. He remains constant and faithful, neither his power nor his love is diminished by the passage of time, and in these respects he stands over against his creatures and they are able to look to him for salvation and for the conservation of whatever values have been painfully realized through human struggle and effort.

But that is only part of the truth. Many human beings who have been active in the realization of value have testified that it was not simply by their own efforts and struggles that their achievements came about and that their actions were evoked and sustained by the spirit of God in their midst, inspiring them through divine grace. They have believed that God himself has been engaged in the struggle, and that he is not just an observer, untouched by it all, but an active participant. Especially for any religion which attaches importance to history and holds any eschatological belief, it is natural to believe that God is himself in the events of history and is concerned about their outcome.

Again, it would seem that the truth cannot lie exclusively on one side alone. God is both eternal and temporal. There is a sense in which everything is already fulfilled in him, and it is the vision of all things subjected to God, *sub specie aeternitatis*, that has acted as a powerful source of hope and confidence among human beings engaged in the struggle for a better world. Yet, if the struggle is real, it must be real for God, too. If he really cares about the outcome, every step forward must increase his satisfaction and so contribute to his perfection. Though the language is certainly bold, it does not seem to me entirely wrong to say with Eriugena that God is actually making himself in the temporal world; or, in the words of a modern philosopher, Whitehead, that while God in his primordial nature is eternal and perfect, he is in his consequent nature temporal and shares in the 'creative advance of the world'.

I come finally to the problem of evil in dialectical theism. This is not a seventh dialectic in which one recognizes the opposition of good and evil in God. The reason for saying this is that evil is not something affirmative – it is essentially negative, a distortion of the good and parasitic on the good. It is true that most of the thinkers considered earlier in this book, from Plotinus to Whitehead, have been accused by some of their critics of not taking evil with sufficient seriousness. But what would it mean to take evil with more seriousness than they have shown? Would it not mean setting up a dualism in which evil is given positive ontological status as a realm of Satan over against the kingdom of God? This would surely be a reversion to mythology. Evil is not co-ordinate with good, but the absence and sometimes the perversion of good. I say 'perversion', because just to say that evil is the deficiency of good may well sound too weak, and one has to recognize that deficiency in turn leads to massive distortion. The problem of evil is not, I think, finally soluble, and remains part of the mystery of a reality that must, in the long run, be accounted suprarational. But let me mention three points at which, I think, the tradition of dialectical theism shows itself able to cope with the problem of evil, perhaps better than some rival philosophies.

The first is its frank recognition that God is in a real way immanent in the world process, and this inevitably means that he takes upon himself the suffering of the world and shares it with his creatures. This certainly eases the whole question. On the classical view, God was perfect in power and goodness, and immune from the effects of worldly events. So the question was acute. Why does God permit evil to afflict his creatures? And this question was given an additional sharpness because God himself was taken to be free of any suffering. It is easier to reconcile ourselves to the presence of evil in the world if we know that it causes pain even to God, and that in his temporal aspect, he too has to face it and overcome it.

The second point is the recognition that evil is inseparable from any creation. As soon as God posits another than himself, he has put a limit to his own being, including his power. Furthermore, as Leibniz pointed out, this other could not be perfect, or it would be a second God. That which is finite is necessarily imperfect, for it has deficiencies or lacks which separate it from perfection. We cannot complain that the creation is not perfect, that would be ridiculous. We can, however, ask whether the creation is justified. We might think it is so bad that the primal One would have done better to remain undisturbed in his own ineffability.

The third point, then, is whether the world is worthwhile. Again, Leibniz had some good insights. He pointed out that we can hardly suppose that the world was created only for human convenience, and so we are not in a position to deliver an overall judgment. But he went much further, and claimed that this is the best of all possible worlds. I have pointed out that we misunderstand this if we think it expresses brash optimism or the belief that everything at this moment is ideal. He is simply saying that, having regard to the evils which would inevitably affect any world, we may have faith that this whole world process, if we could see it as a whole, would be the best possible. Perhaps most people do in fact believe this. There are a few who talk about returning their tickets, but this is a rhetoric on which they rarely act. A few unhappy souls find things so bad that they commit suicide, but the vast majority of the human race struggle on with a mixture of hope and resignation, believing that the adventure of life is worthwhile and even trusting that all will be for the best.

XIV

Dialectical Theism and Spirituality

Theology, whether natural theology or a theology which expounds a specific revelation, is an intellectual enterprise – indeed, it has often been called a science, though it is a science with its own methods appropriate to its subject-matter, and very different from the methods of the natural sciences. As a science, theology aims at knowledge – the knowledge of God.

Alongside theology one finds the practice of religion or spirituality, as it is often called. In its broadest sense, this term includes prayer in its many forms, worship, rites and ceremonies, fasting, pilgrimages and many other exercises, designed to strengthen religious faith. Spirituality can be defined in different ways. It could be defined as the discipline of becoming a fully personal human being, and this definition would have the advantage of recognizing that there are sometimes to be found secular spiritualities, for instance, patterns of meditation which do not explicitly refer to God. More often, however, the word 'spirituality' does include a religious reference. It is used mainly by those who believe that the full development of the human being includes a relation to God or holy being. In this case, the aim of spirituality is the same as the aim of theology – the knowledge of God.

So both theology and spirituality have the same end in view. Are there then two ways to the knowledge of God? If so, how are these two ways related to each other? Does theology foster spirituality, or does it criticize it or even, in some cases, kill it? Does spirituality on its side afford any genuine knowledge of God that could be a resource for theology, or is it a distraction from the strict theological task, introducing into theology emotion and longing, and so diminishing its claim to be a science? It was Tillich who warned theologians not 'to fill in logical gaps with devotional material'.[1]

Tillich's caution is a salutary one in many contexts of theological work. But it cannot mean that theology must go its way entirely regardless of spirituality. If theology is finally the study of God, and if God is uniquely different from all the entities which make up the world and which are the objects of the many sciences which human ingenuity has developed, then God cannot be studied in the same ways as the objects of those sciences. It has sometimes been objected to natural theology that it turns God into an object. If I thought this were true, then I would have to wash my hands of natural theology, for I have insisted again and again that God is not an object or a being of any kind. He comes before all existence, as the ultimate mystery of whom we cannot properly say that he is, but must rather say that he lets be. If we look for him among the objects comprised in the universe, we shall not find him. From that point of view, he is nothing, yet a nothing more beingful than any object. To turn God into an object or to develop a natural theology which treated him as an object would be the most thorough perversion imaginable of the knowledge of God. If Tillich was correct in counselling against the introduction of devotional material into theological argument, it is equally correct to counsel against the objectification of God, for this would even more surely defeat the theological enterprise. If God is the source of all, then he must also be the source of the knowledge of himself, and this comes first of all in the practice of religion, not in philosophical or theological reflection. This is why I said clearly at the beginning of this book that there is no 'unaided' knowledge of God, just as there is no 'unaided' knowledge of a human person; though perhaps I should have been more cautious and said that if there is in either case any such 'unaided' knowledge, it would be so superficial and abstract as to be worthless. I cannot deny that I have sometimes been present at discussions on God when he has been treated as an object to be analysed, anatomized and argued about. On such occasions, there have come to my mind the words of Francis Bacon: 'The true atheist is he who handles holy things without feeling.'[2]

I shall try to show that the dialectical theism developed in this book does go hand in hand with a profound spirituality. The possibility of this close relation was already apparent in some of the representative figures whom we considered. Plotinus, Dionysius and Nicholas of Cusa were all subtle thinkers, but they were also mystics who had known spiritual experiences in which they had enjoyed the vision of God. Though Hegel was first and foremost an intellectualist and a severe critic of Schleiermacher's appeal to feeling and religious experience, we have seen that his own conception of speculative philosophy was not far removed from mysticism.[3] Whitehead, again, is primarily philosophical and rationalist, and often severely critical of religion in its concrete institutional forms. Yet he speaks from time to time of the religious 'vision', which is not the product of philosophy, though he believes – rightly, I think – that it needs metaphysical backing.[4] In an often quoted passage, he makes a very high claim for this vision: 'The fact of the religious vision, and its history of persistent expansion, is our one ground for optimism. Apart from it, human life is a flash of occasional enjoyments lighting up a mass of pain and misery.'[5] Heidegger, as we have seen, appears to rate the thinking of the philosopher above the faith of the theologian, but he allows a place to the affects in the apprehension of reality, there are unmistakable echoes of the mystics in his writings, and he compares the conceptualized God of the philosophers unfavourably with what he calls the 'divine God' to whom prayer and hymns can be addressed.[6]

Before we go on to the specific relation between dialectical theism and spirituality, let us return to the more general question, raised at an earlier point and now posed anew by the quotations just made, whether there are two ways to the knowledge of God. The same question may be put slightly differently, by asking whether spirituality is cognitive or non-cognitive. The use by Whitehead and other philosophers of the word 'vision' in connection with religion would seem to suggest that there is a cognitive element involved, even if this cognition needs to be backed up, as Whitehead believed, by some metaphysical argument. There are many other philosophers, of course, who would say that religion is entirely non-cognitive, a subjective affair of the will and emotions which may indeed lead us to see things in a certain way and may promote certain attitudes, but which affords no insight into realities beyond ourselves. On the other hand, of course, practitioners of spirituality sometimes claim a direct vision of God which is more real to them than anything else and beside which the ideas of the philosopher are mere abstractions.

Arguments about the cognitive status of experiences or visions of God obviously already imply some decision about what can be regarded as 'knowledge'. In an empirical age which has been marked by the astonishing success of the natural sciences, it is the knowledge of facts, the knowledge that can be expressed in propositions and organized in systems, that has come to have great prestige, and even to be accounted by some as the only knowledge worthy to be so called. But is this not far too narrow a conception of what constitutes knowledge?[7] There is also a direct personal way of knowing, typified most clearly by the knowledge that one person has of another, but with many other forms besides, such as the knowledge one may have of a tract of countryside over which one has often walked, or the knowledge of some great musical work to which one has often listened. This kind of knowledge is not easily put into propositional form and cannot constitute a logical system. It is different from knowledge of facts, but it cannot be denied that it is genuine knowledge, and knowledge of a very important kind.

The knowledge of God gained in philosophy of religion or in theology approximates to the first of the two types of knowledge distinguished here. It finds expression in propositional language, and the propositions in turn constitute a systematic body of knowledge, so that we sometimes speak of 'systematic theology'. Philosophers of religion and theologians alike use arguments and seek consistency both within their own disciplines and in relation to other disciplines. Admittedly, the theologian will often confess that his language is inadequate and that his 'system' is tentative and open to constant revision. Nevertheless, his aim is to offer an account of God that will be, in the broadest sense, 'scientific'.

If we are to claim cognitive status for spirituality, we must understand it as closer to the second kind of knowledge distinguished above. Even when spirituality makes use of words, it does so in a different way from theology and philosophy. Whereas the latter use third-person language to describe or speak *about* God or the holy, spirituality uses the second-person language of address, especially in prayer to God. Again, while theology aims at conceptualization (though it never quite dispenses with images), the language of spirituality is closer to poetry than to science, and makes free use of image, metaphor and symbol. Theology may try to conceptualize God as 'necessary being' or in some other way, but one could hardly pray or sing a hymn to necessary being. So spirituality is more likely to think of God as shepherd or king or even as spouse, concrete images which are not literally applicable, but which evoke the appropriate personal responses in the approach to God. But eventually spirituality may lead beyond all words and images to a silent adoration which gathers up all the separate images and responses into an inexpressible fullness.

The difference between theology and philosophy on the one hand and spirituality on the other is not that the former are cognitive and the latter non-cognitive, but that both are cognitive in different ways. Theology and philosophy are successful to the extent that they find appropriate words in which to frame their knowledge of God. Spirituality, on the other hand, seems to reach its peak when it leaves words behind and enters into a fulfilled silence. But can there be cognition or any form of knowledge without words? I think there can be. Michael Polanyi called it 'tacit knowledge',[8] and gave many examples, such as the skill of the builder or the skill of the research scientist. To some extent, these skills can be described and set out in books, but what is thus put into words is never exhaustive. There is something more that is unspecified and, however much we refine our language, unspecifiable. That is why the training of a builder or scientist cannot come simply out of books but needs the living teacher-student relation, everything that is tacitly conveyed through example and personal intercourse. The great bulk of our knowledge is, admittedly, conveyed in words, but our knowledge is not exhausted by what can be put into words. The activity of thinking, which, among other things, includes the creative opening up of new knowledge, races ahead of language, so to speak. Under the pressure of creative thought, language develops new words, new meanings, new modes of expression, as it tries to keep pace with these tacit insights. In this process, language expands and becomes more accurate and more sensitive, yet it always lags a step or two behind. It is in some such way that we may understand the relation between the theologico-philosophical quest for God and spirituality. Spirituality is like the thought that leaps ahead of language. There is, in Paul's way of putting it, a 'spiritual discernment' (ὁ δὲ πνευματικὸς ἀνακρίνει μὲν πάντα).[9]

Can we make clearer what this discernment is, so as to strengthen the case for a cognitive dimension in spirituality? It is the capacity to intuit things as not just a collection of items fortuitously thrown together but in their unity and interconnectedness. This is what some pyschologists have intended by the German word *Gestalt* – literally 'form', and I have already on a number of occasions stressed the fundamental role of form, without which no understanding of anything would be possible, and I have also linked form with what we call 'mind'. We could also compare spiritual discernment with aesthetic perception. When we look at a picture, we do not perceive it simply as a multi-coloured piece of canvas; we perceive its 'composition', the way in which all its parts are interrelated so as to convey a meaning. A human face is perhaps the outstanding instance of what I intend. We do not see a face as a mere physical object or even as part of a body, but as the expression of a person, revealing the inner life and attitudes of that person. Our perception of the face includes an intuitive grasp of its unity and meaning as the face of a person.

There is a parallel here to the discernment of God. In an early chapter, I speculated that in primitive religion natural phenomena might be perceived as more than merely natural phenomena, as expressing a unity and presence which is taken to be God or a god. Something very similar, but at a much more sophisticated level, appears in the spirituality of Wordsworth and many other poets. There is a vision (to use Whitehead's word) of a unity and wholeness pervading all things, and not a dead unity but one that pulsates with a life somehow akin to our own and which we call 'spiritual'. Among philosophers of religion who seem to hold some such view is H. A. Hodges, whose view I have already quoted, that the 'foundation of theism is not a speculative guess or inference or theory, but an imaginative vision of existence'.[10] Elsewhere he claims: 'The mystic is one who sees the deep-seated unity which things have by their common derivation from and utter dependence on the Ultimate, and who wishes to be drawn experientially nearer to the centre of that unity than he is now.'[11] In epistemology, Hodges adhered to a fairly strict empiricism, but apparently this did not prohibit him from acknowledging the possibility of an intuitive religious vision. A similar case is that of Ian Ramsey, a man with a scientific training whose outlook was close to empiricism, but who did not seem to think that this was inconsistent with the recognition that in and around some empirical event there might take place what he called a 'cosmic disclosure'. In his own words, this is 'a situation which takes on depth to disclose another dimension, a situation where I am in principle confronted with the whole universe, a situation where God reveals himself'.[12]

How are we to judge the claim that in and through some particular event or constellation of events someone has intuitively perceived a spiritual unity in which all things cohere and which may be called 'God'? On the one hand, it does seem to me probable that it was in such experiences that the idea of God originated or, at any rate, began to take shape, for there may have been an antecedent *a priori* germ of the idea. But the question is not how the idea originated, but whether it is true to reality. What is the epistemological status of the vision or disclosure that some people claim to have perceived in religious experience? We might think it only fair to accept it until or unless it is shown to be illusory. On the other hand, we might think that if there is any doubt on such an important matter, then those who make the claim must try to find for it some metaphysical or ontological backing in a philosophy of religion. The experiences I have mentioned would fit in most comfortably with a philosophy of religion stressing the divine immanence, for the events associated with these experiences are not miracles in the popular sense of the word, that is to say, interventions of a transcendent divine power, but simply ordinary events which can be given a natural explanation but which nevertheless become disclosive or revelatory events, lighting up vast tracts of nature and history beyond themselves. Yet, in speaking of immanence, I am far from suggesting any kind of pantheism. The God who discloses himself *in* the events of this world, not just *through* their instrumentality, is at the same time a God who transcends the merely natural. As one writer on spirituality has remarked with great common sense, 'I cannot see how anyone, gazing at flowers and trees, ducks and geese, and even a few million square miles of desert or a herd of wild elephants, could possibly mistake all this for God Almighty. But any of it might manifest and disclose him.'[13]

Spiritual discernment leaps ahead in its intuitive perception of God. Philosophy and theology come along behind as second order enterprises, which analyse, conceptualize and evaluate what is already there in religion. Men and women are already praying, worshipping and communing with God before they have clearly thought out what they are doing or have satisfied themselves about the validity of it all. They may well think that no validation is needed. But in fact philosophical and theological reflection invariably follow. Often they are required to justify beliefs and practices, but they may also come to criticize them, for spirituality has a tendency to run to luxuriant growth and sometimes needs to be pruned back.

A very good example of the relation between spirituality and theology is afforded by the place of the Blessed Virgin Mary in Christianity. Theological reflection on Mary and her place in the scheme of salvation was a relatively late development. Only within the last two centuries has there been an attempt to give definite formulation to the dogmas of her conception without sin and her assumption into heaven. It must be a question whether mariological dogmas would ever have been formulated at all for theological reasons, had it not been for the spur of Marian spirituality to encourage theological reflection. The place of Mary in Christian spirituality was securely established long before there was any theological speculation about her. From a very early time prayers and intercessions were directed to Mary, while hymns were composed and sung in her honour.[14] While the motivation behind the upsurge of Marian devotion was no doubt largely the recognition of her indispensable place in the economy of salvation, it surely also must have been the need to find a place for the feminine in Christian spirituality. Thus, as devotion to Mary grew and established itself, it was necessary for theology to develop appropriate doctrines which would supply a justification for the devotions. It is a very clear case of *lex orandi, lex credendi*. However, the case of Mariology is especially interesting because it shows us theology not only in its reflective and supportive role, but also exercising a critical function. Already in the fourth century Bishop Epiphanius found it necessary to restrain the excesses of Marian devotion in his diocese by declaring: 'Mary should be honoured, but the Father and the Son and the Holy Ghost should be adored. Nobody should adore Mary.'[15] This anticipates the later theological distinction between worship in the fullest sense and veneration. The saints are worthy of veneration, but this is different in kind from the worship due to God alone. Here we see the development of theological distinctions which are indeed sympathetic to Marian spirituality but which also act as a check on the exuberance of devotion to Mary, for there would come a point at which the honours paid to a finite human person would become idolatrous. In recent times, Vatican II encouraged devotion to the Virgin and claimed that 'this cult is altogether special', but it also declared that 'it differs essentially from the cult of adoration' offered to deity, and warned against excesses.[16]

The example given makes it clear that spirituality leads and intellectual reflection follows, that the *lex orandi* is more fundamental than the *lex credendi*. Truths of faith are intuitively discerned before they are formulated as doctrines and incorporated into theology. But spirituality needs theological reflection if it is not to run riot. On the other hand, theology and philosophy of religion become intolerably dry and lose all interest if we turn them into purely academic exercises and separate them from the life of the spirit. From the Enlightenment onward, there have been theologians and philosophers who have tried to construct purely rational theologies. But even if a religion within the limits of reason alone could not be faulted on intellectual grounds (and this is doubtful), it would still fail through sheer dullness. It has nothing of the outgoing recklessness of trust and adoration that belong to the spiritual quest for God. The quest for the knowledge of God in theology and philosophy must not be separated from the quest for God in spirituality. As we noted at the beginning of this inquiry, Lord Gifford himself did not think of lectures given on his foundation as a disinterested academic exercise, but believed that the knowledge which they seek 'lies at the root of all well-being',[17] that is to say, of human flourishing which is precisely the end of spirituality.

I wish now to turn to the specific topic of the relation of dialectical theism to spirituality, and to a particular kind of spirituality, namely, mysticism. There are several reasons for choosing mysticism for this discussion. First, we have already noted that several important representatives of dialectical theism, from Plotinus on, have also been mystics, and this may testify to an inner connection between their philosophy and their spirituality. Second, mysticism is often taken to be the highest reach of spirituality. If the mystic, in his moment of rapture, has an unclouded vision of God, what more could there be? Other forms of religious experience could in fact be regarded as stages towards the mystical vision. Third, mysticism has been studied both critically and sympathetically by many philosophers, and the arguments both for and against its cognitive status have been explored. That status has not been established, but neither has it been overthrown. The verdict is the Scottish one of 'Not proven', and I think one would agree with Frederick Copleston that 'unless there is good reason for thinking it probable that mystical writers are lying or suffering from delusions, it is much more reasonable to accept their testimony than not to accept it'.[18]

Mysticism itself, however, comes in several forms. There is a mysticism that looks out upon nature and is seized with the profound unity of all things in the cosmos, to such an extent, perhaps, that distinctions between individual things virtually disappear. More typical, perhaps, is the mysticism that turns inward to the very centre or ground of the self, and finds that this is not an isolated self-contained entity but is continuous with a universal spirit pervading all things. This mysticism is itself of more than one kind. Some mystics use imagery to express their experiences. Erotic imagery is perhaps the commonest; for instance, the use of the Song of Solomon among Christian mystics. This is not surprising, for marriage and the sexual relation is the most intimate union or communion between finite human beings, and is well suited to represent that union of the soul with God which is in itself ineffable. But there are other mystics who eschew imagery, and whose experience of union with deity seems to be more intellectual and even impersonal, in the sense of being unemotional.

This last-named type of mystic is well exemplified by Meister Eckhart and it is his work that we shall consider. He had the advantage of being an able philosophical theologian as well as a mystic, so that his theological opinions were fairly clearly set forth. We can see in him both the strengths of a spirituality related to dialectical theism and its more questionable aspects which brought him into conflict with the ecclesiastical authorities and resulted in proceedings against him for heresy, still going on when he died in 1328.[19]

What is characteristic of mystical spirituality is that it is founded on the affinity between God and the human soul. The soul has come from God and, figuratively speaking, it 'remembers' its origin in God and seeks to return to God. Obviously, this type of spirituality coheres with a theology which stresses divine immanence; indeed, in some cases the stress on immanence is pushed very close to pantheism. The 'feel' of this kind of spirituality is different from that of the spirituality that goes with the conventional or classical theism. It is, I venture to say, more affirmative and more intimate than is possible when the stress is laid one-sidedly on divine transcendence and sovereignty. In the latter case, there may indeed be a deep sense of the reality of God and an attitude of awe and reverence, yet there is a danger that this may become too much like the homage paid to an exalted ruler. Again, the underlying model of the sovereign God tends to make prayer be understood as petition addressed to an external power on whose almighty will everything depends. By contrast, the mystic who finds the Spirit of God within the depths of his own being will consider himself not so much to be praying to an external power as rather letting God's Spirit pray within him. The mystic, however, is not one-sidedly immanentist in his understanding of God and is acutely aware of the final mystery and incomprehensibility of deity. So he too knows the meaning of awe, but it is an awe quite different from the homage paid to a superior power – it is the awe that is amazed and struck dumb by the vision of divine love, well expressed by Joseph Addison when he wrote:

> Transported with the view, I'm lost
> In wonder, love and praise.[20]

This is reflected in the fact that the mystic, when he tries to image the relation to God, if he attempts it at all, is more likely to think of God as spouse than as king or judge. Inevitably, however, this encourages a boldness of language which minimizes the difference between God and the creature and pushes in the direction of pantheism.

Meister Eckhart gave a central place to what he called *Abgeschiedenheit* in the soul's approach to God. The word is usually translated 'detachment', but this should not be understood in a merely negative way. It is the kind of detachment that sees all finite things in their relation to God, and refuses to be enslaved by any one of them. It is therefore better understood as serenity than as renunciation. In his treatise 'On Detachment', Eckhart says that 'true detachment is nothing else than for the spirit to stand as immovable against whatever may chance to it, of joy or sorrow, honour, shame and disgrace, as a mountain of lead stands before a little breath of wind'.[21] This is what brings a human being into the greatest likeness to God. It does not mean a withdrawal from the world, but rather seeing things in their true perspective and valuing them aright. So Eckhart could write: 'no person in this life may reach the point at which he can be excused from outward service. Even if he is given to a life of contemplation, still he cannot refrain from going out and taking an active part in life.'[22]

The return of the soul to God appears to take place in two stages. The first is the birth of God in the soul, or the birth of the Son or Logos in the soul. A person who has practised detachment is ready for this intimate entry of God into the centre of his life. The union is so close that it is a kind of deification of the human soul. 'If my life is God's being,' says Eckhart, 'then God's existence must be my existence and God's is-ness (*Istigkeit*) is my is-ness.'[23] The language here could hardly be exceeded for boldness, but Eckhart does exceed it when he says later: 'The Father gives birth to his Son without ceasing; and I say more: he gives birth to me, his son and the same Son. I say more; he gives birth not only to me, his son, but he gives birth to me as himself and himself as me and to me as his being and nature.'[24] These are the words of a God-intoxicated man that seem to have reached or transgressed the limits not only of orthodoxy but even of sanity, yet the idea that through baptism the Logos is born in the soul of the believer is one that reaches far back into patristic theology,[25] and the New Testament itself recognizes that the believer becomes a son, albeit a son by adoption. If we are to take the most charitable reading of Eckhart, we may accept that he also distinguished between the begetting of the eternal Logos who is one with the Father by nature, and the birth of that Logos in the souls of those who are adopted as children. But we shall return to this in a moment.

In the meanwhile, we must look at the second stage in the soul's pilgrimage, a stage even more startling than the first. This second and final stage is the break-through. We must become detached even from our images of God and break through to the ineffable divine essence. That is what is meant by Eckhart's often quoted words about 'man's last and highest parting, when for God's sake he takes leave of God'.[26] In Christian terms, it would mean going beyond the persons of the Trinity to the one essence of Godhead, an essence which is an absolute unity in which all distinctions have disappeared. At this point too the unity of the soul of the believer with God is realized. This teaching about a God beyond God has both ancient and modern parallels, in Dionysius, Tillich, Jaspers and others. It would be hard to reconcile it with Christianity, since the mediatorial role of Christ seems to have been eliminated. Eckhart scholars are divided as to whether the Meister has at this point toppled over into pantheism. But although his language may have been badly chosen, we cannot doubt the depth of his experiences, and it was certainly not his wish to institute a heresy. 'I can be in error,' he said, 'but I cannot be a heretic, for the first belongs to the intellect but the second to the will.'[27]

Perhaps his position, if not the language in which he expressed it, will seem more defensible if we look at the theology of creation which lay behind it. Just as the return to God is in two stages, so the original coming forth from God was twofold. For these two moments, Eckhart uses the two words *bullitio* and *ebullitio* – literally, a 'boiling' and a 'boiling over'. The boiling is a process of emanation and so of differentiation within the deity itself. The primal source (the Father, or perhaps the unitary essence) gives birth to the Logos and the Spirit, much as in the triad of Plotinus or the trinity of Christian theology. But it is part of Eckhart's teaching that along with the begetting of the Logos there took place the creation of the world of finite beings, so that the world too is co-eternal with God. But the world was produced by *ebullitio*, so that there seems to be a clear division here. The world is not a direct emanation of God but a lower level of existence dependent on God and created by him – a 'boiling over'. The question becomes especially acute when we consider the human soul. As we have seen, Eckhart sometimes speaks as if the soul were itself divine, and one of the charges brought against him was that he taught that there is something uncreated in the human soul.[28] Certainly his language sometimes suggests this, but he himself denied the charge. If one recognizes that the complex notion of creation cannot mean simply 'making', and that there may be degrees of participation by God in what he brings forth, as implied by the distinction between *bullitio* and *ebullitio*, Eckhart's teaching could be understood as a variety of what we have been calling 'dialectical theism' rather than a lapse into pantheism. Actually, some such dialectic seems to be required to explain the paradoxical conjunction in the human being of his unmistakable finitude with his equally unmistakable hankerings after the infinite. An affinity, though not an identity, of the human spirit to the divine Spirit, would seem to be a prerequisite of the mystical experience. We should remember, too, that Eckhart had much to say about the operation of divine grace in initiating and sustaining the relation of God and man.

Like other mystics, indeed, like all religious people, Eckhart sometimes found that when he looked for God, he was not there. This absence of God is no doubt in part due to human sin and blindness, but is it not due in part also to God's occasional withdrawal of himself? Eckhart thought so. 'The vision and experience of God', he wrote, 'is too much of a burden to the soul while it is in the body, and so God withdraws intermittently, which is what Christ meant by the saying, "A little while, and you shall not see me; and again, a little while, and you shall see me." '[29] Heidegger's view that Being is sometimes more, sometimes less, manifest, is perhaps an echo of the mystic.[30] We have seen that the finitude of the world makes evil inevitable, and evil itself is an obscuration of God. Further, the being of God could not be fully manifested on the level of finite being, so that even 'revelations' remain, at the same time, a veiling of deity. Eckhart's insight enables us to see the importance of this for spirituality. If God were always clearly manifest, there would be no need to seek him and the spiritual pilgrimage would come to an end. If he were always absent, we would give up the quest through sheer discouragement. As happens also in some of our deepest human relationships, the lover reveals himself enough to awaken the love of the beloved, yet veils himself enough to draw the beloved into an ever deeper exploration of that love. In the love affair with God (if we may so speak) there is an alternation of consolation and desolation, and it is in this way that the finite being is constantly drawn beyond self into the depths of the divine.

XV

The Theistic Proofs Reconsidered

In the preceding chapter we were considering the relation between theology or religious philosophy and spirituality; more especially, the relation between dialectical theism and mysticism. We had to face the question whether there are two ways to the knowledge of God – the way of intellectual reflection which we follow in theology and the philosophy of religion, and the way of spirituality where knowing is scarcely to be distinguished from loving. We have seen, too, that spirituality leads the way in the knowledge of God (if indeed there is such knowledge). Men and women claim to know God in religious experience before they engage in the critical questioning through which their alleged knowledge might be validated or invalidated. Even if one were to allow that there is a *prima facie* case for the cognitive claims of mysticism and of religious experience in general, this would not release one from the reflective task of trying to provide a justification of these claims on intellectual grounds. The ¹aims are not self-authenticating, for many people have in fact denied them, and philosophers who have studied the experiences of the mystics are divided about the question of its cognitive status. William James speaks of the 'noetic quality' of mystical experiences and says that they 'seem to those who experience them to be also states of knowledge' or 'states of insight into depths of truth unplumbed by the discursive intellect'. Yet, because of their ineffability, he also says that 'mystical states are more like states of feeling than like states of intellect'.[1] W. T. Stace cannot accept that the mystic has any 'objective' knowledge, but seems willing to recognize an 'inter-subjective' knowing.[2] But these words 'objective' and 'inter-subjective' are slippery terms here. If God is quite other than any finite object, he cannot be known as an object, and so there cannot be 'objective' knowledge of him as there is of objects within the world. If 'objective' here is simply intended to mean a reality that is more than a mere item in the subjective consciousness of an individual, then we might want to substitute for it the expression 'inter-subjective'. But this, too, is ambiguous, for it might mean either something which is apprehended by several subjects, all of whom might be mistaken; or it might be understood in a more pantheistic sense as a universal spirit to which many subjects find themselves related in their inner being.

James and Stace were both quite sympathetic to mysticism, and other philosophers have passed unambiguously negative judgments about its cognitive claims. Bertrand Russell, for instance, while acknowledging that mysticism may have certain emotional values, denies that it can provide anything worthy to be called knowledge. 'Insight, untested and unsupported, is an insufficient guarantee of truth.'[3] I do not think that one could or should evade the challenge expressed in these words.

Of course, I could claim that already I have done a good deal to meet the challenge. The claims of religious experience have not been presented as mere untested insights, but in the context of a philosophical framework which I have designated 'dialectical theism'. This has been expounded in considerable detail both in its historical forms and in a contemporary form, and many reasons have been adduced in its support. I have tried to fulfil the promise made near the beginning of stating a theistic philosophy as an interpretation of reality as a whole, as it presents itself to us human beings, and to show that this interpretation is more coherent and better accords with experience than rival interpretations. But I have now reached a point at which I must argue more directly for the truth of the positions which I have espoused. It is here that we shall come closer to the older forms of natural theology, and especially to the so-called 'proofs for the existence of God'. Do these venerable arguments, so often stated, so often refuted and so often restated, still retain any validity? And, in any case, how would one relate them to dialectical theism, since, in their traditional forms, they seem to visualize what I have called 'classical' theism?

But just before we turn to the traditional proofs or arguments, let me preface them with a brief consideration of what may be called the argument from religious experience. We have agreed that 'untested insight' cannot of itself guarantee the reality of God. But the very occurrence of the claim to have a direct awareness of God is a piece of evidence that cannot be just ignored. We may brush aside what we call 'untested insight', but if many people are claiming to have the same or similar insights, and if we can collate and classify and examine these insights, then we are dealing no longer with some naive claim but with a carefully examined and ordered presentation of evidence. The argument is based on the phenomenology of religious experience. It describes such experience in all its varieties and draws attention to recurring patterns that seem to be widely distributed among different individuals and different cultures. It takes account, too, of the ways in which these experiences have been interpreted, and again draws attention to recurring patterns. It may draw attention also to analogies between religious experience on the one hand and other forms of experience, such as interpersonal experience, aesthetic experience, moral experience and so on. I do not say that this argument could stand alone – it needs the support of the more 'metaphysical' and rational arguments of traditional natural theology. But it makes its own contribution to the cluster of arguments which together constitute a cumulative case for the reality of God.

Let us turn then to the traditional arguments, and first of all to the so-called 'ontological' argument, first proposed by Anselm. He defined God as 'something than which nothing greater can be thought' (*aliquid quo nihil maius cogitari possit*).[4] The expression 'nothing greater' here means 'nothing more perfect'. God is the most perfect reality that can be conceived, the sum and unity of all perfections, and this definition does seem to express what most people understand by the word 'God'. According to Anselm, even the atheist has this idea of God in his mind, otherwise he would not be able to deny God. The next step in the argument is the claim: 'But surely that than which a greater cannot be thought cannot be only in the understanding (*in intellectu*). For if it were only in the understanding, it could be thought to exist also in reality (*in re*) – which is greater [than existing only in the understanding.]'[5] The assumption here is that existence or reality is a perfection, like goodness and the other perfect qualities that are supposed to belong to God. But many philosophers have believed that this is a fatal flaw in the argument. Kant pointed out[6] that existence is not another predicate, like goodness and the rest. To say of anything that it exists is not to ascribe to it another attribute in addition to whatever attributes it already possesses, but to assert that it is a reality. You can imagine a hundred dollars with all the attributes belonging to real dollars, but nothing you can imagine will make them real. You cannot make an inference from idea to reality. This criticism made by Kant seems to me to be valid. But apart from this, one might say that Anselm's argument involves a *petitio principii*. In the premisses of his argument, he is already assuming the reality of 'something than which nothing greater can be thought', though it is precisely the reality of this that he is supposed to be proving.

In recent years, attention has shifted to a second form of the argument, in which Anselm claimed that the very idea of God carries with it the *necessity* of his existence. 'You exist so truly that you cannot even be thought not to exist.'[7] Criticism of this form of the argument has lacked clarity because the critics have for the most part been empiricists who have not sufficiently distinguished between the 'existence' of objects within the world, to be established by pointing to empirical instantiations, and the 'existence' or 'super-existence' of God, who is not an object in the world and who is the source or condition of existence rather than an existent entity, in the usual sense. But even if the critics have failed to quash the ontological argument, so that it still has its champions in the twentieth century, there are relatively few people today who would accept its validity. Even one of its most distinguished defenders, Charles Hartshorne, makes a rather limited claim for the ontological argument. It is the claim that 'empirical evidence cannot adjudicate the central religious question; to show this, rather than to furnish a sufficient proof of theism, is the main function of the ontological argument'.[8]

I think, however, that the argument is important in another way as well. It draws attention to the fact that the human being has an *a priori* idea of God. Perhaps this idea arises from his awareness of his own imperfection and finitude, which logically brings with it the idea of a reality not subject to these imperfections. This in turn implies that the search for deity arises out of the very constitution of the human being. Of course, that 'innate' idea of deity may well be, to begin with, vague and confused. Descartes put this point about the idea of God already present to the mind very well when he wrote: 'It is certain that I no less find the idea of God, that is to say, the idea of a supremely perfect being (*un être souverainement parfait*), in me, than that of any figure or number, whatever it is.'[9] It is an important point that human beings, even atheists, have this idea of God in their basic stock of ideas, just as I also thought it important to note that religious experience is widespread among human beings. But just as religious experience might turn out to be illusory, so the *a priori* idea of God might turn out to be incoherent. We note, for instance, that Anselm's definition in terms of 'something than which no greater can be thought' is not identical with Descartes' 'supremely perfect being'. Both expressions would need a lot of teasing out before we could see what are the resemblances and differences between them, and whether they stand for coherent concepts. Descartes' description might seem to fit what I have criticized as the monarchical conception of God. However, these considerations may suggest to us that our general procedure has been correct, in beginning from a fairly general notion of God and then seeking to develop from it a more detailed coherent concept, what we have called a dialectical concept of God. I have been trying to show that this concept is more coherent and more satisfying both intellectually and religiously than such rival views as atheism, pantheism and even classical theism.[10] But while the idea of God is *a priori*, as Hartshorne maintained, empirical considerations cannot be ignored, and it is in fact not always easy to know where the *a priori* ends and the *a posteriori* begins.

The ontological argument for the existence of God is by far the best known of the *a priori* approaches to the question, but it is not the only one. I propose now to attend to another *a priori* argument which has been grossly neglected but which has, I think, considerable interest and fits in well with the type of theism which I have been expounding. I mean the henological argument, the argument based on the idea of unity (τὸ ἕν). Although in earlier chapters we have not come across any formal statement of this argument, we have on a number of occasions encountered the concept of unity, beginning with Plotinus' concept of The One, and with echoes in Nicholas of Cusa, Eckhart, Leibniz, Whitehead and other thinkers who have come to our notice.

Going back to Plotinus, we find him teaching that the idea of unity is just as fundamental or even more so than the idea of being. If we were confronted with a sheer multiplicity of phenomena, a moving flux of individual items, we could know nothing at all, we could not know that anything existed. There has to be some stability amidst the flux. We recognize beings as beings because they have a certain identity which allows them to persist through time, that is to say, a certain unity. In this sense, it is not false to say that unity is as fundamental as being or even precedes it. Let us remind ourselves of Plotinus' actual words: 'If unity is necessary to the substantial existence of all that is – and nothing exists which is not one – unity must precede being and be its author.'[11] So the idea of unity is present in every perception, for every object is seen as having a unity or identity which allows us to recognize it as that object and no other.

But although each particular being has a unity in itself, it does not exist in isolation. It is related to other beings, and we have seen that among most of the philosophers considered in earlier chapters there was a strong doctrine of internal relations. This means that each existing object is influenced in its character by these relations to other objects, and influences them in turn. Plotinus mentioned this especially in the case of souls or selves: 'If the soul in me is a unity, why need that in the universe be otherwise? And if that, too, is one Soul, and yours and mine belong to it, then yours and mine must also be one.'[12] The relations that bind together souls in one are presumably spiritual relations, typified by love, but internal relations appear at all levels. Everything is what it is because of its relations to everything else. We may remember Cusanus' claim that the human foot can be understood only when we see it in relation to the entire human body and beyond that in relation to the total environment in which human beings live.[13] In Leibniz' teaching about the monads, each of which mirrors the universe,[14] and in Whitehead's doctrine of prehensions, according to which every entity grasps and is grasped by every other entity,[15] we see how the unity which depends on relations is built up into the concept of an organic universe.

These remarks are already pointing us to a third kind of unity, the unity of the whole. We have begun from the base, as it were, from individually existing beings, each with its own unity, to constellations of such beings bound together in larger unities by their internal relations to each other, and from there to the idea of the *uni*verse as an organic whole. But if we had been possessed of a divine or, at least, superhuman wisdom, we might have begun with the whole and descended to the particular items within it, for the relations are reciprocal. If the whole is what it is because of the parts, the parts are what they are because of the whole. In Plotinus, it is The One that already hides within itself the seeds of all finite beings, or if one prefers a modern philosopher, in Whitehead it is the primordial nature of God that contains the eternal objects, the sum of possibilities that can achieve their actuality in the temporal stream of becoming.

Because the henological argument has not been discussed to

anything like the same extent as the ontological argument, it has not assumed forms of comparable definiteness. One recent exponent, however, Herbert Richardson, has stated it in a form which visualizes three levels of unity roughly comparable to those distinguished in the three preceding paragraphs. We may be surprised when he tells us that 'unity is a complex notion'.[16] This sounds paradoxical, but we have to remember that by 'unity' is not meant simply arithmetical unity. Even numerical unity can be understood only in relation to multiplicity. If we think also of the internal or constitutive unity of anything, we see that this too implies a plurality. This unity is the coherence of a plurality, in such a way that the unity and plurality belong dialectically together. To quote another writer on the subject: 'Unity is not to be considered as an abstract determination independent of multiplicity, but as a positive dialectical relationship in which multiplicity in its various modes is always an intrinsic element of unity.'[17]

With his understanding of unity as a complex notion implying an intrinsic plurality, Richardson distinguishes the three following forms of unity: 'the unity of any denumerable individual, or *individuality*; the unity of any two or more individuals when taken together, or considered as one thing – *relationality*; the unity of any or all relationalities considered as complete, or *wholeness*.'[18] Obviously, this analysis corresponds quite closely to the distinctions made above. But Richardson develops these thoughts in an interesting way. Each of the three types of unity, he believes, gives rise to its own ways of understanding and speaking, in fact, to three categoreal systems. One of these is appropriate to individual beings, another to relations, a third to wholes. But the mind does not rest content with three systems of explanation. It seeks an inclusive unity, a 'unity of unities', in Richardson's phrase. This unity of unities Richardson is prepared to call 'God' – and perhaps he has as much right to apply the name of God to this all-embracing unity as Aquinas had to the concepts that emerged from the five ways. From a philosophical point of view, the understanding of God as the ultimate unity seems to make a lot of sense. From a religious point of view, we may recall Paul's assertion about Jesus Christ: 'He is before all things, and in him all things hold together.'[19] Here the rather abstruse philosophical principle of unity is given concreteness in being identified with Jesus Christ.

There is, as I have said, no stereotyped form of the henological argument. Though he does not use the terminology, Karl Jaspers seems to move along similar lines in many of his writings. He talks of 'the unremitting urge for unity' and says that man 'presses toward the fundamental unity which alone is being and eternity'.[20] One of his favourite words is the 'comprehensive' or the 'encompassing' (*das Umgreifende*). The dualism of the subject confronting the object is to be overcome in a comprehensive unity which is neither subjective nor objective. But since all our thinking is governed by the subject-object dichotomy, the all-encompassing reality is strictly ineffable. This ultimate transcendence eludes our thinking (just as Richardson too supposed that the unity of unities eludes the categories appropriate to the several lower unities). We can speak of transcendence only in 'ciphers', as Jaspers calls them. Even the name of God is not adequate. The one God and the personal God are alike ciphers, and it is significant that Jaspers speaks highly of Eckhart: 'The Godhead is unthinkable . . . Being, God, Creator – these are already conceived in categories that do not fit the Godhead. We have to transcend all definitions, including the idea of God.'[21] Yet presumably this most inclusive of unities is not of a lower order than any of the unities which it encompasses, including spiritual unity. The ultimate unity, as Jaspers seems to believe, may be incomprehensible so that it transcends even spirit, but it cannot be lower, and because of this the unity of unities is rightly called 'God'.

We turn now to the *a posteriori* arguments for the existence of God, and first to the cosmological argument, which itself takes several forms. What is essential to the cosmological argument is the conviction that the cosmos or universe points beyond itself to some more ultimate reality as its ground, and this more ultimate reality is claimed to be 'God'. The question which leads into the cosmological arguments is the one framed by Leibniz, 'Why is there something rather than nothing?' or, as somewhat differently put by Heidegger, 'Why are there beings at all, rather than just nothing?'[22] We have already noted the objection that these formulations, especially that of Leibniz, may be too indefinite, and have noted how Milton Munitz rephrased the question to meet such objections: 'Is there a reason for the world's existence?'[23]

But even if one has put the question into a more adequate form, there would still be the objection that the question is superfluous. We do not need to ask about a reason for the world's existence. Obviously, inquiry in any field can only go so far, then it strikes against that which is sheerly given and beyond which it cannot go. Is not the universe itself just the basic given? Why should we look for any reality more ultimate than the world itself? Does it make sense to ask about a reality which transcends the cosmos? And even if it does, would there be any way of answering the question? Does it help to introduce the word 'God', or does this simply push the question further back, so that one is then required to ask about the provenance of God himself, so that one is then involved in an endless regress, which might suggest that it would have been better to stop at the universe.

There are, of course, many replies that can be and have been made to these and similar objections to asking whether there is a reality more ultimate than the cosmos and on which the cosmos depends for its existence. In the end of the day, it is unlikely that the replies will ever satisfy the objectors, and equally unlikely that the objections will ever abolish the question about a reason for the world's existence. No positivist ban will prevent some people, perhaps most people, from wondering about the 'why' of the world, and no alleged answers, whether they come from natural theology or from revelation, will win the acceptance of all the doubters. But perhaps that is exactly how it has to be if religion is to flourish and the search for deity continue.

We look for proofs of God's existence and wonder impatiently why he does not unmistakably show himself and put an end to all our uncertainties. But it may be that Pascal, Kierkegaard, Heidegger and others who have called in question the whole enterprise of proving that there is a God are correct. They have usually suggested that faith is made even more insecure by so-called 'proofs', the cogency of which we begin to doubt when they are no more plainly before our minds. But even if someone hit on a proof that could not be doubted, would that not also be the end of faith? Faith would have become unnecessary and the search for deity would have ended because we had found the object of the quest. But how absurd! For what we had found would not be deity. The true deity is always ahead of us and we never catch him up with even our most ingenious and subtle arguments. Is this not part of God's love affair with his creatures, so to speak? He brushes past us, we glimpse him, we cannot doubt his reality. But we cannot grasp him or pin him down or turn him into another item in the catalogue of human knowledge. This is another illustration of the way in which philosophical argument and spirituality are intertwined in the search for God. In the face of our arguments, God withdraws, and we are reminded of Meister Eckhart's application of the text: 'A little while and you shall not see me; and, again, a little while and you shall see me.'[24]

But at the moment we are concerned with the alleged proofs of God's reality, and in particular with the cosmological argument. Any object or event that we encounter within the world is contingent, that is to say, it depends on other objects or events, without which it either would not be or would be different. The human mind is characterized by a desire to know, so it raises questions about these objects and events and seeks to understand how they have come about. We follow back the links that connect one thing with another, but no matter how far we go, we always arrive at other objects and events that are themselves contingent and raise further questions. Are we embarked on an infinite regress through an endless ocean of contingencies, so that we can only point to this 'ocean', whether we want to call it 'universe' or 'multiverse', and say that this is the ultimate source from which everything arises? Or would we have to say that the universe too is contingent and points beyond itself to a more ultimate ground? After all, the planet earth is no less contingent and no more necessary than any object or event upon the earth; the solar system is no less contingent than any of its planets; the galaxy is no less contingent than the solar system. If we can ask about the 'why' of the most trivial event, we can ask about the 'why' of the universe; we can even ask, with Leibniz and Heidegger, 'Why are there beings at all, rather than just nothing?' But at that point, a decisive break in the questioning has taken place, for the Leibniz-Heidegger question cannot be answered in terms of some other being, as all the questions up to that point can be. It can be answered only in terms of a reality of another order which is a 'nothing' within the universe and which is designated by such ciphers as 'God' or 'being' or 'transcendence'.

But even if we grant that the universe itself is contingent and would seem to have no more necessity or aseity about it than any constituent fact within it, how can we venture to ask about its 'why' or how would we know in what direction to look? Are the expressions 'God', 'being' and 'transcendence' not just ciphers but empty words? I think one could look beyond the universe only if there were something in the universe that points beyond it, only if immanent within the universe there are traces of that more ultimate reality of another order on which the universe depends. Furthermore, I think we can be quite specific in saying where this pointer to transcendence is to be found. It is to be found in the human being, which is itself a being in process of transcendence. The heart of the cosmological argument for God turns out to be what I have elsewhere called the 'anthropological' argument. Within the cosmos and brought forth by the cosmos there is a being whose horizons are not limited to the cosmos and who has the temerity to ask, 'Why are there beings at all, and not just nothing?' The being who asks this question is by nature the ontological being, that is to say, the being who cannot rest in his quest for reality. Bernard Lonergan has seen the essence of human transcendence precisely in the capacity for asking questions and for *keeping on* asking questions until one comes to a final answer.[25] Since man is himself a product of the universe, we can say that in and through this product, the universe is questioning itself, transcending itself and pointing beyond itself.

After asking his question, 'Why is there something rather than nothing?' Leibniz makes a very odd comment. He says: 'For nothing is simpler and easier than something.'[26] What does this mean? It means, I think, that what is fundamental in human experience and what motivates the human desire to know is not, as some have suggested, the shock of non-being but rather, the shock of being, the fact that there is something, indeed, quite a lot of things, rather than nothing. That anything at all exists excites wonder. We cannot help looking for a sufficient reason to account for this existence. Radhakrishnan remarked that 'the contemplation of sheer nothing-ness as a possibility leads to the perception that any kind of existence requires an absolute being'.[27] This may be true, but it is not just 'any kind of existence' that confronts us but this universe which has brought forth the microcosmus, the human being who in miniature mirrors the whole universe and who by his questioning expresses the universe's own testimony to a reality more ultimate than itself.

As soon as we begin to talk not just about the fact *that* there exists a cosmos but about *what kind* of universe it is, we are beginning to move from the cosmological argument for God to the teleological argument, or the argument from design. There was a time when this was considered to be the strongest of all the theistic proofs, but, as I acknowledged at the very beginning of this book, that time is long past and the arguments of Paley and others strike us nowadays as simplistic and misguided. Hume had already pointed out that the world is more like an organism than an artefact; that is to say, any design we might perceive in it has arisen from an immanent source rather than a transcendent designer, while the theory of evolution showed that what superficially looks like purpose may be alternatively explained as natural selection. So the teleological argument has taken some hard blows.

In spite of the severe criticisms that have been made of it, the teleological argument continues to be advanced, and not always by unsophisticated persons. The difference between contemporary upholders of teleology and older ones is that whereas the latter chose particular instances of what they supposed to be purpose, the former are more likely to appeal to a wide area of interlocking facts. This is the line taken by F. R. Tennant, who held that 'cosmic teleology' is the one empirical argument for theism. He agrees that the separate fields of facts to which the older teleologists made their appeal do not demand teleological explanation and that an alternative account can be given. But, he claims:

> Causal explanation and teleological explanation are not mutually exclusive alternatives; and neither can perform the function of the other. It is rather when these several fields of fact are no longer considered one by one, but as parts of a whole, or terms of a continuous series, and when for their dovetailing and interconnectedness a sufficient ground is sought, such as mechanical and proximate causation no longer seems to supply, that divine design is forcibly suggested. Paley's watch is no analogue of the human eye; but it may none the less be an approximate analogue of nature as a whole.[28]

So the appeal now is to the order, intelligibility and development of the world as a whole. Tennant points out that there could be a collection of existents and happenings which could not be considered a universe or cosmos, 'even to the extent of any one existent being comparable to another or behaving in the same way twice'.[29] Some philosophers might reply that even in such a chance collocation of particles some kind of order would naturally arise and, given a sufficiency of time, the universe we know might come about. To this I think it might be replied that there will only develop that degree of order that is already potentially inherent in the original material. In the case of our own universe, even a hydrogen atom is a highly structured and organized entity, both internally and with respect to its possibilities for entering into complex wholes. If on our planet there has occurred the remarkable development from inanimate matter to rational life, that can only be because the result was already potentially there in the beginning. 'In the beginning was the word.'

Of course, this is compatible with an immanent teleology and does not call for an external designer who at appropriate moments forms protein molecules or whatever might be required. What we know of the course of evolution suggests rather that the cosmos itself, so to speak, is trying out its own possibilities. But this would not be incompatible with the type of theism being advocated in this book, a type in which God is as truly immanent in the process as he is transcendent of it. As I noted in my discussion of Whitehead,[30] there is a form of naturalism which is not at all reductionist, for it calls for a greatly enriched conception of nature as not merely physical but spiritual as well and pervaded by the immanent pole of the divine being as he shares in the creative advance of the world. It seems to me that what residual value there is in the teleological argument offers support to dialectical theism, though not, I should say, to classical theism.

The result of this survey of the traditional theistic arguments is pretty much what we expected. These arguments fall far short of proof, and we may be glad of that since it was pointed out that a proof would be quite unproductive from the point of view of spirituality. But we started out on this exploration of the proofs because the claims of spirituality to have knowledge of God are not self-authenticating, and need the backing of rational argument. So how can we now appear to be expressing satisfaction that proofs are unattainable? This looks like a rather blatant case of turning necessity into a virtue. However, I have only said that the arguments fall far short of proof, not that they are worthless. As Jaspers says, 'The arguments for the existence of God do not lose their validity as ideas because they have lost their power to prove. They amount to a confirmation of faith by intellectual operations.'[31] As Hume seemed prepared to admit, the evidence for is somewhat stronger than the evidence against, but even if it were much stronger, it would not produce believers. The function of the proofs is to show that the search for deity is not the vain pursuit of an illusion but a rationally defensible quest.

XVI

Dialectical Theism and Ethics

What are the implications of dialectical theism for ethics? We have seen that it encourages a mystical form of spirituality. But does it also have consequences for our moral values and policies of action? Before I attempt to answer this question, it is desirable that I should say a few words on a prior question. What, in general, is the relation of a theology or a religious faith to the moral life?

Traditionally, morals and religious belief have been closely associated with one another. Admittedly, there have been exceptions. Especially in modern times, there have been men and women of high moral calibre who have disclaimed any religious convictions. On the other hand, there have been religions which have had little influence on morality, and even some which practised inhuman and degrading rites. But, on the whole, religion and morality have gone together, and, though it might be hard to demonstrate, many people have believed that the decline of religion must lead eventually to the decline of morality also.

But have we now come to a parting of the ways? Many contemporary philosophers seem to think so. Perhaps it was appropriate that in earlier times morals should be backed up by the sanction and authority of religion, but is this any longer of importance? Religion seems to have little authority left to it in secularized societies. As for sanctions, few people, I suppose, still hold to the traditional ways of understanding heaven and hell as respectively the reward and punishment for a good or bad life. Since the Enlightenment, too, there has been a concern for the autonomy of the human being, as one who must order his life in accordance with his own reason and conscience, rather than in conformity with rules imposed by some external authority. Has the human being then become sufficiently adult, so that morals can stand on its own, without any appeal to religion? The separation of morals and theology might be beneficial to religion also, for too often it has been regarded as a kind of auxiliary to the moral life and we have forgotten that religion has a value of its own.

The prevailing tendency is to separate morals from religion, and if this is regarded as desirable, then we need not pursue the question about dialectical theism and ethics, for ethics would be independent of any theological beliefs. But not all philosophers are happy about the secularization of morals. Basil Mitchell, for instance, notes 'the dissatisfaction of certain sensitive minds with prevailing patterns of secular morality. What they look for in them and do not find is a standard that transcends the *de facto* preferences of individuals and societies, by which these may be judged'.[1] The words are taken from a book in which he engages in a searching critique of some typical secular model philosophies. I think myself that there are strong ties between religion and morality, and that at least some of these ties are essential rather than simply accidents of history. At the same time, I recognize the importance of human autonomy and responsibility, and do not think that morality can be securely based on an external authority. But even if we say that the basis of morality is to be found in human nature itself, we have then to ask the question about human nature. Is it to be understood simply in terms of biology, sociology and psychology? Or is there a theological dimension here that cannot be omitted without impoverishment and distortion? It is worth recalling that Kant, while arguing strongly for the autonomy of morals against any heteronomous view, was also clear that morality is not merely a human invention or a social contrivance, but has its ground in objective and universal rational structures. This has to be pointed out in order to make clear that to claim that morality is finally grounded in God does not commit one to the somewhat naive and anthropomorphic view that moral laws are the commands of God. That would only be the case if God were conceived as an entirely transcendent source of a heteronomous authority. But if we think of God as the immanent rationality which we know in our own being, the law of God is also the law of our own nature, and the antithesis between autonomy and heteronomy is abolished.

Unfortunately, Kant himself seems to waver, as I noted in an earlier discussion.[2] According to W. G. de Burgh, 'when Kant addressed his mind to questions of religion, he invariably conceived God as a transcendent creator, moral governor and judge'.[3] This certainly seems to be how God appears in Kant's moral argument for the existence of God. I did not consider this with the other traditional arguments for theism, for it seemed better to defer it to the point where we are considering the specific question of the relation of theology and ethics. Kant holds that in an ideal world, happiness would be proportionate to virtue. 'Accordingly, the existence of a cause of all nature, distinct from nature itself, and containing the principle of this connection, namely, of the exact harmony of happiness with morality, is also postulated.'[4] This ultimate cause is, of course, God. Here it rather looks as if God is being brought in as a *deus ex machina* to ensure that virtue gets its just reward. But we could say that such a role for God is just as undignified as that of intervening in the workings of the planetary system to iron out any irregularities. There is, however, another way of reading Kant. If we take moral obligation, the sense of 'oughtness', with absolute seriousness, does this not lead us to affirm that this is a morally ordered world? We all have the experience of knowing or feeling that we *ought* to do this or that. It may well be that in each particular case we can relativize that sense of obligation and point to its social conditioning. But we can ask, Why *ought* we to do anything whatever? What is moral obligation as such? What is the secret of its ultimacy, so that we know that we cannot do anything else, without betraying or even destroying ourselves at the deepest level? Do we not have a pointer here to the deepest reality?

Of course, to speak of a 'morally ordered' world is to speak of something less than or other than a personal transcendent God. It could be interpreted in terms of an immanent rationality, present both in the universe and in the human mind. Perhaps Kant could be interpreted along these lines. However, to speak even of an immanent moral or spiritual principle in the cosmos is nearer to theism than to atheism, and is certainly far from any reductionist naturalism.

But can any validity be attached to these moral arguments? I know that there have been many new and subtle formulations since the time of Kant, but in such arguments there is a very serious danger of begging the question. The argument begins from attributing full seriousness, if not actual ultimacy, to moral obligation; and if one begins from there, then the conclusion is bound to contain, if not a personal God, at least a moral and spiritual order as the deepest reality that there is. It is true that we seem to experience an ultimacy in the sense of moral obligation. That is why most people[5] believe that moral value takes precedence above all the other values which they seek to realize. But moral experience, like religious experience, may be too variable and too open to subjective interpretations to be an infallible guide to the nature of reality. To the serious moral agent, nothing seems more important than the pursuit of the right and the good, and their final realization demands a morally ordered world. But it is not impossible that the world is unjust; even perhaps, as some have ventured to say, absurd. Like all the other theistic arguments, the moral argument is not decisive, though it adds new considerations to the cumulative case. But, as a practical rather than a theoretical argument, perhaps the suasion of the moral argument is in the first instance practical. It forces us to face the question whether, if there is no God, everything is permitted. It is again the question whether an unmitigated atheism must not inevitably work itself out in nihilism. The case for grounding morality on a religious philosophy is not theoretically decisive, but there are strong practical grounds for assenting to it.

However, many questions of detail are still left open. Is the reality upon which morality is supposed to be founded a personal transcendent God, or an impersonal immanent moral order? The first of these alternatives might seem to be pushing us back in the direction of that monarchical deity, here conceived as lawgiver and judge, a conception of which we have been very critical in earlier chapters. On the other hand, can there be an impersonal moral order, or does not the very notion of morality imply personality? I suppose that ideas like 'nemesis' and 'karma' do suggest an impersonal, almost automatic or mechanical process, that achieves a measure of justice in the world. But by a 'moral order' we would normally assume something that is at least personal, though it might be suprapersonal. But the contrast between a transcendent personal God and an immanent impersonal order is too stark. We may find that dialectical theism, occupying as it does a place which is different from those of either classical theism or pantheism, is able to resolve some of these oppositions.

We have already seen that dialectical theism encourages a type of spirituality which finds its highest expression in the mysticism of persons like Meister Eckhart. Now, some writers on religion[6] have made a sharp distinction between mystical religion and prophetic religion, and have seemed to imply that only prophetic religion is in earnest about morality and sets forth clearly the ethical demands of a religious faith. The contrast between the two types gets elaborated in various ways. It is claimed, for instance, that mysticism leads to pantheism and so to quietism and moral inaction, while prophetic religion recognizes the one transcendent God who stands over against the world as its creator, lawgiver and judge, though also as one who is gracious and merciful. Only such a transcendent, personal God, it is claimed, can sustain human beings in the quest for righteousness, and we are pointed to the example of ancient Israel which developed both the purest monotheism and the loftiest ethics among the nations. It is also said that the spirituality of the mystic is individualistic. The mystic retires into himself and seeks his own salvation, while prophetic religion looks out on the world and proclaims God's demand for social and political righteousness. Again, the message of the Hebrew prophets is cited as an illustration. Mystical religion is further charged with being static. It accepts the existing order of things, does not take evil with sufficient seriousness, and believes that a vision of perfection is already to be had by those who have eyes to see. We have indeed touched on some of these points in discussing Plotinus.[7] Prophetic religion, on the other hand, is said to be eschatological. It looks for the transformation of all things into a new, redeemed order, and as such it is able to supply a hope and dynamic to encourage and energize moral endeavour. Finally, the mystical type of religion is charged with being a human effort to grasp God. The mystic often talks of the ascent to God and describes ways of rising to the contemplation of the divine, while the prophet speaks of human sin and impotence, and sees the only remedy for this situation in a gracious condescension of God to man.

The contrast between prophetic and mystical religion, as stated by Oman and others, and as I have just summarized it, is, I think, very much oversimplified and exaggerated. In the first place, one must challenge the assumption that mysticism is allied to pantheism. No doubt this is true in some cases, but our own concern has been with the mysticism that emerges in relation to dialectical theism, and we have seen again and again that this is far removed from pantheism, though it certainly does allow more weight to the concept of divine immanence than does classical theism. As for the claim that mystical religion is primarily individualistic, this too can be challenged. It is surely odd that mystics are accused at the same time of losing themselves and letting themselves be absorbed in a larger whole! Ideally, the mystic does not cease to be the person he or she is, but the boundaries of his personality become, as it were, porous to a reality beyond his own. Again, to say that the universe of the mystic is static and unchanging is a generalization which cannot be uncritically accepted. In the cases we have considered in the earlier parts of this book, we have seen that there has been an attempt to do justice to both time and eternity, to encourage moral striving for the betterment of the world in time and history while at the same time cherishing the vision of a world that is already perfected in God. Let me now try to spell out these points in greater detail, and I think it will be found that dialectical theism, with its associated spirituality, sustains an ethic which need not fear comparison with the one which we associate with classical theism.

The first thing to say about the ethic implied by dialectical theism is that it is a *natural law* ethic. Nowadays, natural law seems to be just about as unpopular as natural theology. Actually, I think that they stand or fall together, and I am committed to both of them.[8] In the present context, I wish to emphasize two points about a doctrine of natural law. The first is that such a doctrine claims that the basic ethical insights are in principle available to any rational human being, whatever his religion or ideology, just as natural theology makes the claim that there is similarly available a basic knowledge of God. In this first sense, natural law doctrine stands opposed to any attempt to tie ethics to some specific revelation. It would be implacably opposed, for instance, to Barth's claim that ethics is a branch of Christian dogmatics, just as natural theology would be opposed to the same theologian's teaching that there is no genuine knowledge of God outside of the biblical revelation. A second point about natural law is that it locates ethical norms in 'nature', understood both as 'human nature' and as that wider 'nature' within which human life is set. This wider 'nature' would perhaps be better called 'reality', in the metaphysical sense of the term. I do not say 'God', for, as we have seen in our discussion of Kant, there might be some immanent rationality of the cosmos at the basis of morality, and this would hardly qualify as 'God'. Yet, for most believers in natural law, the wider 'nature' or 'reality' would not be 'mere nature', that is to say, nature understood in reductionist terms, as if morality in turn were explicable biologically. Indeed, catholic theologians, who regularly teach a doctrine of natural law, would see it as founded ultimately on the nature of God. In this aspect, natural law doctrine contrasts with those religious ethics which see the moral law as the command of God. The latter found morality on the divine will, rather than the divine nature.

We can recognize the coherence of a doctrine of natural law with dialectical theism if we remember how often we have come across the thought that man is a microcosm, reflecting in himself the structure of the universe, and even in some way mirroring God, as a being made in the divine image and participating in some measure in the being of God. The human being, in virtue of his human constitution, transcends towards God, and already in this lies the basic motivation and directedness of moral striving. The great advantage of such a theory is that it transcends that opposition between autonomy and heteronomy which has been a bone of contention since the time of Kant, and has seemed to many people to make a religious ethic incompatible with the recognition of human freedom. Dialectical theism, by turning away from the notion of the monarchical (and sometimes oppressive) God, must also turn away from any idea that the moral law rests on the commands of the divine will, yet precisely in so doing is able to rehabilitate a truly religious ethic, in which the free human conscience and practical reason reflect on the level of the finite the spiritual nature of the God from whom they have come. God's nature (the way he is, if we may so speak) is not a foreign nature, so that a religiously founded ethic would be heteronomous. Rather, if we may recall Eckhart's bold words, 'God's isness is my isness',[9] I fulfil myself and fulfil the moral demand by finding myself in God.

While dialectical theism leads very readily into a doctrine of natural law, it is only fair to remember that not all versions of classical theism deny natural law, or equate the moral law with the command of the divine will. In particular, Thomas Aquinas had a well developed doctrine of natural law. As we have noted,[10] he had also a doctrine of divine immanence, but this was not much developed. Perhaps it is only when immanence receives the stress accorded to it in what we call 'dialectical theism' that the firm foundations of a natural law doctrine are allowed to appear.

I pass on to a second implication of dialectical theism for ethics, namely, that it encourages a morality that transcends the individual human being. In making this claim, I am contradicting the assertion that a mystical spirituality has the opposite effect, and encourages the concern with individual salvation. Let me remind the reader of some noble words of Plotinus: 'If the soul in me is a unity, why need that in the universe be otherwise? And if that, too, is one Soul, and yours and mine belong to it, then yours and mine must also be one.'[11] Could there be any stronger statement of the solidarity of all human beings, whose lives are intertwined with one another within the universal Soul to which they all belong? It is true that the mystic (or, at least, many mystics) begins by retiring into himself or herself, but it is a misunderstanding to think of this as individualism, for the mystic discovers in the very core of his or her own being that it is linked to the being of God and so to the being of all men and women. He realizes that his self is no impenetrable atom but stands open to God and to other finite selves, yet without being simply absorbed or merged in them. The mystical relation is made possible only by the dialectical rhythm of identity and distinction.

This deep sense of solidarity with all spiritual beings makes dialectical theism with its mystical spirituality no less concerned for the well-being of society – indeed, of the whole human race – than is prophetic religion. There is, however, a difference at this point. The ethic of dialectical theism (and in this too it has affinities with the Thomistic ethic) is an ethic of virtue and character, that is to say, it understands morality as the formation of persons and the building of human community rather than the performance of actions. Prophetic religion, on the contrary, perceives morality as the doing of right actions. This leads to a somewhat episodic view of morality as a series of demands. The extreme development of this point of view is the so-called 'situation ethic' which breaks the moral life up into a plurality of discrete situations, each of them unique and unrepeatable. Stanley Hauerwas has described such an ethic as 'a natural development of a theological tradition that provided no means to develop an ethic of character'.[12] An ethic of character brings far more stability and continuity into the moral life, and clearly it is more closely tied to a spirituality, understood as personal formation. The relation between character and action is, however, a complex one. Character itself seems to be partly formed by habitual action, but there comes a time when the formed character is itself the source of the action.

One also has to take into account here the influence of beliefs upon action. I would claim that belief in a God who is immanent in his creation, including finite moral agents, so that he is the very lure of their transcendence, encourages a responsible pursuit of moral goals, understood as our co-working or synergism with God, and this does in fact accomplish more in building up moral individuals and a moral community, than the belief that moral laws are the heteronomous commands of a transcendent deity who demands obedience rather than offering mystical communion. Incidentally, the objection that mysticism leads to quietism or moral inaction is another accusation that cannot stand up and rests on misunderstanding. As we have seen in our discussion of Meister Eckhart, the serenity and detachment of the mystic do not mean that he is indifferent to the concerns of the world around him. He is never delivered from the demands of practical morality, and his contemplation of God should have the effect of making him more sensitive to moral obligations rather than indifferent to them. Even the notion of detachment (*Abgeschiedenheit*) from worldly things is not to be understood in negative terms as renunciation. It is rather, as was said before, seeing all things in the light of God and in their unity under God, and this means using the things of the world without becoming enslaved to them. I shall return to this point when we consider what is needed for an environmental ethic.

Meanwhile, let us pass to another topic, the claim that a mystical spirituality consorts with a static view of the world, while prophetic religion is eschatological and encourages the hope of a radical transformation. I think this objection would have force in the case of philosophies which treat time as an illusion, believing that the events which appear to the senses are a mere surface-play, as it were, if not actually illusion. For such philosophies, the reality is unchanging. It is complete and perfect at any moment, if only we have eyes to see it. But this sounds more like some form of pantheism than like dialectical theism. The latter acknowledges a temporal dimension in God and a real historical unfolding of the divine in history. Thus, an eschatological element is incorporated into it, as we have seen in the case of Heidegger,[13] and the incentive to strive by moral effort after a good that is 'not yet' is certainly present. Properly understood, dialectical theism is even further removed from pantheism than it is from classical theism, and its mystical spirituality must not be given a pantheistic interpretation. Even in the case of Meister Eckhart, where admittedly there are some inclinations towards pantheism, surely the full and final vision of God still lies ahead, for we have seen that in his earthly existence, the mystic is sometimes more, sometimes less aware of God: 'A little while, and you will not see me; and, again a little while and you will see me.'[14]

I have tried to show then that dialectical theism and its accompanying mystical spirituality have important implications for ethics, and indeed provide the outlines of a religiously based ethic that is more satisfying than one based on classical theism. The reason for its being more satisfying is that it avoids one-sidedness, and incorporates into its structures both sides of certain dialectical truths. Thus it acknowledges the importance of human striving and the reality of human freedom, transcendence and autonomy, while at the same time acknowledging that it is immersion in God that directs and motivates this striving. The moral law here is a natural law, founded in the divine nature and reflected in human nature. All this seems to make more sense than the idea that the moral law is the command of a transcendent God imposed heteronomously upon creatures from whom he is 'wholly other', a command, moreover, which they have no capacity to obey except by 'grace alone' (*sola gratia*), while this grace, in turn, seems to be also external and has to be 'infused' from outside. Dialectical theism tries to give full weight to all the complex and often conflicting factors that enter into the structure of the moral life, and I think it succeeds in this better than do either the traditional theological ethics or a purely secular ethic.

These are, of course, large claims to make. The only way in which they could be substantiated would be take an actual ethical problem and to show that dialectical theism has more to contribute to its solution than either a secular ethic or one based on classical theism. The problem I propose to take as an example is one of the most serious facing us today – the environmental problem.

This is a peculiarly modern problem, and though it has been building up for about three centuries, only in the second half of the twentieth century have people really become concerned about it, for by this time it has assumed critical proportions. For many thousands of years, the human race lived in the most intimate relations with the surrounding non-human nature. Man's experience of nature was ambiguous. On the one hand, it might appear benign, and he depended upon it for all the necessities of life. As we have noted, the earliest gods were probably the great powers of nature, on which human life depended. But nature could be hostile as well as benign. Human life was a constant struggle for survival, wresting a meagre living from nature in the face of many dangers, such as flood, drought, storm, wild animals, disease and so forth. About three hundred years ago, with the rise of the scientific mentality, all this began to change. On the one hand, nature was progressively stripped of such numinous qualities as it still possessed. It came to be understood more and more in purely material and mechanical terms, a gigantic system of particles and forces quite indifferent to the human race and its needs – a race which it had brought forth more or less by accident. The scientific method of inquiry brought for the first time an understanding of how this system works, and with it the possibility of predicting events and bringing them under human control. One very obvious example of this was the discovery of the causes of diseases, then the methods for controlling and even eliminating these causes, with the result that human life today is far more secure and free from pain than it was even a few decades ago. Better health is only one aspect of the amazing changes that science and technology have brought about in the conditions under which human beings live in this world. We talk nowadays about the 'affluent society', because for millions of people the old struggle for survival has been left behind and their lives are surrounded by comforts and conveniences of which their ancestors of two or three generations ago never dreamed. Admittedly, there are still larger numbers of human beings who do not enjoy these benefits, but it is assumed that the scientific and technological revolution will increasingly spread from the west across the entire globe.

The dreams of the Enlightenment have already been fulfilled to an extent that would astonish the eighteenth-century *savants*, and, superficially, there seems to be no end in sight to this 'progress'. Yet, as it goes on, we become more and more aware of the ambiguity of what is happening and we question more and more whether it is rightly called 'progress'. The most obvious threat arises from the fact that some of this technological effort has been diverted into military purposes, and that an increasing number of countries are in possession of weapons so destructive that they make the whole future of humanity very precarious. It is hard to believe that sooner or later there will not arise a situation in which some human being or group of human beings will, in desperation, unleash death on an unprecedented scale. It might be replied that science and technology are in themselves neutral, and that we have the responsibility to see that they are used for good purposes, not bad. But this may be too simplistic. Some writers, such as Herbert Marcuse, have questioned the alleged neutrality of science and technology. These are not 'value-free' inquiries, but are guided, like all human activities, by certain 'interests' of which people may be only dimly aware. Acquisitiveness and aggression are among the motives that make for technological expansion, but these are not only motives, they are also consequences generated by technology, for technological advance has become something self-propagating and already largely withdrawn from human control. So the question is whether the very mentality which it produces is not one that encourages concupiscence and competition, and so a diminution of more genuinely human qualities. The ambiguity of this whole situation has been brought home to us very forcibly by the realization that earth's resources are not infinite, and that the combination of a number of factors – diminishing supplies of scarce materials, increased demand of a burgeoning population no longer checked by diseases, the side effects produced by industrial waste, and so on – together pose a threat which may be less dramatic than that of nuclear warfare but which will be no less dangerous and may be much more difficult to overcome. We have reached the position where the human race can survive only through refinements and expansion of technology, yet where every such refinement or expansion exposes us to new perils.

So great nowadays is the popular faith in the omnipotence and beneficence of technology that the immediate response to the environmental crisis has been to seek to cure it by new and better technology – for instance, more efficient use of energy, safer insecticides, and so on. These may be palliatives with some limited value, but there is an inherent absurdity in trying to devise techniques for the control of techniques. The problem of technology is not itself a technological problem. To revert to Marcuse for a moment, he thinks that the dominance of technology has produced a generation of men and women so preoccupied with facts that they have lost the sense of what he calls 'essences and norms'[15] by which facts are to be assessed and priorities established. This may remind us of Heidegger's belief that in our concern with the beings, we have forgotten being.

Of course, Marcuse's talk of 'essences and norms' may strike many people as very old-fashioned, though this may just be an index to the extent to which our minds are in fact dominated by a positivistic obsession with physical fact. There are many other people willing to recognize that we must seek a wider, more holistic view of things. Early in this book,[16] we noted that reductionism is necessary to the progress of science; that is to say, certain limited areas have to be selected for study, and even within these areas, only certain phenomena are to be taken into account. But we also saw reason to believe that while reductionism is methodologically useful, there is no justification for turning it into a metaphysical principle. Our contemporary problems with technology and the environment are in no small measure derived from our habit of dividing things up and treating them in isolation (the habit of abstraction) so that we lose sight of the whole and of the interrelatedness of all its parts.

Obviously, what I have just been saying underlines the need for a philosophy of nature, broader than any of the special sciences. It also supports the idea of a religious ethic, for the modern secular view of the world as a collection of atomic facts cannot yield ethical principles adequate to the kind of problems raised by the environmental issue. A doctrine of creation is perhaps the only foundation on which to base a satisfactory ethic to guide the technological revolution. At least, this doctrine teaches that man did not create and does not have the absolute disposal of the material world. But I would want to go further, and say that even if one introduces a doctrine of creation, the particular form of the doctrine taught by classical theism will not instil a sense of restraint and responsibility in the handling of material things. In classical theism, the creation is quite external to God, it is wholly 'dedivinized', and some people at least have taken this to be just as much an incentive to the unrestrained domination and exploitation of nature as any secular ethic could be. But the religious alternative to classical theism is not pantheism or any romantic idolizing of nature, such as might stand in the way of science or of a sane technology. The alternative is the kind of dialectical theism developed in this book. In all the forms of it which we have considered, it has stressed the organic structures of nature and encouraged a holistic view; and in teaching that God is as truly immanent in the world as he is transcendent of it, it leads to a respect for the dignity and beauty of the created order, such as will discourage reckless and wasteful exploitation. It may even suggest – as we noted when discussing Leibniz – that man is not necessarily the be-all and the end-all of creation, or the measure of all things. This dialectical theistic philosophy has built into it a practical dialectic of appreciating as well as appropriating, of using without abusing. This is the true *Abgeschiedenheit*.[17]

XVII

Dialectical Theism and Theology

In an earlier chapter, I asked about the implications of dialectical theism for spirituality. We found that while it is supportive of prayer and of the quest for God, it tends especially to a form of mysticism, exemplified in the spirituality of Meister Eckhart who, in the eyes of some critics, can scarcely be reckoned an orthodox Christian. In the present chapter, I shall raise more directly the relation of dialectical theism to Christian theology. This question is, of course, closely connected with the question of the relation of natural theology in general to Christian theology. Christian theologians themselves give different answers. The tradition of Calvin and Barth finds no place for a natural theology, not so much because God has not revealed himself in his creation as because human minds, through their fallibility and sinfulness, cannot recognize the testimony of the creation to God and proceed rather to project idols of their own imagining which can only be misleading and a corruption of the truth of God. On the other hand, the tradition of Christian theology which runs from Aquinas to Rahner does admit a natural knowledge of God, and while holding that this natural theology is imperfect and abstract, regards it as a propaedeutic to the concrete revelation of Christianity. To quote Rahner: 'It is only if man stands before God always and of necessity and on every presupposition, even, then, as sinner, as turned away from God and deprived of the free gift of divine life – "by nature", then – that he is that being who has to come to terms with revelation, who has the power to perceive revelation, for whom the failure to perceive revelation involves not merely deficiency but guilt.'[1] Although I would not express myself quite as Rahner does, and although I have said that the boundary between natural and revealed theology is blurred, I have more sympathy with the Aquinas-Rahner tradition than with the Calvin-Barth one. I recognize that there is a natural theology independent of the Christian revelation, I believe that it has validity, and I have tried to show that it takes the form of what I have called 'dialectical theism'. But I would certainly agree that this natural theology is in itself abstract and philosophical, and that something far more concrete is required if it is to make a wide appeal to human beings and to function as a creative spiritual force in the lives of ordinary people. It is perhaps not going too far to say that natural theology seeks embodiment or, if you like, incarnation, in a concrete faith and predisposes to the acceptance of such a faith. Natural theology may provide a philosophical framework and an intellectual defence for some concrete faith, though it may also raise critical questions for that faith and lead to its rethinking at certain points.

Natural theology could be brought into relation to any number of concrete historical theologies as these have developed out of the major religions of mankind, and in the final chapter we shall in fact consider whether dialectical theism can play a part in promoting dialogue and understanding among the several religious traditions. But for the moment we are concerned with the case which is likely to be closest to most of my readers – the relation of natural theology to Christian theology. And when I say 'natural theology', I have in mind the dialectical theism which has emerged in our studies as the most convincing form of natural theology. How then does this dialectical theism relate to Christian theology? Is its conception of God compatible with the Christian doctrine of God? Does dialectical theism provide a philosophical framework from which one might go on to the concreteness of Christian faith?

Before attempting to answer these questions, I should perhaps defend the introduction of such questions at all. This is supposed to be a work on natural theology, and I think it may be claimed that I have been heedful of Lord Gifford's instruction that lecturers on his foundation should not appeal to any specific revelation. Where in earlier chapters mention has been made of Christian doctrines, this has been by way of illustration, rather than by way of an appeal to an authoritative standard. In bringing Christian theology more definitely into the argument in this present chapter, I am not meaning to depart from the constraints of natural theology. It seems to me that it is a matter of interest to ask how far the natural theology or doctrine of God that was set out in Chapter XIII is compatible with the understanding of God that is held by many people in

Western countries where the influence of Christian theology has been paramount. I am not saying that Christian theology is to be the norm by which our natural theology is to be assessed. On the contrary, I might even want to suggest that some elements in the traditional Christian doctrine of God may call for revision in the light of our studies of dialectical theism. In the first instance, all that I am seeking to do is to compare the two positions, noting both similarities and differences. I will not, however, conceal from my readers that I hope to find more similarities than differences.

At first sight, this must seem to be a vain hope. Is not the God of the Bible and of Christian theology much closer to the God of classical theism, which has indeed been thought out largely by Christian thinkers? The transcendence of the Judaeo-Christian God over the creation, his image as king, lawgiver and judge, his providential rule over history and his absolute disposition of events, his otherness and qualitative difference from the creatures – all this seems to be in flat contradiction to the ideas we have met in dialectical theism, such as emanation, immanence, passibility. Again, what about the role of Jesus Christ as mediator? Does not dialectical theism simply by-pass him and encourage the mystical quest for a direct encounter with deity?

What, for instance, is there in common between the God of Plotinus and the God of the Old Testament, the God of Abraham, Isaac, Jacob and their successors? If we take the God of Plotinus to be the triad of The One, the Mind and the Soul (as I think we should), then this God is so deeply involved in the cosmos that he quite lacks the transcendence and freedom of the God of the Hebrews, as well as perhaps infringing the monotheistic principle. On the other hand, if we identify the God of Plotinus more narrowly with The One (though this is surely a mistake), then this ineffable impersonal mystery seems even further removed from the highly personal and even passionate God of the Bible.

Here, of course, we are explicitly talking about the God of Old Testament religion. Is he simply to be identified with the God of Christian faith and theology? If so, then the attempt to show that there is an affinity between the God of dialectical theism and the God of Christianity seems bound to fail. There is no doubt, of course, that the God of Christian faith stands in continuity with the God of the Old Testament – we are talking about the same God. We can agree with Rahner that for the men of the New Testament, 'the prophetic monotheism of the Old Testament is the foundation of their knowledge of God'.[2] But is it not also the case that the understanding of God was profoundly altered by the revelation in Jesus Christ, for if Christ is indeed the manifestation of God in the finite, then his way through the world from the stable to the cross revolutionizes the understanding of God, and invests him with a humility, passibility and involvement with the creation which were not obvious (though they may to some extent have been latent) in the Old Testament. The trouble is that Christians have been very slow to Christianize their understanding of God and seem to have a habit of lapsing back into the pre-Christian monarchical conception of God. The possibility that dialectical theism is compatible with a fully Christian understanding of God cannot be lightly dismissed. Let us remember, too, that dialectical theism does not deny the transcendence of God or most of the attributes which he had in classical theism and Christian theology, but simply asks that the properties ascribed to him should be understood dialectically, that is to say, each property is qualified by its opposite, and God himself, in accordance with the logic of the infinite, is understood as *coincidentia oppositorum*.

But what is this 'fully Christian understanding of God' that we have just mentioned? How close is it to the understanding of God in the Old Testament or in classical theism? How profound were the changes in the understanding of God brought about by the new revelation in Christ? We shall have to make a much more careful study of the Christian conception of God before we can properly answer the question about its compatibility or incompatibility with dialectical theism.

I have quoted Karl Rahner as saying that for the writers of the New Testament, 'the prophetic monotheism of the Old Testament is the foundation of their knowledge of God'. This quotation is taken from a long and carefully argued article by Rahner, entitled '*Theos* in the New Testament'.[3] Rahner's article would appear to rule out any attempt to understand the God of the New Testament in terms of dialectical theism, just as much as the Old Testament God. In fact, Rahner's conclusion is that when the New Testament writers mention God (ὁ θεός), they almost invariably have in mind the transcendent monotheistic deity of the Old Testament, never the trinitarian God of later Christian theology but the Father, the first person of the Trinity (as he was to become).[4] It is true, of course, that the beginnings of trinitarian doctrine are present in the New Testament,[5] and I shall have more to say about this in a moment, but the linguistic point made by Rahner seems well established, namely, that in the New Testament God (ὁ θεός) is understood as the same God who was known in the Old Testament.

I said that the usage is almost invariable. As Rahner points out, there are a few cases where the expression θεός is applied to Jesus Christ. Certainly, Jesus was not called 'God' in the earliest days of Christianity. For his first disciples, he was a prophet or a rabbi, certainly a human being. Even when he was hailed as messiah, that title, however exalted, was still a human title. It was only very slowly and one might even say, reluctantly, that Christian writers and preachers, steeped as they were in Jewish monotheism, began to apply God-language to Jesus. There is quite a bit of controversy among New Testament scholars over the question of whether Jesus is explicitly called 'God' in that collection of writings. In a famous essay, Bultmann claimed that 'neither in the synoptic gospels nor in the Pauline epistles is Jesus called God; nor do we find him so called in the Acts of the Apostles or in the Apocalypse; only in the deutero-Pauline literature do we find some such passages; and, moreover, the interpretation of them is disputed'.[6] He admits only one 'undoubted' case where Jesus is designated or, rather, addressed, as God – the confession of St Thomas in which he exclaims, 'My Lord and my God!'[7] How much theological weight can be placed on an isolated emotive utterance of this kind is questionable. Raymond Brown is prepared to go considerably further than Bultmann in recognizing passages in which Jesus is called God.[8] He claims three clear instances, and five more that are probable. The three clear instances are the confession of Thomas, already noted in connection with Bultmann, then the statement that 'the Logos was God' at the beginning of John's Gospel,[9] and the citation of a psalm in the Epistle to the Hebrews which implicitly has the effect of calling Jesus God.[10] John Fenton has drawn attention to another passage overlooked by Bultmann and Brown, the giving to Jesus in Matthew's Gospel of the appellation 'Emmanuel', translated 'God with us' (μεθ᾽ ἡμῶν ὁ θεός).[11]

It may seem strange that on such a central issue as the divinity of Jesus Christ one has to hunt around in the New Testament in order to find a handful of passages which are themselves susceptible of various interpretations. There is no denying that overwhelmingly the meaning of 'God' in the New Testament is to be taken in a transcendent and monotheistic sense. Yet, although one is still a very long way from Nicaea and Chalcedon and further still from the Athanasian creed, there are already stirrings which point towards these later developments. After all, 'God' (and its equivalent in other languages) was not a specifically Christian word. Not only was there a God of the Jews but many pagan deities besides. At an early stage in its existence, the Christian church had to face the question whether the simple expression 'God' was sufficiently explicit for the new understanding of God that had come about through the revelation in Jesus Christ. The uncertain and hesitant ascriptions of the name of 'God' to Jesus in the New Testament may be taken as evidence of the extent to which thinking about God had been influenced by the new revelation in Christ, so that when the Christian spoke of God, he was thinking of Christ at the same time. The development of christology went hand in hand with the rise of the doctrine of the triune God, and the rise of that doctrine in turn means the movement away from a stark transcendent monotheism in the direction of a dialectical theism. It is the dialectic or paradox of a God who is three in one and one in three, and this is associated with the dialectic or paradox of the god-man.

We see the transition in progress at an early date in a passage from Paul. He wrote: 'Although there may be so-called gods in heaven or on earth – as indeed there are many "gods" and many "lords" – yet for us there is one God, the Father, from whom are all things and for whom we exist, and one Lord, Jesus Christ, through whom are all things and through whom we exist.'[12] This is one of the earliest attempts to specify the Christian God and to distinguish him from the many 'gods' and 'lords' worshipped in other cults. Admittedly, Jesus is not called 'God' in this passage, but he is brought into a very close relation to God the Father. This is because he had brought to Christians a new understanding of God so profound that from then on they were determined not to speak of God without reference to Christ, or of Christ without reference to God. No doubt, of course, they were still far from understanding the relation in the full Nicene sense. Nothing is said here about the Holy Spirit who was destined to become the third person of the triune Godhead. The Holy Spirit is never explicitly called 'God' in the New Testament, though his divine provenance is understood. So one might ask whether the New Testament points in the direction of a binitarianism rather than a trinitarianism. There may indeed have been a transitional binitarianism on the way to trinitarianism, and certainly there was no clear distinction between the Holy Spirit and the spirit of Jesus or even the risen Christ, but this transitional binitarianism is not to be understood as a deliberately formulated doctrine (as binitarianism would be in a modern Christian theologian) but rather as an accidental stage on the way to the conception of the triune God.

It is not our business to trace the details of the development, but it can be confidently asserted that the Christian understanding of God moves from a conception virtually identical with that of the Old Testament to the doctrine of the triune God, three persons and one substance or essence. That is, in effect, a development from the monarchical conception of God to a dialectical conception. The most obvious dialectic in the Christian Trinity is that between unity and multiplicity or differentiation. The one substance of the Godhead is not monolithic, but contains differentiations of relation among the persons. Of course, we took note that even in ancient Hebrew religion, the use of a plural noun for 'God' suggested some kind of diversity within the unity. In fully developed Christian trinitarian doctrine, the dialectical conception of God includes many contrasts. Because God is the Son and the Spirit as well as the Father, we can say that he is temporal as well as eternal, passible as well as impassible, immanent as well as transcendent and so on.

It is usually claimed that while natural theology can establish the reality of God, it is only the Christian revelation that can lead us on from there to the doctrine of the triune God. Certainly, the specifically Christian doctrine of the triune God is tied to a particular religious history, and the three persons of the Father, the Son and the Holy Spirit are so closely bound up with and defined by that history that this doctrine is something quite specific and peculiar to Christianity. Nevertheless, when we were discussing the triadic conception of deity found in Plotinus, I raised the question whether any natural theology must not assume a triadic form and present us with a triune God. If this is so, then the triunity of God may be claimed to belong to natural theology. We have seen many evidences to suggest that triunity belongs to the very dynamics of deity, and that while the specific details of the Christian doctrine of the Trinity arise out of the Christian revelation, the triune form of deity comes from natural theology and is common to many religions and religious philosophies.

Christian theologians used to be puzzled by the occurrence outside of their own tradition of threefold conceptions of God. They called these *vestigia trinitatis*, 'traces of the Trinity', and sometimes supposed that they represented the vague and imperfect recollection of some primaeval revelation. Few people would hold such a theory nowadays, but the alternative is to acknowledge that reflection on the idea of God leads towards a triune conception, which must therefore be accounted part of natural theology. Confirmation of this may be had from an unexpected quarter. Karl Barth is the great modern theologian of revelation, and an implacable opponent of natural theology. Yet when he comes to expound the doctrine of the triune God as the foundation for his dogmatic theology, he derives the doctrine not from the content of the specific Christian revelation but from a formal analysis of the idea of revelation in general. To quote Barth's words: 'The ground, the root, of the doctrine of the Trinity . . . lies in revelation.' [13] If God reveals himself, then this event of revealing has a threefold form, which Barth describes by the terms revealer, revelation and revealedness, and it is on the basis of this analysis that he articulates Father, Son and Holy Spirit as the three 'modes' in his terminology of the one Godhead. I do not myself think that Barth's language is very helpful, and his teaching about the triune God is unclear, but it does seem to me that that teaching is derived from an analysis of the pure concept of revelation, not from the content of the Christian revelation.

If my argument up to this point is valid, then I have shown not only that, in spite of initial appearances, dialectical theism is compatible with the Christian understanding of God, but also that it leads towards a conception of God as triune and so provides a philosophical framework for the Christian dogma of the Trinity.

We have taken note that the development of the doctrine of the triune God went hand in hand with the development of christology. If the Trinity is one fundamental dogma of Christian theology, the incarnation is another. Trinity and incarnation are together the most distinctive items in Christian belief. Our next question then is whether dialectical theism coheres with a doctrine of incarnation as well as with the doctrine of the triune God.

We have already touched on the development of the Christian understanding of Jesus Christ. We cannot trace this in detail, but, as in the case of trinitarian teaching, the main outline is clear enough. To begin with, Jesus was probably regarded as a prophet, and Schillebeeckx has shown that the concept of 'prophet' had within itself great potential for development. [14] At some point, this prophet came to be accepted as messiah. As yet, he remained still a purely human figure, but his association with God was so close and he had had such a profound effect on people's understanding of God that more and more there was a pressure to identify him with God. At first this was done in what would later have been considered an 'adoptionist' way: the man Jesus was adopted or raised up to be Son of God. The early preaching of Peter, which may well be representative, shows us this stage of development. He declared: 'Let all the house of Israel therefore know assuredly that God has made him both Lord and Christ, this Jesus whom you crucified.'[15] An adoptionist christology, however, is affected by an inner instability which prevents it from remaining merely adoptionist. For how could a human person manifest the being of God so fully as to be acclaimed 'both Lord and Christ', unless God himself in his coming forth from himself into the finite realm had descended into that human person? So adoptionism leads into a full doctrine of incarnation. Adoption and incarnation are not, as has often been supposed, rival theories. They are complementary. Thus in the relatively late Gospel of John Jesus is proclaimed in a fully incarnational setting: 'The Word became flesh and dwelt among us.'[16]

This idea of incarnation is highly compatible with dialectical theism. It implies an ultimate source, in itself hidden and incomprehensible, whether we call this source the Father or Being or Beyond-being or whatever. But we could know nothing about this source and it could not rightly be called either 'source' or 'Father' if it did not come out to relate itself to what is other than itself, if it did not communicate itself by uttering its 'Word'. As we have seen in earlier discussions, the creation is not merely external to God, but God in a real sense puts himself into the creation and expresses himself in it. But this does not mean that he diffuses himself uniformly through the creation. Perhaps there are some forms of pantheism which teach that God is uniformly present and immanent in everything, but it is hard even to make sense of such an idea. In any case, dialectical theism is not pantheism, and though it does teach an immanence of God in the cosmos, it recognizes that God is not and indeed cannot be equally immanent or equally expressed in everything. As far as this planet is concerned – and for the present we need not worry about any others – only the human being, possessed of freedom, intelligence, creativity and the drive to transcendence, could serve as the embodied reality through which God's Word might be concretely uttered. Only the human being, made in the image of God, could serve in the highest degree for

God's self-communication. As we have learned from Eriugena, the human being is both the recipient of theophanies and himself a theophany. Thus, if we accept that God does emerge from his aseity to dwell in his creation, we are already predisposed to accepting a doctrine of incarnation.

I have already claimed that the idea of the triune God is one that can be derived from natural theology, in advance of that particular trinity known through the Christian revelation. Am I now making a similar claim for the idea of incarnation, and, if this is so, am I not carrying the claims of natural theology far beyond what is reasonable? I do indeed believe that within the framework of theism, and especially of a dialectical theism which stresses God's immanence, temporality, passibility and knowability alongside his transcendence, eternity, impassibility and incomprehensibility, then some form of incarnation is implicit in the dynamics of this situation. That may help to explain why other religions besides Christianity have taught doctrines related to the idea of incarnation, just as they have also taught the threefold being of God. However, I should make it clear that all that could be gathered from natural theology would be a general idea of incarnation, perhaps not very different from the Hegelian idea of a general incarnation of the divine spirit in the human race. Nothing would or could be said about the specific Christian claim that the Word became flesh in the particular human being, Jesus of Nazareth, or in the Christ-event of which he was the source and centre in a concrete occasion.

In an earlier part of the book, we passed in review eight representative figures whose religious philosophies illustrated the major features of what I have been calling 'dialectical theism'. I deliberately omitted Kierkegaard from these representative figures, because he was quite specifically a Christian thinker who did not practise an abstract natural theology but prized the particular expression of truth that he found in Jesus Christ. Nevertheless, his emphasis on paradox is clearly related to dialectic and to the *coincidentia oppositorum*, and though he was a severe critic of Hegel, there is considerable affinity between the two. I want now to work from the other side, as it were, and to show that Kierkegaard's thinking about the incarnation points towards a dialectical theism.

There is a well-known parable told by Kierkegaard about a powerful king who loved a humble maiden. How is the king to elicit from the maiden a true love that will be free from the homage that she owes to him as king?[17] He could raise her to a rank equal to his own, but that would be an artificial and external act, testifying to power rather than love. Or he could, as in the fairy-tales, disguise himself as a beggar and win her love as such, but true love cannot be based on deception.[18] If the union cannot be brought about by the elevation of the maiden or by a pretence, there is only one possibility, a real descent on the part of the king.

> In order that the union may be brought about, God must therefore become the equal of such a one, and so he will appear in the likeness of the humblest. But the humblest is one who must serve others, and God will therefore appear in the form of a *servant*. But this servant-form is no mere outer garment, like the king's beggar-cloak, which therefore flutters loosely about him and betrays the king . . . It is his true form and figure. For this is the unfathomable nature of love, that it desires equality with the beloved, not in jest merely, but in earnest and truth. And it is the omnipotence of the love that is so resolved that it is able to accomplish its purpose. The servant-form was no mere outer garment, and therefore God must suffer all things, endure all things, make experience of all things.[19]

We must notice that the servant-form is 'no mere outer garment' but God's 'true form and figure'. Perhaps one could interpret this in a 'death of God' sense, as some have interpreted (though probably wrongly) Hegel,[20] that God has fully poured himself out into the creation and emptied himself of his transcendent otherness. I do not think that this is what Kierkegaard meant, but clearly he did mean to disavow the monarchical view of God. Indeed, later in the same book, he states what he takes to be the essential meaning of Christianity: 'We have believed that in such and such a year God appeared among us in the humble figure of a servant, that he lived and taught in our community, and finally died.'[21] In other words, God is not the celestial monarch that he has been represented to be, even in classical theism, but a God deeply involved in the strivings and sufferings of his creatures, so that he would be better represented in servant-form. Kierkegaard's language, of course, is dramatic and pictorial, and has its own one-sidedness, but it would not be unfair to claim that just as dialectical theism draws us towards a concept of incarnation, so Kierkegaard's reflections on incarnation point us towards a form of dialectical, not to say paradoxical, theism.

But is not someone like Meister Eckhart a far more typical representative of dialectical theism than Kierkegaard, and have we not seen that Eckhart seemed to think rather lightly of incarnation and to recommend a direct mystical approach to God, in which not only the mediator Jesus Christ seems unnecessary but even the persons of the Trinity disappear as the soul loses itself in the divine essence which is like a wilderness without distinctions? He writes, for instance: 'Sometimes I have spoken of a light that is uncreated and not capable of creation and that is in the soul. I always mention this light in my sermons, and this same light comprehends God without a medium, uncovered, naked, as he is in himself.'[22] This is one of the passages in which Eckhart comes nearest to a pantheistic identification of the soul with God, a view which led to his condemnation by the authorities.

But this imageless, intellectual and somewhat abstract mysticism is not the only view found in Eckhart, still less does it represent the views of other adherents of dialectical theism. To show another side of Eckhart, let me quote a parable which he tells. It is not so charming as Kierkegaard's, indeed, it has a touch of the macabre, but it is making essentially the same point.

> There were a rich husband and wife. Then the wife suffered a misfortune, through which she lost an eye, and she was much distressed by this. Then her husband came to her and said: 'Madam, why are you so distressed? You should not distress yourself so, because you have lost your eye'. Then she said, 'Sir, I am not distressing myself about the fact that I have lost my eye; what distresses me is that it seems to me that you will love me less because of it.' Then he said, 'Madam, I do love you.' Not long after that he gouged out one of his own eyes and came to his wife and said: 'Madam, to make you believe that I love you, I have made myself like you; now I too have only one eye.' This stands for man, who could scarcely believe that God loved him so much, until God gouged out one of his own eyes and took upon himself human nature.[23]

Like Kierkegaard, Eckhart can speak of God's humbling himself and of his suffering with his creatures, and of his making himself equal with the beloved, and these truths he sees set forth especially in the incarnation. Still, it cannot be denied that there is a wide gap between Kierkegaard's *existential* apprehension of the incarnation and Eckhart's *mystical* understanding of it. For Kierkegaard, incarnation is quite definitely and specifically the incarnation of the Word in Jesus Christ. For Eckhart, incarnation often has a much more general sense. It is the birth of God in the soul that has prepared itself through emptying out worldly attachments. It is, of course, entirely in accordance with Christian teaching to believe that all the faithful are adopted to be the children of God and that Jesus Christ is to be regarded not simply as an individual but as the prototype of a new humanity. Nevertheless, this new humanity is believed to have its origin in Christ and to be entered through incorporation into him. Meister Eckhart may have believed this, and in fact he denied having taught that there is a divine uncreated element in the human soul through which one relates directly to God. But even his staunchest admirers admit that his language was quite ambiguous and that he sometimes writes as if the birth of God in the soul is a natural human capacity apart from Christ. Yet even this ambiguity has its value, since it permits us to see an affinity between Christian mysticism and the mysticism of non-Christian religions.

I did say in an earlier chapter[24] that mysticism is the form of spirituality which seems to go most naturally with a dialectical theism, and I took Eckhart's mysticism as an example. Many Christian theologians, however, have been hostile to mysticism. Some have seen it as an arrogant attempt on the part of the human being to ascend up to God, others have seen it as a distraction from what they consider to be the more important prophetic and ethical expressions of Christianity. Some of these suspicions may have been awakened, especially in view of what has been said about the ambiguities in Eckhart's mysticism. Thus even if it is conceded that dialectical theism relates affirmatively to Christian theology in respect to the doctrines of the triune God and the incarnation, there may be a lingering suspicion that its close historical associations with mysticism are evidence of a final incompatibility with Christianity. But I do not think that such suspicions are justified.

Let us agree that there is a mysticism which, at least in its language, seems to lay all the stress on man's ascent to the divine and even claims an identity of the human soul with God, as a divine spark – and let us agree also that such language is not absent from Eckhart. Nevertheless, to concentrate on this is a onesided reading. The typical mystic has much to say also of grace and of the divine initiative. It is God who comes to the soul before we seek him and it is he that draws us out of ourselves. It is the coming down of the divine that enables the rising up of the human. Moreover, whatever may be the case with Meister Eckhart, there are many Christian mystics who use consistently Christian language in all this. Adolf Deissman did not hesitate to attribute what he called 'Christ-mysticism' to the apostle Paul and speaks of the paradox of the 'I – yet not I' which repeatedly flashes out of his letters. 'Paul,' he says, 'was not deified nor was he transformed into spirit nor did he become Christ . . . But he was transformed by God, he became spiritual and he was one whom Christ possessed and a Christ-bearer.'[25] Surely this kind of mysticism offers no offence to Christianity. And it is so far from diminishing the prophetic and ethical impact of Christianity that it is rather its seed-bed. For is it not this immersion in God as known in Christ that inspires the practical living out of Christianity?

XVIII

Dialectical Theism and the World Religions

While this book has been written with the conviction that natural theology, in the sense explained in the first chapter, is a valid enterprise, I have several times drawn attention to its limitations. Not only does it never rise above a certain level of probability,[1] it also suffers from abstractness and generality and even a kind of artificiality when compared with the rich concreteness of a theology that has arisen out of one of the great historical religions of the world. Thus I even went so far as to say that natural theology seeks its embodiment or even its incarnation in some faith that is tied to a particular manifestation of the divine.[2] But to express the matter in this way could be misleading, if it were taken to mean that religious thinkers first arrive at a general natural theology and then go on to the formulation of some particular tradition. The sophisticated undertaking of natural theology comes after the formulation of particular theological traditions, even if it expresses in a schematic and generalized way the beliefs that are logically prior to the particular formulations and that can be exposed by stripping these formulations down, so to speak. On the other hand, this does not mean that natural theology should replace the concrete theologies of the various religious traditions. This may have been the ideal of the Enlightenment, perhaps of Kant when he wrote *Religion within the Limits of Reason Alone*, but such a theology would be so formally rationalistic and so lacking in imagination and poetry that its appeal would be limited to very few people and it could never exercise the influence that belongs to the concrete teachings of, say, Christianity or Hinduism. When Lord Gifford expressed his desire that the lectures which he founded should be made available to a wide public and declared his belief that natural theology has an important contribution to make to human well-being,[3] we would, I think, misunderstand him if we supposed that he had any wish to replace the concrete theologies based on revelations or supposed revelations with an abstract philosophical understanding of religion. I take him rather to have been meaning that the study of natural theology would enable those who assented to Christian or some other revealed theology to come to a more critical and therefore intellectually more secure grasp of the concrete faith which they held. For natural theology, by exposing the fundamental beliefs which in any concrete theology are clothed and covered over with the language of dogma and even mythology, makes these beliefs more accessible to evaluation and lets their reasonableness (or unreasonableness) be more clearly seen. Thus in the preceding chapter I tried to show that the central Christian dogmas of the triune God and the incarnation of the word, both of them highly paradoxical and initially implausible, are philosophically defensible in the light of natural theology, or, at least, that form of natural theology which I have called 'dialectical theism'.

In the present chapter I again want to strip down, as it were, the concrete religious traditions 'to examine the underlying natural theology, but with a different purpose from what I had in the previous chapter. There my motive was to show the compatibility of dialectical theism with Christian dogma. In the present chapter, I wish to broaden our field of view. Christianity is one among half a dozen or so great world religions which together number as their adherents the great bulk of the human race. At first sight, what may strike us most forcibly is the great differences between these faiths. Yet we must also be impressed by similarities and recurring features. At least some of the differences turn out to be accidental, arising from different cultural and historical modes of expression, though the underlying ideas may be very close. The question is, whether there is a basic natural theology concealed within the several concrete theologies of the major world religions, and whether this basic natural theology – if indeed there is one – can be understood in terms of dialectical theism. If we are pointed towards an affirmative answer to this question, then another function of dialectical theism would be to promote dialogue among the world religions, by drawing attention to deep-lying essential convictions that are common to the different traditions.

I do not, of course, want to exaggerate what could be achieved along these lines. The very idea of dialogue implies that there are differences to be sorted out as well as similarities to be exhibited. The simplistic belief that the great religions are all saying much the same thing is, in the end, inimical to better relations among them, for it lacks respect for the distinctive characteristics of each tradition. The Buddhist ideal of humanity, for instance, is different in important respects from the Christian ideal, and neither of them is served by an over-hasty identification or by minimizing the differences. A worthwhile dialogue, leading to better understanding on both sides, can take place only if careful attention is paid to the differences as well as to the similarities.

In the present discussion, it is the idea of God in the different traditions that calls for study. But precisely in this matter the difficulties seem most acute. We often hear it said, somewhat naively, that the great religions are different ways to the one God, but a moment's reflection shows us the difficulty in making such a claim. For instance, to return to the contrast between Christianity and Buddhism, the former recognizes a personal God while the latter, in its original form, is often held to be atheistic or to recognize as its ultimate an impersonal cosmic principle. Thus it is doubtful if even the word 'God' (or its equivalent in other languages) is common property to the religions, or God himself their common concern. I have suggested elsewhere[4] that perhaps the expression 'holy being' would be a less prejudicial way of expressing that ultimate reality which all the religions seek. The word 'God' may be too concrete and too heavily laden with personal connotations. It is the word which Western people use for holy being, but in their minds it is inevitably coloured by associations derived from the family of religions which they know best – I mean, Christianity, Judaism and Islam. The religions of further Asia would for the most part think of holy being in different ways. But there can be only one ultimate. So either that Western conception of God, derived from Semitic sources and understanding holy being in concrete personal terms, is mistaken, or else the conceptions prevailing in further Asia are mistaken, or else, in spite of the apparently irreconcilable opposition between the two views, which perhaps reaches its highest pitch when someone contrasts theistic Christianity with allegedly atheistic Buddhism, there is the possibility of a more comprehensive concept which would be able to embrace both Eastern and Western conceptions of holy being. To express this in another way, we could say that there is still another dialectical opposition in God in addition to those we have considered earlier. This final dialectic is the opposition of personal and impersonal.

Although I have not explicitly discussed the dialectic of personal and impersonal, we have had glimpses of it in the studies of some of the representatives of dialectical theism. Many of them entertained the idea of a 'God beyond God', if we may use the expression. In the teaching of Plotinus, The One which is incomprehensible and ineffable stands above both Mind and Soul, and is so wholly other in its ultimacy that even the name of 'God' is not appropriate.[5] Dionysius the Areopagite spoke of the 'thearchy', which he explicitly claimed to be not only 'beyond being' and 'beyond intellect' but even 'beyond deity', and it seems that the very persons of the Trinity lost their distinctness in the inexpressible unity of the thearchy.[6] In somewhat different terms, Meister Eckhart described the highest reach of the mystical consciousness as the 'breakthrough' in which the soul penetrates beyond the persons of the Trinity to achieve union with the single undifferentiated essence of deity.[7] In more recent times, Heidegger has rejected the idea of a personal creator God in favour of the ontological difference between the beings and wholly other being, and has posited as the ultimate a transpersonal event which can be described only as 'It gives'.[8] Among modern theologians, Tillich has popularized the idea of 'God above God' which he calls 'the content of absolute faith' and which, he says, 'transcends the theistic idea of God'.[9] As he somewhat ironically remarks, 'God became "a person" only in the nineteenth century.'[10] He explains this remark by referring to the fact that after Kant reality was divided into two spheres – a self-regulating nature, where physics is supreme and God is superfluous, and the realm of personal beings, ruled by moral law, where alone there is a place for God. Still, even if we were to agree with Tillich that the explicit affirmation that God is a person is a relatively recent one (for the traditional application of the term 'person' to the hypostases of the triune God had a different and less clearly defined sense), it cannot be denied that in the Judaeo-Christian tradition, God had always personal attributes.

What, then, are we to say of this strong tendency among the exponents of dialectical theism to turn away from, or, at least, to qualify profoundly, the idea of a personal God? Three points are, I think, worth noticing.

The first is that among the examples I have quoted (and they are only a selection) there appear to be two distinct ways in which the thinkers concerned have come to the idea that the ultimate reality of God lies beyond the personal, or, if one prefers to speak in such a way, that there is God beyond God. The first of these ways is most clearly illustrated by Plotinus. In common with other dialectical thinkers, he recognizes a triune God, and he places the impersonal, incomprehensible, wholly other character of God in the most primordial of the divine hypostases, what he calls 'The One'. The other possibility is best seen in Meister Eckhart. For him, the ultimate and ineffable reality is not the most primordial hypostasis (the Father) but the one essence of Godhood which is common to all three hypostases. This first point may strike the reader as somewhat academic, but it is of interest as reflecting a longstanding difference between East and West in the understanding of the triune God and it is not without some practical consequences.

The second point is that when one denies that God is a person, it is almost automatically assumed that he must be impersonal in the sense of 'sub-personal' or 'less than a person', perhaps a mere life-force, *nisus, élan* or however it might be described. But this is not the only possibility. God, in the depth of his Godhood, may be suprapersonal. To say that God is not a person can be understood in a Dionysian sense as meaning that he is 'beyond personhood' or 'more than a person'. These are not meaningless phrases, for personhood, as we know it, is essentially imperfect and subject to limitations. For instance, our experience is never completely unified, we never have a total recall of our past, and for the most part our minds grasp things discursively, point by point, rather than intuitively in their totality. F. H. Bradley paid considerable attention to such questions, and suggested that the immediacy of feeling affords some clue to the nature of an experience transcending our own and to which the adjective 'suprapersonal' or 'superpersonal' would be appropriate. He speaks of an experience characterized by 'a unity higher than all relations, a unity which contains and transforms them', and claims that 'of the manner of its being in detail, we are utterly ignorant, but of its general nature we possess a positive though abstract knowledge'.[11] This language from a philosopher is reminiscent of the negative theology of Dionysius and others, though Bradley seems willing to allow a more affirmative understanding of God than were some of the mystics, at least in their explicit statements. However, Bradley is critical of those religious people who insist on the 'personality' of God in such a manner that they really turn God into another finite self with the same mode of existence as they have. God is not a person, but this is no lack or deficiency, for he is supra-personal.

This leads to a third point: although God transcends the category of personality, nevertheless we can and must address him and talk of him in personal terms. For although God is transcendent, he is also immanent in his creation, and in that creation, personal beings stand higher than any other kind of entity. As we have seen in an earlier chapter, the human being, endowed with personhood, is the recipient of God's manifestation in the finite (his 'theophanies') and is at the same time the adequate medium for such a theophany (incarnation).[12] So to say that God transcends the personal is not to deny that he includes personality. If it is incorrect to say that God is a person, or that he is good or wise or beautiful, it would be even further from the truth to say that he is less than a person or bad or foolish or ugly. As I have insisted more than once before, though we may not know what these various words mean when applied to God, we at least know in what direction to look. To return for a moment to F. H. Bradley:

> With regard to the personality of the Absolute we must guard against two one-sided errors. The Absolute is not personal, nor is it moral, nor is it beautiful or true. And yet in these denials we may be falling into worse mistakes. For it would be far more incorrect to assert that the Absolute is either false or ugly or bad, or is something even beneath the application of predicates such as these. And it is better to affirm personality than to call the Absolute impersonal. But neither mistake should be necessary. The Absolute stands above, and not below, its internal distinctions. It does not eject them, but it includes them as elements in its fullness. To speak in other language, it is not the indifference but the concrete identity of all extremes. But it is better in this connection to call it superpersonal.[13]

These reflections, then, may suggest to us that the conception of a personal God in Western religions and the conception of an impersonal ultimate in some of the Eastern religions may not be such an absolute difference between them as it seems at first sight. Personal/impersonal is one more dialectic within the divine *coincidentia oppositorum*, and like the other dialectics, this one is not to be dismissed as mere contradiction. Both sides have their right, and, with proper care for the context, both sides deserve to be given expression, both liturgically and theologically. As in all dialectic, sometimes one side of the opposition receives greater emphasis than the other, and there may be good reasons for a particular emphasis in a particular historical tradition, but neither side can totally vanquish the other, and should not be allowed to do so. If a predominantly impersonal (or suprapersonal) conception of God seems remote and even cold, that may be less of a distortion than the warm pietistic personal devotion, which can reduce deity to human dimensions and may finally evaporate in romantic emotion.

I think we shall find that in all the great religions of the world, personal and impersonal ideas are intertwined in their several conceptions of deity (God or holy being) and that beneath the concrete symbols developed in their histories, we can discern the contours of dialectical theism. Obviously, if this could be made explicit, the way would be opened to constructive dialogue between traditions which, on the surface, might seem to be very far apart. The only way to make it explicit is to review the major traditions and to show the dialectical elements that are latent in each of them. Clearly, we can do this only in the most sketchy and provisional way, but it will be enough to show that there are many paths leading in this direction we have indicated, and that these are well worth exploring.

We begin with Christianity, and we can treat this tradition briefly, since I have already devoted a whole chapter to showing the compatibility of dialectical theism with Christian doctrine. It goes without saying that the Christian conception of God is overwhelmingly personal. This is fully understandable, seeing that Christianity inherited the Jewish conception of God and, moreover, believed that God had given the definitive revelation of himself in the form of a human person. Yet, over against this, has to be set the fact that Christian reflection on the God who had manifested himself in Jesus Christ led to the doctrine of the Trinity, three persons in one substance or being. Some theologians have taken that word 'person' in its modern sense, and have constructed a 'social' trinity, but it is hard to see how such a view can avoid lapsing into tritheism. On the other hand, it is equally hard to see how the Trinity can together constitute a 'person', as Barth seems to claim, while acknowledging that this way of talking has been devised as a modern safeguard against naturalism and pantheism.[14] Furthermore, theological reflection needs to introduce such impersonal expressions as 'self-subsistent being'. *Pace* Pascal, Ritschl, *et al.*, the responsible Christian thinker cannot be content to use only biblical images of God drawn from personal life, for to call God 'Father' or 'King' and, even more, 'Maker of heaven and earth', is to venture, whether one wishes or not, into assertions about what is real and what is unreal, and these assertions can only be clarified and assessed by putting them into ontological language. Christianity is certainly committed to the belief that God is not less than personal and has revealed himself in personal form, but equally it is not committed to the belief that personality exhausts the being of God and the history of its own theology shows that it has been necessary to deploy a whole battery of impersonal ontological and metaphysical terms in order to say what has to be said about God as the ultimate beginning and end of all things.

When we turn from Christianity to its nearest neighbour among the religions, Judaism, it might seem more difficult to point to any personal/impersonal dialectic in God, for Judaism and the ancient Hebrew scriptures have no doctrine of a trinity, and in the central tradition of this faith, God is one, personal and transcendent.

But alongside that central tradition, even in the Old Testament, there are secondary elements which modify the central body of teaching. God is certainly one – this is a fundamental affirmation. Yet, as we have noted,[15] the usual Hebrew word for God is a plural form, suggesting some distinctions within deity. In some of the ancient narratives, God seems to alternate with the 'angel of the Lord' who was identified by some of the Christian Fathers with the Word or *Logos* and was named by some Jewish sectaries 'little Yahweh', so that he has something of the character of a second God or an emanation of Yahweh.[16] The Old Testament speaks also of the 'Spirit' of God, while in the wisdom literature, which represents a more reflective and even contemplative stream of Hebrew religion alongside the predominant prophetic stream, wisdom becomes a kind of divine hypostasis which has been with God from the beginning.[17] Of course, the language may be merely metaphorical, but it contains the seeds of a conception of God in which stark unity has been modified. Again, God is certainly personal in the Old Testament, and the language is frequently anthropomorphic. Yet, as Rudolf Otto showed, the God of the Old Testament is also a mysterious being, possessed of numinous, that is to say, non-rational and non-personal, qualities, which are more fundamental than the rational and moral qualities which are ascribed to him at a more developed stage of the religion. Otto mentions the prophet Isaiah, a man with the most serious ethical concern, as nevertheless equally aware of the mysterious depths of God, whom he typically calls 'the holy one of Israel'.[18] (The Hebrew word for 'holy', *qadosh*, means literally 'separate'.) Curiously, it is a very anthropomorphic expression, the 'wrath of God', which seems to symbolize most vividly the non-rational, non-personal depth of deity. Finally, the God of the Old Testament is certainly transcendent, but he can be near as well as far and he is deeply concerned for his people. We find one prominent Jewish scholar, Leo Baeck, declaring that here there is no foundation for 'the conflict between transcendence and immanence'.[19]

When we pass from the Old Testament to Judaism, the tendencies described become intensified. We have already noted that at the beginning of the Christian era, Philo of Alexandria was bringing together biblical teaching and Greek philosophy.[20] He bestowed on God the impersonal name of ὁ ὤν, 'He who is', declared his essence to be unknowable, introduced mysticism and posited the *Logos* as the intermediary between God and humanity. The greatest Jewish thinker of the Middle Ages, Maimonides, taught a negative theology. Among the Jewish sects, mysticism flourished – first among the Kabbalists, and then in less esoteric form among the Hasidim of Eastern Europe, who, in turn, had a profound influence on the most famous Jewish philosopher of modern times, Martin Buber.[21] Buber tells us how his own initial attraction to mysticism eventually gave way to the personalist philosophy for which he is well-known. But when Buber confronts the question whether God is a person, He gives this strongly qualified answer:

The description of God as a person is indispensable for everyone who like myself means by 'God' not a principle (although mystics like Eckhart sometimes identify him with being) and, like myself, means by 'God' not an idea (although philosophers like Plato at times could hold that he was this); but who rather means by 'God', as I do, him who – whatever else he may be – enters into a direct relation with us men in creative, revealing and redeeming acts, and thus makes it possible for us to enter into a direct relation with him. The ground and meaning of our existence constitutes a mutuality, arising again and again, such as can subsist only between persons. The concept of personal being is indeed completely incapable of declaring what God's essential being is, but it is both permitted and necessary to say that God is *also* a person.[22]

This carefully weighed statement by the leading exponent of the I-thou philosophy does not seem to me incompatible with the views of F. H. Bradley, quoted above, and gives hope that the Jewish concept of a personal God has within it a dialectic that can make possible a constructive dialogue with those Eastern religions whose concept of holy being is apparently impersonal.

Before we leave the Western/Semitic family of religions, we must consider the youngest and perhaps the most vigorous among them, Islam. The case here is different from what we find in either Judaism or Christianity. It is true that again we have one God, but his unity is so strictly interpreted that anything like the Christian belief in a triune God is excluded, and likewise his transcendence is stressed to such an extent that any sense of his personality is greatly weakened. God is said to have seven attributes: life, knowledge, power, will, hearing, seeing, speech.[23] These attributes do seem, for the most part, to be the characteristics of a person, and the last three appear to be quite anthropomorphic. But they are interpreted in ways which would rigorously exclude any anthropomorphism. God hears, sees and speaks, but in ways quite different from our human ways of hearing, seeing and speaking, and incomprehensible to us. This God is even more numinous than the God of the Old Testament. The difficulty in relating him to the ways of understanding holy being in the further Asian religions is therefore quite different from what we encountered in the cases of Judaism and Christianity. A true dialectic is always complex, sometimes tortuous, and if we find a dialectical analysis working out too mechanically, it is probably mistaken. In the case of Islam, the problem is not to generate an impersonal element, for Allah has already been removed to such a transcendent height that he is effectually depersonalized. The problem is rather to bring him near, so that a closer relation is possible.

Such a relation has been realized in Sufi mysticism, the corrective which Islam has supplied from its own resources. According to J. S. Trimingham, 'early Sufism was a natural expression of personal religion', called forth in 'reaction against the external rationalization of Islam in law and systematic theology'.[24] The God of Islam had always been called 'merciful' and was believed to be nearer than anything else, but Sufism, with its mystical practice and sense of the immanence of God, gave these beliefs a new vividness. The Sufis called God *al-Haqq*, 'the reality', and, at least to begin with, this appellation probably referred to the reality of a God known directly in experience rather than to the abstract idea of metaphysical reality.

When we move on to the religions of India and the Far East, we find a different situation. Here, impersonal conceptions of holy being are dominant, and these are combined with a strong sense of immanence, even to the point of pantheism. But the dialectic inherent in the idea of deity comes into play, in the opposite direction from what we found in the Judaeo-Christian tradition, and now personal conceptions of God emerge as correctives to the prevailing impersonalism (or, it may be, suprapersonalism). Let me briefly give examples.

The religion of India has taken innumerable forms, and within these the dialectic of personal and impersonal is clearly to be seen. The two sides of the dialectic are represented by two great classical philosophers of India, Shankara and Ramanuja. Shankara represents the predominant trend, which is monistic and impersonal. These ideas go back to the early Vedic hymns. One famous Vedic hymn[25] speaks of a primal Absolute, of which one could not say either that it existed or did not exist, or that it breathed or did not breathe. The gods are later than this Absolute and represent aspects of it. According to Shankara, human souls too are parts of the Absolute, though sin may blind us to this truth. There is nothing real besides the Absolute, even the world of nature is *maya*, a surface-play which is not far from illusion. The Absolute is impersonal, though perhaps one could say that it is spiritual, and through retribution and rebirth, it exercises a moral government. Salvation is achieved by realizing one's unity with the Absolute.

In all this, one can see resemblances to Plotinus, Eckhart and other Western thinkers considered earlier in this book, but Shankara's doctrine is far more one-sidedly monistic than any of the Western teachings. Ramanuja, dissatisfied with this impersonal monism, taught the relative independence of nature and of the human soul, thus allowing sufficient space betwen the souls and God for the possibility of personal devotion (*bhakti*). In the popular Hinduism of the present time, personal devotion to Krishna has a prominent place. Krishna is an incarnation or descent (*avatar*) of the high god Vishnu, but though he is Vishnu in human form, something of the impersonal and numinous otherness of the god remains in the background, as one sees from the theophany in the *Bhagavadgita*.[26]

Buddhism began as an offshoot from Hinduism, and it has often been said that the original Buddhism was atheistic. That would depend, of course, on what qualifies as 'theism', and we have seen that the charge of atheism has often been made without adequate grounds.[27] The Buddha did not deny the reality of the gods, but he did seem to conceive the ultimate reality in a quite impersonal way. Still, we might say, as we did in relation to Shankara, that the ultimate, though impersonal, was none the less spiritual and moral. It was a process involving judgment, retribution, rebirth and, for those who became enlightened, salvation. But such an austere doctrine does not satisfy the religious instinct for worship and communion. The Buddha himself was soon being venerated, even in the older (*Theravada*) form of Buddhism. In the later (so-called *Mahayana*) Buddhism, personal devotion to buddhas and boddhis-attvas proliferated. In Japan today, a popular figure is the Amida Buddha, who, having gained his own salvation, vowed not to accept it until he had brought all to salvation: 'In case I attain the ultimate goal of buddhahood, I vow to receive all human beings who think of me one to ten times or more, sincerely wishing to be received into my pure land. Until I have fulfilled this vow, I will not become a buddha but will remain a buddha-to-be (*boddhisattva*)'.[28] Another popular figure, whose features are to be seen all over Japan, is the compassionate Kannon, who has a female form and is said to be modelled on an eighth-century empress of China.[29] These and similar developments are not to be attributed simply to popular demand for what Kierkegaard called 'a nice human God',[30] but have their roots in the dialectic of deity and can be philosophically defended, as we learned from the passages quoted earlier from the writings of Bradley and Buber.

Turning finally to religion in China, we find that the personal/impersonal dialectic has sorted itself out into the two distinct indigenous religions of that country. Confucianism and Taoism. These are very different and have often been in conflict, but they have also been closely intertwined and each has made its essential contribution.

In Confucianism, the rational and the humanistic prevail. Indeed, it looks very much like 'religion within the limits of reason alone', and it was for this reason that all things Chinese were admired in eighteenth-century Europe. The Confucian God or Heaven is no doubt real, but like the God of deism he is kept discreetly in the background. Anything savouring of mystery or of the numinous is eschewed. With Taoism, it is quite different. The Western mind can hardly begin to understand what Taoism is, especially as experts disagree over the translation of the basic texts. The word *tao* itself has many meanings in Chinese philosophy, and is, of course, used also by Confucius. In Taoism, *tao* refers to the ultimate cosmic principle, but even to call it *tao* is somehow to do it violence, for it is strictly ineffable, though in mystical ecstasy one can come into relation with it. Perhaps the nearest equivalent is The One of Plotinus. Within the universe, the dialectical forces of *yin* and *yang* (male and female, day and night, summer and winter) are continually at work, and the *tao* maintains them in unity and harmony. The ideal for human beings is the quietist one of conforming to the rhythm of the universe. Since in China it has usually been considered permissible to profess more than one religion at a time, we may suppose that the ideal would be to combine the reasonableness and humanity of the Confucian tradition with something of the depth and spirituality that have come from Taoism.

The result of this survey of the understanding of deity or holy being in the great religions is encouraging. I have confined myself to the half dozen major religious traditions because their long persistence and the large number of their adherents is evidence of their inherent spiritual value. In spite of all their differences, we find them pointing to a spiritual source which is recognizably the same in each, a dialectical unity of opposites which constitutes the fullness of being, even if in particular traditions one side or other is exaggerated while something else is diminished. This fullness of being is deity, the goal and inspiration of our own human transcendence. It is attested not only by the several religious traditions but by the reflections of natural theology, and we can understand why Lord Gifford claimed that the knowledge which comes from such reflections 'lies at the root of all well-being'.

Notes

Chapter I The Idea of Natural Theology

1. David Hume, *Dialogues concerning Natural Religion*, Hafner Publishing Company 1969, p. 94.
2. Ibid., pp. 42–3.
3. I am assuming that his occasional suggestions that philosophical scepticism accords well with religious faith are ironical.
4. Hume, op. cit., p. 31.
5. Immanuel Kant, *Critique of Pure Reason*, ET Macmillan 1929, p. 29.
6. Ibid., p. 532.
7. Immanuel Kant, *Critique of Judgment*, ET Clarendon Press 1928, Part II, p. 52.
8. Immanuel Kant, *Critique of Practical Reason and Other Works on the Theory of Ethics*, ET Longmans Green 1883, pp. 220ff. The 'other works' include *Groundwork of the Metaphysic of Morals*, quoted below.
9. A. S. Pringle-Pattison, *The Idea of God*, Oxford University Press 1920, p. 35.
10. Kant, *Critique of Practical Reason*, p. 200.
11. Ibid., p. 17, n. 2 (see above, n. 8). My point about the relation between respect and reverence is illustrated by the fact that T. K. Abbott, whose translation is quoted here, gives 'respect', while H. J. Paton in his translation of the *Groundwork* (Harper Torchbooks 1964) gives 'reverence'. The German word is *Achtung*.
12. Kant, *Critique of Judgment*, Part II, p. 131.
13. Immanuel Kant, *Religion within the Limits of Reason Alone*, ET Harper Torchbooks 1960, p. 142.
14. Ibid., p. 163.
15. Ibid., p. 179.
16. Keith Ward, *Holding Fast to God*, SPCK 1982, p. 5.
17. The quotations which follow are taken from the pamphlet, 'Gifford Lectureship: Extracts from the Trust Disposition and Settlement of the Late Lord Gifford', issued for the guidance of lecturers.
18. Thomas Aquinas, *Summa Theologiae*, Ia, 8, 3.
19. Perhaps I should also explain why some philosophers and theologians have been omitted, apart from the obvious limitations of space and the balance of the argument. Augustine and Aquinas, though both greatly influenced by neo-Platonism, seem to me to belong definitely in what I have called 'mainline theism'. On the other side, Spinoza and Schelling are far too close to pantheism. Kierkegaard's concept of paradox might qualify him as a dialectical theologian, but he is too much an individual to be included under any classification.

Chapter II   Towards a Concept of God

1. G. D Kaufman, *An Essay on Theological Method*, Scholars Press 1975, p. 9.
2. A. R. Peacocke, *Creation and the World of Science*, Oxford University Press 1979, p. 115.
3. See below, pp. 139–52.
4. F. Copleston, *Religion and the One*, Search Press 1982, pp. 6–7.
5. Deut. 6. 4.
6. Isa. 55. 8–9.
7. Ex. 3. 14.
8. P. Weiss, *The God We Seek*, Southern Illinois University Press 1964, p. 157.
9. Martin Luther, *The Book of Concord*, ET Fortress Press 1959, p. 365.
10. Thomas Aquinas, *Summa Theologiae*, Ia, 13, 11.
11. Anselm, *Proslogion*, ET SCM Press 1974, p. 93.

Chapter III   A Critique of Classical Theism

1. For the use of the expression 'classical theism' by a critic, see Schubert Ogden, *The Reality of God*, Harper and SCM Press 1966; by an advocate, see H. P. Owen, *Concepts of Deity*, Macmillan 1971. Quotations from St Thomas all come from the *Summa Theologiae*. I have used the bilingual edition, edited by Thomas Gilby, OP, 60 volumes, published by Eyre and Spottiswoode and McGraw-Hill 1964–76.
2. See above, p. 11.
3. Ia, 2, 3.
4. See below, p. 90.
5. Ia, 2, 3.
6. Ibid.
7. Ibid.
8. Ibid.
9. See below, p. 162.
10. See above, p. 18.
11. Vol. II of the Gilby edition, Appendix 4, pp. 186–7.
12. See above, p. 18.
13. Ia, qq. 45–6.
14. Ia, 46, 1.
15. For a fuller discussion, see my book, *Thinking about God*, ch. 13, 'Creation and Environment', SCM Press and Harper 1975.
16. Ia, 105, 5.
17. D. F. Strauss, *The Life of Jesus Critically Examined*, ET Swan Sonnenschein, London 1906, p. 39.
18. Ibid., p. 40.
19. W. C. Dampier, *A History of Science and its Relations with Philosophy and Religion*, Cambridge University Press 1942, p. 188.
20. In H. W. Bartsch (ed.), *Kerygma and Myth*, ET SPCK 1957, p. 5.
21. E. L. Mascall, *The Openness of Being*, Darton, Longman & Todd 1971, p. 162.
22. Ia, 12, 4.

Chapter IV Alternatives to Classical Theism

1. J. Macquarrie, *In Search of Humanity*, SCM Press 1982 and Crossroad 1983, especially Chapter XX.
2. E.g., in my *Three Issues in Ethics*, SCM Press and Harper & Row 1970, pp. 16–17.
3. See above, p. 29.
4. John Bowker, *The Religious Imagination and the Sense of God*, Oxford University Press 1978, p. 260.
5. Ibid., p. 274.
6. J. N. Findlay, *Ascent to the Absolute*, Allen & Unwin and Humanities Press 1970, p. 205.
7. See below, p. 61.
8. See below, p. 141.
9. P. Masterson, *Atheism and Alienation*, Gill & Macmillan 1971, p. 1.
10. The most sustained argument (not always convincing) to show the atheistic consequences of Descartes' *cogito* is set forth in Cornelio Fabro, *God in Exile: Modern Atheism*, ET Newman Press 1968. The path which leads from Descartes to Nietzsche is characterized as follows by Heidegger in *Nietzsche*, ET Harper & Row 1982, Vol. 4. p. 28: 'Western history has now begun to enter into the completion of that period we call the *modern*, and which is defined by the fact that man becomes the measure and the centre of beings. Man is what lies at the bottom of all beings; that is, in modern terms, at the bottom of all objectification and representability. No matter how sharply Nietzsche pits himself time and again against Descartes, whose philosophy grounds modern metaphysics, he turns against Descartes only because the latter still does not posit man as *subjectum* in a way that is complete and decisive enough. The representation of the *subjectum* as ego, the I, thus the egoistic interpretation of the *subjectum*, is still not subjectivistic enough for Nietzsche. Modern metaphysics first comes to the full and final determination of its essence in the doctrine of the Superman (*Übermensch*), the doctrine of man's absolute preeminence among beings. In that doctrine, Descartes celebrates his supreme triumph.'
11. See note 1 to this chapter.
12. Stewart Sutherland, *Atheism and the Rejection of God*, Blackwell 1977.
13. Ninian Smart, *The Concept of Worship*, Macmillan 1972, pp. 10–11.
14. E. Haeckel, *The Riddle of the Universe*, ET Watts 1929.
15. Charles Hartshorne, *Creative Synthesis and Philosophic Method*, SCM Press 1970, p. 270.
16. See above, pp. 27–8.

Chapter V Classical: Plotinus

1. The critical edition of the *Enneads* by P. Henry and H. R. Schwyzer is published under the title *Plotini Opera* by Oxford University Press in the series 'Oxford Classical Texts', 1964–83. All six *Enneads* are published in a version edited, with French translation, by E. Bréhier: *Plotin: Ennéades*, seven volumes, Bude, Paris, 1924ff. Porphyry's *Life* and *Enneads* I–III in the Henry-Schwyzer text with English translation by A. H. Armstrong are published in 'The Loeb Classical Library': *Plotinus*, three volumes, Heinemann and Harvard University

Press 1966ff. Stephen MacKenna's complete English translation, *Plotinus: The Enneads*, was first published in five volumes by The Medici Society, 1917ff. A single volume edition of this translation, revised by B. S. Page, was published by Faber & Faber in 1969. Elmer O'Brien has provided a translation with notes of ten of the principal tractates in *The Essential Plotinus*, Hackett Publishing Company 1964. In my quotations, I have followed the translations sometimes of MacKenna, sometimes of Armstrong, sometimes of O'Brien, but have standardized the translation of key terms.

2. A. H. Armstrong, *The Architecture of the Intelligible Universe in the Philosophy of Plotinus*, Cambridge University Press 1940, p. 26.

3. W. R. Inge, *The Philosophy of Plotinus*, Longmans [3]1928, vol. I, p. 7.

4. II, 3.

5. III, 1, 3.

6. II, 9, 17.

7. I, 3.

8. See the chapter 'The Origins of Dialectic' in L. Kolakowski, *Main Currents of Marxism*, Clarendon Press 1978, Vol. I, pp. 9–80.

9. VI, 6, 13.

10. II, 1, 1.

11. W. R. Inge, op. cit., vol. II, p. 131.

12. Deut. 6. 4.

13. See J. A. Lyons, *The Cosmic Christ in Origen and Teilhard de Chardin*, Oxford University Press 1982, p. 91.

14. Wisd. 7. 25.

15. Gen. 1. 7; 1. 16; 1. 26, etc.

16. Gen. 2. 7; Ps. 33. 6; 104. 30; Ezek. 37. 9.

17. John Macquarrie, *Principles of Christian Theology*, SCM Press and Scribner, [2]1977, pp. 217–8.

18. A. H. Armstrong, op. cit., p. 43.

19. V, 5, 6.

20. VI, 9, 1.

21. V, 2, 1.

22. V, 3, 11.

23. V, 6, 6.

24. VI, 7, 32.

25. IV, 8, 6.

26. V, 2, 1.

27. H. P. Owen, *Concepts of Deity*, Macmillan 1971, pp. 61–5.

28. It is difficult to find a good English equivalent for νοῦς. I have used here the hendiadys 'Mind or Intellect', and have generally used 'Mind'. Inge prefers 'Spirit', while MacKenna translates the word as 'Intellectual Principle'.

29. V, 1, 4.

30. Ibid.

31. W. R. Inge, op. cit., vol. II, pp. 39–40.

32. V, 1, 3.

33. IV, 3, 9.

34. IV, 4, 18.

35. IV, 9, 1.

36. VI, 9, 6.

37. Augustine, *Confessions*, VII, 9, 14.
38. See V, 1, 7; V, 5, 3; V, 8, 13.
39. E. O'Brien, op. cit., p. 90.
40. V, 9, 2.
41. I, 4, 8.
42. V, 5, 5.
43. *Life*, 23.
44. VI, 9, 11.
45. VI, 9, 8.
46. II, 3, 16.
47. III, 2, 17.
48. VI, 5, 7.

Chapter VI   Patristic: Dionysius

1. Acts 17. 34.
2. The principal extant works of Dionysius are four treatises: *The Divine Names* (DN), *The Mystical Theology* (MT), *the Celestial Hierarchy* (CH) and *The Ecclesiastical Hierarchy* (EH). These writings are contained in vols. III and IV of J. P. Migne, *Patrologia Graeca*. I shall refer to them by the abbreviations shown in brackets. There is a critical edition of CH by G. Heil, with French translation by M. de Gandillac and introduction by R. Roques, in the series Sources Chrétiennes: Denys l'Aréopagite, *La hierarchie celeste*, Les Editions du Cerf 1970. There is an English translation by C. E. Rolt of DN and MT, published by SPCK 1920, and frequently reprinted. There are older English translations of the writings of Dionysius, but these are long since out of print.
3. A. Harnack, *History of Dogma*, ET, Williams & Norgate 1898, Vol. IV, p. 340.
4. L. Bouyer, *Le Père invisible*, Les Editons du Cerf 1976, p. 326.
5. Ibid., p. 325.
6. CH vii, 2.
7. See above, p. 67.
8. CH vii, 2.
9. A. J. Ayer, *Language, Truth and Logic*, Gollancz [2]1946, pp. 85–6.
10. DN v, 8.
11. DN xi, 6.
12. DN iv, 20.
13, DN vii, 2.
14. DN ii, 7.
15. K. Jaspers, *Philosophical Faith and Revelation*, ET Harper & Row 1967, p. 151.
16. DN xiii, 3.
17. DN xiii, 3.
18. DN iv, 10.
19. DN iv, 1.
20. DN iv, 13.
21. T. J. J. Altizer, *The Gospel of Christian Atheism*, Westminster Press 1966, p. 103.
22. DN i, 2.

23. DN i, 1.
24. A. Farrer, *The Glass of Vision*, Dacre Press 1948.
25. P. Tillich, *Dynamics of Faith*, Harper 1958.
26. I. T. Ramsey, *Models and Mystery*, Oxford University Press 1964.
27. CH ii, 3.
28. MT ii.
29. CH iii, 2.
30. CH iii, 2.
31. EH i, 4.

Chapter VII   Mediaeval: Eriugena

1. The collected works of Johannes Scotus Eriugena, edited by H. J. Floss, are contained in Vol. CXXII of J. P. Migne, *Patrologia Latina*. My references are to the columns and sections of this volume and these are also printed in the margins of the other editions about to be mentioned. Eriugena's principal work, *On the Division of Nature*, is known both by its Latin title, *De Divisione Naturae*, and by the Greek title, *Periphyseon*. The critical edition, with English translation, is by I. P. Sheldon-Williams: Johannes Scottus, *Periphyseon*, The Dublin Institute for Advanced Studies, 1968ff. Unhappily the editor died after publishing Books I and II. He left Book III in an advanced state of readiness, and it has been brought out by Professor John J. O'Meara, who states that it is intended to publish Books IV and V in due course. There are critical editions of two other works, with French translations, edited by M. Edouard Jeauneau: Jean Scot, *Homélie sur le prologue de Jean* (1969) and *Commentaire sur l'évangile de Jean* (1972). Both are in the series Sources Chrétiennes, published by Les Editions du Cerf, Paris.
2. 508D–509A (unless otherwise stated, all references are to *Periphyseon*).
3. See Sheldon-Williams, 'Introduction' to Book I, p. 5.
4. 441B–442A.
5. 615D.
6. 442A.
7. 526D–527A.
8. 517C–518A.
9. 524D.
10. 621A.
11. 621B.
12. 622A.
13. 621B.
14. 677C.
15. 459B–C.
16. 461B–C.
17. 426C–D.
18. 482A–B.
19. 487B.
20. Thomas Aquinas, *Summa Theologiae*, Ia, 13, 11.
21. 455C.
22. 729A.
23. 469A.

24. 453A.
25. 632D.
26. 683C–D.
27. 487B.
28. 607B.
29. 454C.
30. 680D–681A.
31. 449D.
32. 733B.
33. 768B.
34. 570A–C.
35. 579A.
36. 572B.
37. John J. O'Meara in *The Mind of Eriugena*, ed. J. J. O'Meara and Ludwig Bieler, Irish University Press 1973, p. xiii.
38. 519B and D.
39. 683C.
40. *Homily*, 284B.

Chapter VIII　Renaissance: Cusanus

1. Frederick Copleston, SJ, *A History of Philosophy*, Doubleday (Image Books) 1963, Vol. III/2, p. 37.
2. For *De docta ignorantia* and *Apologia*, I have made my own translations from the Latin text edited by Paul Wilpert: Nikolaus von Kues, *Werke*, Vol. I, Walter de Gruyter & Co. 1967. I shall hereafter refer to these works as DI and Ap. I have consulted the English and French translations of DI, the former by Germain Heron, OFM: Nicholas Cusanus, *Of Learned Ignorance*, Yale University Press 1954; the latter by L. Moulinier: Nicholas de Cusa, *De la docte ignorance*, Librairie Felix Alcan 1930. I have used the English translation of *De visione dei* (hereafter VD) by E. G. Salter, with introduction by Evelyn Underhill: Nicholas of Cusa, *The Vision of God*. The original edition was published by J. M. Dent and E. P. Dutton in 1928; republished by Frederick Ungar Publishing Co. in 1960. For *De non aliud*, I have used Jasper Hopkins' edition, which includes the Latin text (according to Wilpert), English translation, introduction and notes: Nicholas of Cusa, *On God as Not-other*, University of Minnesota Press, Minneapolis, 1979 (hereafter NA).
3. DI, I, 22.
4. N. Thulstrup, *Kierkegaard's Relation to Hegel*, ET Princeton University Press 1980.
5. NA, p. 29.
6. VD, p. 75.
7. DI, I, 3.
8. DI, I, 11.
9. DI, I, 25.
10. Plato, *Apology*, 21.
11. DI, I, 1.
12. DI, II, 13.
13. Ibid.

14. C. A. Campbell, *On Selfhood and Godhood*, Allen & Unwin 1957, p. 13.
15. DI, I, 2.
16. DI, I, 4.
17. DI, II, 1.
18. DI, I, 5.
19. DI, I, 13–23.
20. DI, I, 5.
21. DI, I, 7.
22. DI, I, 19.
23. See above, p. 103.
24. DI, I, 21.
25. DI, I, 23.
26. See above, p. 102.
27. NA, pp. 35, 41.
28. NA, p. 141.
29. VD, p. 26.
30. VD, p. 49.
31. VD, p. 36.
32. DI, II, 4.
33. Ap, *'Per hoc enim, quod omnia sunt in deo ut causata in causa, non sequitur causata esse causam.'*
34. DI, II, 5.
35. DI, II, 12.
36. DI, II, 7.
37. DI, III, 3.
38. DI, III, 4.

Chapter IX Enlightenment: Leibniz

1. *Essais de theodicée sur la bonté de Dieu, la liberté de l'homme et l'origine du mal* was published in 1710. I have used the English translation by E. M. Huggard: *Theodicy – Essays on the Goodness of God, the Freedom of Man and the Origin of Evil*, by G. W. Leibniz, Routledge & Kegan Paul 1951. I refer to it in the notes as *Th*. *La monadologie* was written in 1714 and published posthumously. I have quoted (with minor changes) from the translation by Robert Latta contained in *The Monadology and Other Philosophical Writings*, by G. W. Leibniz, Oxford University Press 1898. I refer to this volume in the notes as *M*.
2. *Th.*, p. 53.
3. *Th.*, p. 64. Kant's remarks on organism, dating from eighty years after Leibniz' book, are worth quoting: 'An organized being is not a mere medicine. For a machine has solely motive power, whereas an organized being possesses inherent formative power and such, moreover, as it can impart to material devoid of it – material which it organizes. This, therefore, is a self-propagating formative power, which cannot be explained by the capacity of movement alone, that is to say, by mechanism.' (*Critique of Judgment*, ET Oxford University Press 1952, Part II, p. 22).
4. *M.*, p. 219.
5. *M.*, p. 50.
6. *Th.*, p. 128.

7. See above, p. 20–21.
8. *M.*, p. 235.
9. *M.*, p. 276.
10. *M.*, p. 235.
11. *New Essays in Philosophical Theology*, ed. A. Flew and A. McIntyre, SCM Press 1955, pp. 47ff.
12. E. L. Mascall, *The Openness of Being* (Gifford Lectures), Darton, Longman & Todd 1971.
13. *Th.*, p. 127.
14. *Th.*, p. 238.
15. *M.*, pp. 243–4.
16. See above, p. 63.
17. *M.*, p. 243 n. 75.
18. See *M.*, p. 222 n. 15.
19. *Th.*, p. 88.
20. *Principles of Nature and Grace*, Section 7, in *M.*, p. 415. The French original of this section reads as follows:
Jusqu'icy nous n'avons parlé qu'en simples *Physiciens*: maintenant il faut s'elever à la *Metaphysique*, en nous servant du *Grand Principe*, peu employé communement, qui porte que *rien ne se fait sans raison suffisante*, c'est à dire que rien n'arrive, sans qu'il soit possible à celuy qui connoitroit assés les choses, de rendre une *Raison* qui suffise pour determiner, pourquoy il en est ainsi, et non pas autrement. Ce principe posé, la première question qu'on a droit de faire, sera, *Pourquoy il y a plustôt quelque chose que rien?* Car le rien est plus simple et plus facile que quelque chose. De plus, supposé que des choses doivent exister, il faut qu'on puisse rendre raison, *pourquoy elles doivent exister ainsi*, et non autrement (G. W. Leibniz, *Die Philosophischen Schriften*, ed. C. I. Gerhardt, Georg Olms, Hildesheim 1961, Vol. vi, p. 602).
21. See above, pp. 90 and 120.
22. H. A. Hodges, *God beyond Knowledge*, Macmillan 1979, p. 89.
23. M. K. Munitz, *The Mystery of Existence*, Appleton-Century-Crofts 1965, p. 34.
24. M. K. Munitz, op. cit., p. 5.
25. M. Heidegger, *Introduction to Metaphysics*, ET Yale University Press 1959, p. 1.
26. See below, p. 158–9.
27. *M.*, p. 267.
28. See above, p. 40.
29. *M.*, p. 266.
30. *Th.*, p. 267.
31. *Th.*, p. 286.
32. *Th.*, p. 248.
33. *Th.*, pp. 252, 341.
34. *Th.*, p. 138.
35. *Th.*, p. 228.
36. *Th.*, pp. 135–6.
37. *Th.*, p. 142.
38. *Th.*, p. 216.

39. Voltaire, *Candide, ou l'optimisme,* in *Contes Philosophiques,* Nelson, Paris 1936. See also *Zadig ou la destinée,* in the same volume, pp. 33–125.
40. *Th.,* pp. 371–2.

Chapter X　Nineteenth Century: Hegel

1. See above, p. 44.
2. J. N. Findlay, *Hegel: A Re-examination,* Collier Books 1962, p. 26.
3. Charles Taylor, *Hegel,* Cambridge University Press 1975, p. 51.
4. Quotations in the text are taken from standard English translations of Hegel' works. I have used the following abbreviations in the notes:
ETW　*On Christianity: Early Theological Writings,* ET Harper Torchbooks 1961. German originals, 1795–1800.
PM　*The Phenomenology of Mind,* ET Allen & Unwin 1931. German original, 1807.
L　*Logic* (from 'The Encyclopedia of the Philosophical Sciences'), ET Oxford University Press 1892. German origin, 1817.
PH　*The Philosophy of History,* ET Dover Books 1956. German Original, 1830–1.
LPR　*Lectures on the Philosophy of Religion,* ET Routledge & Kegan Paul, 3 vols., 1895. German original, 1832.
5. *ETW,* p. 71.
6. *ETW,* p. 146.
7. S. Kierkegaard, *Concluding Unscientific Postscript,* ET Oxford University Press 1945, p. 182.
8. *ETW,* pp. 256–7.
9. *ETW,* p. 266.
10. See above, p. 27.
11. *PM,* p. 71.
12. *ETW,* p. 230.
13. *ETW,* p. 185.
14. *LPR,* III, p. 24.
15. See above, p. 61.
16. *PM,* p. 86.
17. *L,* p. 180.
18. *PM,* p. 208.
19. *PM,* p. 68.
20. *PM,* pp. 75–6.
21. *PM,* pp. 554–5.
22. *PM,* p. 758.
23. See O. Pfleiderer, *The Philosophy of Religion on the Basis of Its History,* ET Williams & Norgate 1887, Vol. ii, pp. 94–5.
24. *PM,* pp. 554–5.
25. *PM,* p. 758.
26. *L,* p. 125.
27. *L,* p. 136.
28. O. Pfleiderer, op. cit., p. 81.
29. See below, p. 161.
30. C. A. Campbell, *On Selfhood and Godhood,* Allen & Unwin 1957, p. 13.

31. *L*, p. 210.
32. *L*, p. 34.
33. *L*, p. 10.
34. See above, p. 123.
35. See above, p. 71.
36. *L*, pp. 350–2.
37. *LPR*, Vol. i, pp. 1–2.

Chapter XI Twentieth Century (1): Whitehead

1. In the notes to this chapter, the following abbreviations are used for Whitehead's philosophical works:
SMW *Science and the Modern World*, Cambridge University Press 1925.
RM *Religion in the Making*, Cambridge University Press 1926.
PR *Process and Reality* (Gifford Lectures), Cambridge University Press 1929.
AI *Adventures of Ideas*, Penguin Books 1942.
IS *The Interpretation of Science* (Selected Essays), Bobbs-Merrill 1961.
2. *AI*, pp. 21, 121.
3. *PR*, p. 3.
4. *PR*, p. 7.
5. *PR*, Preface, p. x.
6. *SMW*, p. 223.
7. *SMW*, p. 151.
8. See above, p. 61.
9. *SMW*, p. 157.
10. *RM*, p. 91.
11. *SMW*, p. 93.
12. *SMW*, pp. 74–5.
13. I think one would need to exclude Hegel and his followers from this stricture, but it is doubtful if Hegel was an idealist in Whitehead's sense of the term, for the latter seems to imply that the idealist denies the reality of the physical world. See above, p. 130.
14. *AI*, p. 222.
15. *IS*, p. 41.
16. *IS*, pp. 39–40.
17. *SMW*, p. 286.
18. *AI*, p. 98.
19. See above, p. 118.
20. *AI*, p. 206.
21. *PR*, p. 26.
22. *SMW*, p. 101.
23. Latta explains the point very clearly. 'The monad, then, has perception, but not necessarily in the sense of consciousness. For consciousness is not the essence of perception, but merely an additional determination belonging to certain kinds or degrees of perception. Conscious perception is called by Leibniz, "apperception" ' (G. W. Leibniz, *The Monadology and Other Philosophical Writings*, Oxford University Press 1898, p. 34).
24. *AI*, p. 186.

25. *SMW*, pp. 105–6.
26. *RM*, p. 79.
27. George F. Thomas, *Religious Philosophies of the West*, Scribner 1965, p. 374.
28. *SMW*, p. 226.
29. *RM*, pp. 44–5.
30. *PR*, p. 28.
31. *AI*, p. 209, also p. 206.
32. John B. Cobb, Jr., *A Christian Natural Theology Based on the Thought of Alfred North Whitehead*, Westminster Press 1965, p. 169.
33. See above, p. 141.
34. *SMW*, p. 27.
35. *AI*, p. 319.
36. *PR*, p. 24.
37. *PR*, p. 489.
38. See *SMW*, p. 105.
39. *PR*, p. 488.
40. See above, p. 93.
41. *PR*, p. 490.
42. See my book, *The Humility of God*, SCM Press and Westminster Press 1978.
43. *PR*, p. 497.
44. *PR*, p. 492.
45. *PR*, pp. 492–3.

Chapter XII   Twentieth Century (2): Heidegger

1. The *Gesamtausgabe* of Heidegger's works is at present in course of publication by Vittorio Klostermann, Frankfurt. An English translation of his works is being published by Harper & Row, but English translations of several important works have appeared from other publishers. In the notes, I have used abbreviations for the titles of individual works, as shown below. I have quoted from English translations where available, otherwise I have made my own translations.

SuZ *Sein und Zeit*, Niemeyer, Halle, 1927; ET, *Being and Time*, SCM Press and Harper & Row 1962.

WM *Was Ist Metaphysik?* Cohen, Bonn 1930; with Introduction and Epilogue, Klostermann 1949; ET with Epilogue in *Existence and Being*, Gateway Books, Chicago 1949.

EM *Einführung in die Metaphysik*, Niemeyer, Tübingen 1953; ET, *Introduction to Metaphysics*, Yale University Press 1959.

H *Brief über den Humanismus*, Klostermann 1947; ET in *Basic Writings*, 1978.

WHD *Was heisst Denken?* Niemeyer, Tübingen 1954; ET, *What Is Called Thinking?* Harper & Row 1968.

IuD *Identität und Differenez*, Neske, Pfullingen 1957; ET, *Identity and Difference*, Harper & Row 1969.

US *Unterwegs zur Sprache*, Neske 1965.

G *Gelassenheit*, Neske 1959; ET *A Discourse on Thinking*, Harper & Row, 1966.

N   *Nietzsche*, 2 vols., Neske 1961; ET, *Nietzsche*, 4 vols., Harper & Row 1979–82.
TuK   *Die Technik und die Kehre*, Neske 1962.
ZuS   *Zur Sache des Denkens* (including the essay, *Zeit und Sein*), Niemeyer, 1969; ET, *Time and Being*, Harper & Row 1972.
PT   *The Piety of Thinking*, ET of various essays on theology and related topics, Indiana University Press 1976.

2. J. R. Williams, *Martin Heidegger's Philosophy of Religion*, Wilfrid Laurier University Press, Waterloo, Ontario 1977, p. 154.

3. See above, pp. 53–4.

4. *US*, p. 96.

5. *IuD*, ET, p. 55.

6. Hans-Georg Gadamer, '*Anrufung des entschwundenen Gottes*', in *Evangelische Kommentare*, Vol. x, 1977, pp. 204–8.

7. A *catena* of some of these passages is included as an appendix to the book *Heidegger et la question de Dieu*, ed. R. Kearne and J. S. O'Leary, Grasset, Paris 1980, pp. 311–36.

8. 'Nur noch ein Gott kann uns retten', in *Der Spiegel*, no. 23, 1976, pp. 193ff.

9. See Francois Fedier in *Heidegger et la question de Dieu*, p. 39.

10. *SuZ*, ET, p. 30.

11. *PT*, pp. 5–21.

12. *SuZ*, ET, p. 272.

13. Ibid., p. 74.

14. Ibid., p. 492, n. iv.

15. Ibid., p. 499, n. xiii.

16. *WM*, pp. 38–9.

17. *WM*, p. 42.

18. *WM*, editions from 1949 onward, pp. 7–23.

19. *EM*, ET, p. 7.

20. *IuD*, ET, p. 62.

21. *EM*, ET, p. 7.

22. *IuD*, ET, p. 72.

23. Blaise Pascal, *Pensées*, no. 737.

24. *N*, ET, vol. 4, p. 26.

25. E. L. Mascall, *The Openness of Being*, Darton, Longman & Todd 1971, p. 141.

26. F. H. Bradley, *Appearance and Reality*, Oxford University Press 1893, p. 5.

27. *US*, p. 109.

28. See above, p. 90.

29. Thomas Aquinas, *Summa Theologia*, Ia, 13, 11.

30. *PT*, pp. 22–31.

31. K. Löwith, *From Hegel to Nietzsche*, ET Doubleday 1967, p. 207.

32. *H*, p. 10.

33. *H*, p. 29.

34. *H*, pp. 36–7.

35. *N*, ET, vol. 4, p. 193

36. Ibid., p. 201.

37. See *WHD* and *G*.

38. See above, p. 157.

39. *ZuS*, FT, p. 8.
40. Ibid, p. 8.
41. *TuK*, p. 46 (following J. R. Williams' translation).
42. *Der Spiegel*, loc. cit., p. 209.
43. *US*, p. 258. On the relation of the event to being, seé also p. 260 n. 1.

Chapter XIII   A Dialectical Concept of God

1. Thomas Aquinas, *Summa Theologiae*, Ia, 13, 11.
2. Ex. 3. 14–15.
3. See above, pp. 32, 90.
4. See above, p. 120, 158, 159.
5. L. Wittgenstein, *Tractatus Logico-Philosophicus*, Kegan Paul 1922, p. 187.
6. See above, p. 260, n. 20.
7. Augustine, *De Trinitate*, V, 10.
8. See above, p. 151.
9. L. Wittgenstein, *Tractatus Logico-Philosophicus*, p. 187.
10. J. Macquarrie, *In Search of Humanity*, SCM Press 1982 and Crossroad 1983, pp. 253ff.
11. See above, p. 20.
12. H. A. Hodges, *God Beyond Knowledge*, Macmillan 1979, p. 175.
13. J. Macquarrie, *Principles of Christian Theology*, SCM Press and Scribner ²1977, p. 219.
14. William Temple, *Nature, Man and God* (Gifford Lectures), Macmillan 1935, p. 129.
15. Karl Barth, *Church Dogmatics: The Doctrine of Creation*, vol. III/1, ET T. & T. Clark 1958, p. 116.
16. Ibid., p. 182.
17. Ibid., p. 183.
18. Ibid., p. 318.
19. Ibid., p. 318.
20. See above, p. 40.
21. F. Nietzsche, *Thus Spake Zarathustra*, ET Dent 1933, p. 3.
22. Isa. 63, 9 (alternative translations have been suggested).
23. See above, p. 150.
24. Ps. 90. 4.

Chapter XIV   Dialectical Theism and Spirituality

1. P. Tillich, *Systematic Theology*, Chicago University Press 1951 and SCM Press 1978, I, p. 106.
2. Francis Bacon, 'Of Atheism', in *Essays or Counsels, Moral and Civil*, Henry Parson, London 1720, p. 98.
3. See above, pp. 134–5.
4. A. N. Whitehead, *Religion in the Making*, Cambridge University Press 1927, p. 71.
5. A. N. Whitehead, *Science in the Modern World*, Cambridge University Press 1926, p. 275.
6. See above, p. 160.

7. See my book, *In Search of Humanity*, SCM Press 1982 and Crossroad 1983, ch. vi, 'Cognition'.

8. M. Polanyi, *Personal Knowledge*, Routledge & Kegan Paul and Harper Torchbooks 1964, *passim*.

9. I Cor. 2. 15.

10. H. A. Hodges, *God Beyond Knowledge* (Gifford Lectures), Macmillan 1979, p. 175.

11. Ibid., p. 106.

12. I. T. Ramsey, *Models for Divine Activity*, SCM Press 1973, p. 4.

13. Martin Thornton, *My God*, Hodder & Stoughton 1974, p. 40.

14. See, e.g., the writings of Gregory Thaumaturgus.

15. Epiphanius, quoted by Ludwig Ott, *Fundamentals of Catholic Dogma*, Mercier Press 1957, p. 216.

16. W. M. Abbott (ed.), *The Documents of Vatican II*, Herder & Herder 1966, pp. 94–5.

17. See above, p. 13.

18. F. Copleston, *Religion and the One*, Search Press 1982, p. 159.

19. Eckhart's works are usually divided into Latin writings, mainly scholarly, and German writings, mainly popular sermons. There has been considerable discussion over the authenticity of some of the writings attributed to him. I have relied here mainly on the English translation with copious notes by Edmund Colledge and Bernard McGinn, entitled *Meister Eckhart: the Essential Sermons, Commentaries, Treatises and Defense* SPCK 1981 (abbreviated C & McG), but have supplemented it with a few passages from R. B. Blakney, *Meister Eckhart: A New Translation*, (abbreviated RBB), Harper Torchbooks 1957.

20. *English Hymnal*, No. 511.

21. C & McG, p. 288.

22. RBB, p. 238.

23. C & McG, p. 187.

24. C & McG, p. 187.

25. C & McG, p. 50.

26. RBB, p. 204.

27. C & McG, p. 72.

28. C & McG, p. 80.

29. RBB, p. 110.

30. See above, p. 166.

Chapter XV   The Theistic Proofs Reconsidered

1. William James, *The Varieties of Religious Experience* (Gifford Lectures), Longmans Green 1952, p. 371.

2. W. T. Stace, *Mysticism and Philosophy*, Macmillan 1960, p. 146.

3. Bertrand Russell, *Mysticism and Logic*, Longmans 1918, p. 12.

4. Anselm, *Proslogion* 2.

5. Ibid.

6. Immanuel, Kant, *Critique of Pure Reason*, ET Macmillan 1956, pp. 505f.

7. Anselm, *Proslogion* 3.

8. C. Hartshorne, *Creative Synthesis and Philosophic Method*, SCM Press 1970, p. 257.

9. R. Descartes, *Meditations* 5.
10. See above, pp. 43–56.
11. See above, p. 62.
12. See above, p. 68.
13. See above, p. 109.
14. See above, p. 113.
15. See above, pp. 144–5.
16. H. W. Richardson, *Toward an American Theology*, Harper & Row 1967 (English edition: *Theology for a New World*, SCM Press 1967), p. 82.
17. L.-B. Puntel, 'Unity', *Sacramentum Mundi*, Herder & Herder 1970, Vol. VI, p. 324.
18. Richardson, op. cit., p. 82.
19. Col. 1.17.
20. K. Jaspers, *The Perennial Scope of Philosophy*, ET Routledge & Kegan Paul 1950, p. 19.
21. K. Jaspers, *Philosophical Faith and Revelation*, ET Harper & Row 1967, p. 269.
22. See above, pp. 120, 158–9.
23. See above, p. 121.
24. See above, p. 197.
25. B. Lonergan, *Insight*, Philosophical Library 1970, p. 635.
26. See above, p. 260 n. 20.
27. S. Radhakrishnan, *Eastern Religions and Western Thought*, Oxford University Press 1939, p. 126.
28. F. R. Tennant, *Philosophical Theology*, Cambridge University Press 1930, Vol. II, p. 104.
29. Ibid.
30. See above, p. 142.
31. Jaspers, *Perennial Scope*, pp. 34–5.

Chapter XVI Dialectical Theism and Ethics

1. Basil Mitchell, *Morality: Religious and Secular* (Gifford Lectures), Oxford University Press 1980, p. 79.
2. See above, p. 9.
3. W. G. de Burgh, *From Morality to Religion* (Gifford Lectures), Macdonald & Evans 1938, p. 156.
4. Immanuel Kant, *Critique of Practical Reason*, ET Longmans Green 1927, p. 221.
5. There have, of course, been artists who believed that beauty ranks above moral value, while Kierkegaard, in *Fear and Trembling*, speaks of the suspension of ethics by religious values.
6. Such as John Oman, *The Natural and the Supernatural*, Cambridge University Press 1931, pp. 405ff.
7. See above, pp. 70–71.
8. See my *Three Issues in Ethics*, SCM Press 1970, ch. 4.
9. See above, p. 195.
10. See above, p. 14.
11. See above, p. 68.

12. S. Hauerwas, *Character and the Christian Life*, Trinity University Press, San Antonio 1975, p. 230.

13. See above, p. 166.

14. See above, p. 197.

15. A recurring expression in *One-Dimensional Man*, Sphere Books 1968.

16. See above, p. 20.

17. See above, p. 195.

Chapter XVII   Dialectical Theism and Theology

1. K. Rahner, *Theological Investigations*, I, ET Darton, Longman & Todd 1961, p. 83.

2. Ibid., p. 99.

3. Ibid., pp. 79–148.

4. Ibid., p. 143.

5. See C. F. D. Moule, 'The New Testament and the Trinity', *The Expository Times*, LXXVIII, October 1976, pp. 16–20.

6. R. Bultmann, *Essays, Philosophical and Theological*, ET SCM Press 1955, p. 275.

7. John 20.28.

8. R. E. Brown, *Jesus: God and Man*, Bruce Publishing Co., Milwaukee 1967, pp. 23ff.

9. John 1.1.

10. Heb. 1.8–9.

11. Matt. 1.23. Cf. J. C. Fenton, 'Matthew and the Divinity of Jesus', *Studia Biblica 1978* ed. E. A. Livingstone, Sheffield 1980.

12. I Cor. 8.5–6.

13. K. Barth, *Church Dogmatics*, I/1, ET T. & T. Clark 1936, p. 357.

14. E. Schillebeeckx, *Jesus*, ET Crossroad and Collins 1979, pp. 479ff.

15. Acts 2.36.

16. John 1.14.

17. Note the allusion to the spirituality which takes the form of homage. See above, p. 194.

18. The allusion is the docetic christologies, in which Jesus only seemed to be man.

19. S. Kierkegaard, *Philosophical Fragments*, ET Princeton University Press 1936, pp. 24–5.

20. See above, p. 132.

21. Kierkegaard, op. cit., p. 87.

22. Meister Eckhart (C & McG), p. 198.

23. Ibid., p. 193.

24. See above, pp. 193ff.

25. A. Deissmann, *Paul*, ET Hodder & Stoughton 1926, p. 153.

Chapter XVIII   Dialectical Theism and the World Religions

1. See above, p. 29.

2. See above, p. 226.

3. See above, p. 13.

4. J. Macquarrie, *Principles of Christian Theology*, SCM Press ²1977, p. 116.

5. See above, p. 69.

6. See above, pp. 74–5.

7. See above, p. 196.

8. See above, pp. 166–7.

9. P. Tillich, *The Courage to Be*, Collins Fontana Library 1962, p. 176.

10. P. Tillich, *Systematic Theology*, Chicago University Press 1951 and SCM Press 1978, I, p. 245.

11. F. H. Bradley, *Appearance and Reality*, Oxford University Press ²1897, p. 470.

12. See above, pp. 233–4.

13. Bradley, op. cit., pp. 472–3.

14. K. Barth, *Church Dogmatics*, ET T. & T. Clark 1936, I/1, p. 403.

15. See above, p. 22.

16. See G. Quispel in F. I. Cross (ed.), *The Jung Codex*, Mowbray 1955, pp. 67–71.

17. Prov. 8.22ff.

18. R. Otto, *The Idea of the Holy*, ET Oxford University Press 1923, p. 78.

19. Leo Baeck, *Judaism and Christianity*, ET World Publishing Company 1961, p. 174.

20. See above, p. 24.

21. For an instructive account of Buber's debt to the Hasidim, see Pamela Vermes, *Buber on God and the Perfect Man*, Scholars Press 1980.

22. M. Buber, *I and Thou*, ET T. & T. Clark ²1959, p. 135.

23. C. R. North, *An Outline of Islam*, Epworth Press 1934, pp. 70–1.

24. J. S. Trimingham, *The Sufi Orders in Islam*, Oxford University Press 1971, pp. 1–2.

25. N. MacNicol (ed.), *Hindu Scriptures*, J. M. Dent 1938, p. 36.

26. *Bhagavadgita*, ET R. C. Zaehner, Oxford University Press 1969, pp. 82ff.

27. See above, p. 43–4.

28. S. D. B. Picken, *Buddhism: Japan's Cultural Identity*, Kodansha International, Tokyo 1982, p. 36.

29. S. Aoyama and T. Irie, *Buddhist Images*, ET Hoikusha Publishing Company, Osaka 1970, pp. 125–6.

30. S. Kierkegaard, *Training in Christianity*, ET Princeton University Press 1944, p. 66.

Index